The New Nationalism
in America and Beyond

The New Nationalism in America and Beyond

The Deep Roots of Ethnic Nationalism in the Digital Age

ROBERT SCHERTZER
and
ERIC TAYLOR WOODS

OXFORD
UNIVERSITY PRESS

Oxford University Press is a department of the University of Oxford. It furthers the University's objective of excellence in research, scholarship, and education by publishing worldwide. Oxford is a registered trade mark of Oxford University Press in the UK and certain other countries.

Published in the United States of America by Oxford University Press
198 Madison Avenue, New York, NY 10016, United States of America.

© Oxford University Press 2022

All rights reserved. No part of this publication may be reproduced, stored in a retrieval system, or transmitted, in any form or by any means, without the prior permission in writing of Oxford University Press, or as expressly permitted by law, by license, or under terms agreed with the appropriate reproduction rights organization. Inquiries concerning reproduction outside the scope of the above should be sent to the Rights Department, Oxford University Press, at the address above.

You must not circulate this work in any other form
and you must impose this same condition on any acquirer.

CIP data is on file at the Library of Congress

ISBN 978–0–19–754783–0 (pbk.)
ISBN 978–0–19–754782–3 (hbk.)

DOI: 10.1093/oso/9780197547823.001.0001

CONTENTS

List of Figures and Tables vii
Acknowledgments ix

1. The (Not So) New Nationalism 1
   THE PUZZLE: THE RISE OF ETHNIC NATIONALISM IN THE WEST 2
   THE ARGUMENT: THE DEEP ROOTS OF THE "NEW" NATIONALISM 5
   SITUATING THE ARGUMENT: FROM FOCUSING ON POPULISM TOWARD FOCUSING ON NATIONALISM 8
   STRUCTURE OF THE ARGUMENT 13

2. Making Sense of Ethnic Nationalism in the West 16
   UNDERSTANDING NATIONALISM 17
   ETHNO-SYMBOLISM: DOMINANT ETHNICITY, CULTURE, AND HISTORY 26
   TYING TOGETHER THE THREADS OF ETHNO-SYMBOLISM TO UNDERSTAND ETHNIC NATIONALISM 35

3. Mapping Ethnic Nationalism in the Age of Twitter 37
   A SCHEMA FOR MAPPING ETHNIC MYTH-SYMBOL COMPLEXES 37
   APPLYING THE SCHEMA: MAPPING ETHNIC NATIONALISM THROUGH SOCIAL MEDIA 44

4. The Foundations and Development of Ethnic Nationalism in America 54
   THE CULTURAL FOUNDATIONS OF AMERICAN ETHNIC NATIONALISM 56
   THE DEVELOPMENT OF ETHNIC NATIONALISM IN AMERICA 68
   HOW DOES THIS HELP US UNDERSTAND THE NEW NATIONALISM IN AMERICA TODAY? 86

5. Donald Trump and the New Nationalism in America 88

THE ROLE OF ETHNIC NATIONALISM AND THE WHITE MAJORITY IN 2016 (AND 2020) 91

DONALD TRUMP'S ETHNIC NATIONALISM 92

DONALD TRUMP'S TWITTER NATIONALISM IN THE 2016 PRESIDENTIAL CAMPAIGN 98

CONTINUITY AND CHANGE IN DONALD TRUMP'S ETHNIC NATIONALISM 110

6. Marine Le Pen and the Ethnic Stream of French Nationalism 113

THE ETHNIC FOUNDATIONS OF FRENCH IDENTITY AND POLITICAL CULTURE 114

MARINE LE PEN AND ETHNIC NATIONALISM IN FRANCE TODAY 128

CONTINUITY AND CHANGE IN MARINE LE PEN'S ETHNIC NATIONALISM 144

7. English Nationalism and the Campaign for Brexit 147

THE ETHNIC FOUNDATIONS OF ENGLISH NATIONALISM 148

BREXIT AND ENGLISH NATIONALISM 160

CONTINUITY AND CHANGE IN THE LEAVE CAMPAIGNS' ETHNIC NATIONALISM 174

Conclusion: The Deep Roots of the New Nationalism 178

THE PERSISTENCE AND ADAPTABILITY OF ETHNIC NATIONALISM IN THE WEST 180

THE FORM AND CONTENT OF THE NEW NATIONALISM IN THE WEST 184

THIS IS NOT THE END 188

Notes 193
References 195
Index 213

LIST OF FIGURES AND TABLES

Figures

5.1 Tweets depicting "the people" as "the silent majority" 102
5.2 Tweets depicting Mexican migrants as dangerous outsiders 105
5.3 Tweets depicting Muslims as a dangerous threat to majority group 108
5.4 Tweets depicting migrants and the establishment as threats to the values and interests of the majority group 109
6.1 Examples of Marine Le Pen's Tweets constructing an ethnic in-group 137
6.2 Examples of Marine Le Pen's Tweets constructing an ethnic out-group 143
7.1 Tweets depicting Turkey and Muslims as Threats 172

Tables

3.1 Schema to Map Ethnic Myth-Symbol Complex 41
4.1 Ethnic Anglo-American Myth-Symbol Complex, Approximately 1750–1820 67
5.1 Key Distinctions in Donald Trump's Ethnic Conception of the In- and Out-Group in His Twitter Communication in the 2016 Presidential Election 111
6.1 Foundational Ethnic Myths of French Identity 127
6.2 Key Distinctions in Marine Le Pen's Ethnic Conception of the In- and Out-Group in Her Twitter Communication in the 2017 Presidential Election 145

7.1 Foundational Ethnic Myths of English Identity   159
7.2 Key Distinctions in the Leave Campaigns' Conception of the In- and Out-Group in Their Twitter Communication in the 2016 Brexit Referendum Campaign   175

ACKNOWLEDGMENTS

We would like to dedicate this book to John Hutchinson, our mentor and friend, who has taught us both so much. We hope the book lives up to his standards, and carries forward his important contribution to understanding of nations and nationalism.

There are many people we would like to thank for their support along the way as we worked on this book. In fact, there are simply too many to name everyone here, but we would be remiss if we did not single out a few people! First, we would like to express our sincere gratitude to our amazing team of research assistants: Timothy Berk, Javier Carbonell Castañer, Alexandre Fortier-Chouinard, Faisal Kamal, Catherine Ouellet and Amedeo Varriale. We would also like to thank our editor David McBride and the team at OUP, along with the peer-reviewers for their insightful suggestions. We are also grateful to the Social Sciences and Humanities Research Council, the British Academy, Leverhulme, the University of Toronto, the University of Plymouth, and the Migration Policy Centre in the Robert Schuman Centre for Advanced Studies at the European University Institute. All of these organizations provided support at various stages of the project.

We would like to end by thanking our families and our significant others, Bronwyn and Helen, for their unwavering love and support.

1

The (Not So) New Nationalism

On January 6, 2021, President Donald Trump of the United States gave a speech at a rally just south of the White House to thousands of ardent supporters. The speech was Trump's last-ditch effort to stop Congress from certifying Joe Biden's victory in the 2020 presidential election. For months, Trump had been repeatedly claiming that the election was stolen from him. In his speech, Trump argued the election was rigged and illegitimate, telling the crowd that "if you don't fight like hell, you're not going to have a country anymore," and that "you have to show strength, and you have to be strong." He urged the crowd to march on Congress: "We are going to the Capitol," we will "try and give them the kind of pride and boldness that they need to take back our country. So let's walk down Pennsylvania Avenue." About an hour later, a mob of supporters breached the security barriers, reached the doors of the Capitol, and stormed inside. The scenes of the siege are now well known: Trump supporters swarming the Capitol; overwhelmed police in retreat; congresspeople, senators, and staffers rushing to hide; the Confederate flag carried through the halls of Congress; supporters adorned with symbols of white nationalism; a man on the floor of the Senate with zip ties; and a noose and gallows erected outside. This was a siege—an insurrection—led by Trump supporters and white nationalists to try and overturn the results of a democratic election. This happened in America.

People watched the surreal event unfold in shock. President-elect Joe Biden summed up the position of many Americans, calling the insurrection an "unprecedented assault" on democracy, and stating that the "scenes of chaos at the Capitol *do not represent who we are*" (emphasis added). These themes were a continuation of how Biden had depicted Trump when he launched his presidential campaign, which he characterized as a "battle for the soul of this nation." Referencing the surge of ethnic nationalism during Trump's tenure, Biden argued that four more years of Trump in the White House would "fundamentally alter the character of this nation." Tapping into a countervailing mythology of America as a liberal, civic nation, Biden argued that "history will look back on

The New Nationalism in America and Beyond. Robert Schertzer and Eric Taylor Woods, Oxford University Press.
© Oxford University Press 2022. DOI: 10.1093/oso/9780197547823.003.0001

four years of this president and all he embraces as an aberrant moment in time." The events that followed the siege on the Capitol seemingly validated Biden's view that the Trump era was an aberrant period in American politics. Joe Biden's win was certified that day, and Donald Trump was banned from social media for inciting violence—a seemingly fitting end to a presidency that had been defined by Twitter. A few days later, Joe Biden was sworn in as president. In his inaugural address, he celebrated that "we"—America—had "endured and prevailed."

In this book, we ask a question: What if Trump's version of America *is* who "we" are? What if it is just as much a part of American political culture as the liberal ideas that Biden claims to champion? What if America—like many other nations in the West—does have a deeply rooted ethnic nationalism? What if Trump and his contemporaries in other Western nations, like the United Kingdom and France, are not aberrations, or exceptions, but a return to the norm?

The Puzzle: The Rise of Ethnic Nationalism in the West

This book is about nationalism. Nationalism has been one of the most powerful forces shaping modern human history. While much denigrated, nationalism has also been instrumental to human progress. It was a driving force behind the Industrial Revolution, the rise of the modern welfare system, and the formation of our international society of states. It has provided the inspiration for anti-colonial and democratic revolutions. But nationalism's bad reputation is also well deserved. At its worst—when it promotes an exclusive, ethnic conception of the nation—it has spurned widespread conflict and misery. This form of nationalism has proven to be a powerful carrier for illiberal and discriminatory ideas. In short, nationalism brings people together, but it also creates barriers that separate them.

Nationalism is often seen as an archaic, regressive ideology whose time has come. At the end of the twentieth century, with the seeming triumph of liberalism over communism, and the memory of the world wars fading, many keen observers declared that nationalism had been cast into the historical dustbin (Fukuyama 1992; Hobsbawm 1990; Kaldor 2004). The last five years—from 2016 through the events on January 6, 2021—have proved these declarations all too wrong.

Over this period, we have seen a resurgence of nationalism. Troublingly, a distinctly *ethnic* variant of nationalism has re-emerged. By defining nations in ethnic and cultural terms, ethnic nationalism hardens the perceived boundaries between who belongs and who does not. Furthermore, ethnic nationalism has increasingly been combined with populism to mount a powerful challenge to the postwar consensus on the value of liberal pluralism and the free movement of goods and people. This pairing of populist and ethnic nationalist ideas is among the most pressing issues of our time: populism venerates ordinary people and vilifies elites, while ethnic nationalism provides an exclusionary definition of "the people" through ethnic and cultural markers (see Bonikowski 2017). This powerful formula has come to be known as the "new nationalism" (*The Economist* 2016).

Among the most puzzling aspects of the new nationalism is the relative success of ethnic nationalists and populists in some of the most liberal and prosperous democracies across the West. The year 2017 was a watershed for these movements. It signaled a clear moment in the rise of nationalism and populism across the West and the globe (Brubaker 2017; Bieber 2018). Marine Le Pen, the leader of the National Front (now National Rally), won a historic second place in the French presidential elections; the Alternative for Germany secured the third-largest share of the vote in the German federal election; and Geert Wilder's Party for Freedom became the second-largest party in the Netherlands' House of Representatives. These inroads built on the referendum held the previous year in Britain, where a majority of voters opted to leave the European Union. But, undoubtedly, the most visible example of the electoral power of the new nationalism occurred outside Europe, with Donald Trump's 2016 presidential win.

Donald Trump's primary and presidential campaign exemplifies how today's politicians in the West are increasingly tapping into ethnic nationalism and populism to find support among the dominant (white) ethnic group in their countries (Schertzer and Woods 2020). Across the West, white ethnic majorities are the backbone of support for this new nationalism. Under the banners of "taking back control" and making the country "great again," ethnic nationalists have gained support from these "silent majorities" by setting their discourse against the perceived threats of liberalism, multilateralism, globalism, elites, and, especially, foreigners and migrants. In doing so, these new nationalists have found remarkable success among white voters.

What explains this phenomenon? Why, in some of the most liberal, diverse, and prosperous countries in the world, are decidedly illiberal, anti-migrant, and protectionist leaders and parties gaining support? This is what we aim to find out in this book. We want to understand two related aspects of the new nationalism:

1. Why is ethnic nationalism gaining currency across the West and reverberating with the white populations?
2. How and why do these movements differ across countries?

By focusing on these two questions, we aim to better understand the causes, content, and consequences of the new nationalism. We focus on culture, institutions, and ideas to unpack the forces shaping the messages, programs, and policies of ethnic nationalists. We think keeping a careful eye on these forces can help us understand why today's movements are winning support from wide swaths of people across the nations of the West.

To answer these questions, we pay close attention to some of today's most "successful" ethnic nationalists. There are many possible avenues to explore the causes and consequences of the new nationalism. We focus on the political communication of three examples: Donald Trump in the United States, Marine Le Pen and the National Front in France, and the Leave campaigners for Brexit in the United Kingdom. We are particularly focused on Donald Trump. He was the harbinger of the new nationalism. His success in 2016 was a shock, for many reasons; most notably, his victory cut against the vision of America as the home of liberal, civic nationalism. But we also need to place Trump's emergence in context. Following his election in 2016, there has been a resurgence of ethnic nationalism across the West. For this reason, we look to other cases as well.

All three of our cases are emblematic of the rise of ethnic nationalism and populism across the West. They are all puzzling instances, as they are exceptions to the norm of pluralist politics in the bastions of liberal democracy. They are also ripe for comparison. The successful breakthrough of ethnic nationalists in the US, UK, and France took place around the same time, over an eighteen-month period. They share many similarities. The leaders used common techniques and patterns of political communication, but there were also some important differences in the content of their messaging.

Our aim in this book is thus to shed light on the rise of ethnic nationalism in America and beyond. But our goal is also broader. We want to demonstrate the value of an approach that focuses on the role played by ethnicity, culture, and history. Foregrounding analysis of these factors is intended to augment existing accounts that focus on socioeconomic forces.

Our examination of the US, UK, and France has both a historical and a contemporary element. This book explores the links between the historically constituted and institutionalized conceptions of ethnic identity and how leaders are tapping into these ideas today, particularly via social media. Uncovering these links requires an in-depth mapping of each nation's constitutive set of ethnic myths, symbols, and cultural repertoires—the set of ideas that depict a nation as an ethnic nation. It also requires an examination of how leaders are using these ideas in their political communication. Social media is a logical medium to track these patterns of political communication. It is a central aspect of contemporary political campaigns and is increasingly associated with the rise and success of ethnic nationalism. This is what we do here: our book examines how historically established ethnic ideas are used today through a systematic analysis of the Twitter communication of Donald Trump over the 2016 primary and presidential campaign, the Leave campaigners (Vote Leave and Leave.EU) during the 2016 Brexit campaign, and Marine Le Pen during the 2017 French presidential campaign.

The Argument: The Deep Roots of the "New" Nationalism

Our argument in this book is straightforward: the "new" nationalism is not so new. Across the West, nationalist and populist leaders are tapping into ideas about the ethnic nature of their communities that are deeply rooted in the historical and cultural foundations of their nation. These roots are strongest in the myths and symbols of dominant ethnic majorities. By drawing from these long-held and institutionalized myths and symbols, the messaging and programs of today's nationalist leaders gain a measure of perceived legitimacy and authenticity. This link to the past helps explain the form and success of ethnic nationalism in the West. In short, to better understand today's resurgent ethnic nationalism, we need to pay more attention to the role of ethnicity, culture, and history.

There are many layers to this argument. One of the primary ones is that culture matters. Culture is often an ill-defined concept, and as a result it is sometimes downplayed in explanations of politics. In contrast, we play up culture. We are particularly focused on the culture of the dominant, white majorities. We adopt a systematic approach that maps and traces its role in the rise of ethnic nationalism in the West. We understand culture as a complex set of shared ideas and practices—mythologies, symbols, rituals, and customs of collective imagining—that serve to define a community. While there are many different strands to a culture, we explore cultural content associated with the intersection of ethnicity and nationalism. To do so, we have created a novel schema that maps the core myths and symbols that define a group *as an ethnic group*. Applying this schema to our three cases shows how an ethnic conception of the nation is established, crystalized, and adapted over time. The remarkable stability and resiliency of this conception of identity speaks to its ongoing influence on political dynamics.

In our view, culture is both a constrainer and enabler of the new nationalism. This perspective stems from our analysis tracing the evolution of a core set of ethnic myths and symbols for the US, UK, and France over *la longue durée*. We argue that one of the key ways that today's ethnic nationalists cultivate legitimacy is by drawing upon these long-established ethno-cultural complexes. This aspect of a nation's culture is thus an important constraint on the political behavior and programs of today's ethnic nationalists: to cultivate legitimacy and reverberate with members of the ethnic majority, a leader and party needs to be seen to reflect, adopt, and protect an ethnic group's culture. Yet by providing nationalists with a ready repertoire to draw upon when they make their appeals, culture also enables their political success. This is not to say that ethnic myths and symbols are unchanging, primordial facets of social life. Rather, they are historical phenomena, and as such they are subject to processes of construction and reconstruction. These processes are accelerated during times of heightened crisis or perceived threat, when myths and symbols are employed and transformed to fit new circumstances. So, while ethnic nationalist leaders are constrained and enabled by culture, they can also play a role in its transformation.

In a similar manner, we argue that ethnicity matters. Arguments about how culture or ideas shape politics can be deterministic and tend to highlight action without actors, and structures without agents (Hall and Taylor 1996, 954; Checkel 1998, 335; Schmidt 2010, 50). In this book, we focus on the agency of dominant ethnic majorities and their self-proclaimed leaders in the rise and success of the new nationalism. We do this by closely tracing the core cultural content of the dominant (white) ethnic groups in the US, UK, and France. We show how the parameters of membership for these dominant ethnic majorities are established, reinforced, and adapted at critical junctures in each country. We also explore how leaders today are tapping into, and reshaping, these cultural features as central themes of their contemporary political programs to gain support from dominant ethnic majorities. Accordingly, by focusing on ethnicity— and particularly on dominant ethnic groups and their purported leaders—we provide an account of how ethnic identity is institutionalized, carried through time, and continues to shape politics.

We are also arguing that history shapes politics today. Considering the origins and evolution of cultural content—adding time as a variable in our analysis (Pierson 2000)—allows us to situate cultural content in its changing context. This historically informed view of culture and ethnic identity can provide a rich understanding of the new nationalism. Even a cursory glance at history shows this is not the first time that ethnic nationalism has found support among the ethnic majorities of the West. We are not just talking here about the most well-known and violent manifestation of ethnic nationalism that took hold in Germany in the twentieth century. There are numerous other examples. As early as the nineteenth century, the "Know-Nothing" movement in the United States found widespread support by railing against the perceived threat that Irish Catholic immigration posed to America's purported Anglo-Saxon and Protestant culture. During the same period, anti-Irish Catholic sentiment was also a widespread and a powerful mobilizing ideology in the United Kingdom.

Ethnic nationalist themes have returned to the political forefront in both countries numerous times since then in relation to new perceived threats, such as postwar migration to Britain from its former colonies, or migration to the US from Latin America. Ethnic nationalism has also been common throughout modern French history. Even after the liberal ideals of the French Revolution had transformed French citizenship, ethnic nationalist notions of who are the "true" French people continued to be widespread, as was made apparent during the infamous Dreyfus affair. Ethnic nationalism has also occurred, and recurred, in Belgium, Spain, the Netherlands, and Italy, among others. Well-documented examples abound throughout the West. In short, ethnic nationalism is a recurring, endemic feature of Western political life. Tracing its evolution over time can help illuminate the linkages between today's ethnic nationalists and their predecessors.

Since we are trying to explain contemporary ethnic nationalism, we also consider seemingly unique attributes of today's politics. One of these is the role of social media in the rise and spread of the new nationalism. As we argue throughout this book, we do not think that social media is a principal driver of the rise and success of ethnic nationalism and populism. Rather, social media is a communications tool: it provides a powerful platform for leaders and parties to broadcast their messages to potential audiences, including ethnic majority groups. Nationalists have long embraced new technologies to spread their message, from the translation of religious texts into vernacular languages, to the advent of the printing press, to the invention of radio and television. As with past iterations, social media provides a new medium to reach massive numbers of people. Like every new medium, it may structure some elements of this communication. It also may facilitate a more direct connection between leaders and supporters, particularly among those whose ideas are not well represented in mainstream venues. But it is an overstatement to attribute the rise of ethnic nationalism and populism to the rise of social media. We need to pay close attention to the *content* of the political communication to understand why it is resonating with people.

These layers of argument rest on a foundation that we need to foreground analysis of nations, nationalism, and national identity to better understand contemporary politics. The puzzling rise of ethnic nationalism in the West is only really puzzling if we see it as an *exception* to the norm. We build an alternative account here, one that highlights how today's ethnic nationalism is built upon long-established ethnic identities in each of our cases. These identities are encapsulated by the ethnic mythologies, symbols, and cultural repertoires at the heart of many nations. In this respect, this book is an argument about the value of an emerging strand of scholarship among those that study nations and nationalism—ethno-symbolism.

Ethno-symbolism is a perspective that highlights how dominant ethnic groups, culture, and history shape the origins and dynamics of nations. It emerged as a middle-ground position in the grand debate on the modernity of nations and nationalism (for an overview, see Smith 1998). Pioneered by Anthony Smith, it has largely been associated with macro-historical narratives on the emergence of nations in the West and beyond (Smith 2009; Hutchinson 2005). As we discuss in the next chapter, this perspective remains somewhat ill-defined despite its considerable explanatory potential. With systematization and further application, ethno-symbolism can provide powerful insights into the continuity and change of ethnic identity in Western nations, including how ethnic nationalism continues to shape politics.

Ethno-symbolism illuminates how dominant ethnic groups institutionalize a set of myths, symbols, and cultural repertoires that define their group as the "true" members of a nation set against outsiders. These ethnic myths and symbols are employed and updated at times of perceived crisis for the majority group, creating logics of appropriateness that propel ethnic nationalist political programs. These ethnic myths and symbols act as a wellspring of ideas about the nature of the political community that leaders can tap into to mobilize people. The historical continuity of this ethnic identity helps explain why today's ethnic nationalism is reverberating with majority groups in the West. Accordingly, an ethno-symbolic lens can help us see how past ethnic myths and symbols put constraints on the content of ethnic nationalist programs today. At the same time, this perspective shows us how these myths and symbols enable the success of ethnic nationalists by providing them with content that has a measure of perceived legitimacy and authenticity as a reflection of the nation's past political culture.

Employing an ethno-symbolic perspective necessitates foregrounding ethnic and national identity in our understanding of the new nationalism. This approach can augment the dominant accounts today that see populism in the West as an exceptional response to shifting structural conditions. By focusing on the role of ethnicity, culture, and history, we can add a thicker layer of analysis to deepen our understanding of the new nationalism.

Situating the Argument: From Focusing on Populism toward Focusing on Nationalism

Our argument builds upon, and seeks to contribute back to, the scholarship that is trying to make sense of the new nationalism. To situate our argument in this literature, it is necessary to discuss how it has treated the relationship between populism and nationalism, as well as the current orthodoxy that attributes the rise of the new nationalism to external, structural drivers like economic inequality.

Most of the work on the new nationalism has focused on the populist bend of today's politics in the West. This is completely understandable. Many new nationalists share a set of characteristics that we associate with populist movements. These characteristics include a political program that venerates the people and vilifies a collection of outsiders from elites to migrants, often pairing these viewpoints with a focus on law and order and an embrace of illiberal positions (Mudde and Rovira Kaltwasser 2017, 5–9; Mudde 2004). The list of the leaders and movements that share these characteristics to varying degrees is considerable: Donald Trump in the US, Nigel Farage and the UK Independence Party and Leave campaigners in the UK, Marine Le Pen in France, Matteo Salvini in Italy, Alternative for Germany, Geert Wilders in the Netherlands, the Austrian Freedom Party, Pauline Hanson in Australia, Viktor Orbán in Hungary, Law and Justice in Poland, Jair Bolsonaro in Brazil, Narendra Modi in India, Recep Tayyip Erdoğan in Turkey, Vladimir Putin in Russia, and Rodrigo Duterte in the Philippines, to name only some of the paradigmatic examples.

Precisely characterizing these leaders and movements is a difficult task, as they combine elements of populism and ethnic nationalism. The rise of these movements and their close cousins has been variously labeled as national populism (Brubaker 2017; Eatwell and Goodwin 2018), populist-nationalism (López-Alves and Johnson 2019), authoritarian populism (Norris and Inglehart 2019), and the populist radical right (Mudde 2016). The constant here is seeing the movements *as instantiations of populism* (Judis 2016; Moffitt 2016; Mudde and Rovira Kaltwasser 2017; Hawkins and Rovira Kaltwasser 2019). The lack of clarity reflects a long-running debate over the definition of populism. But it also reflects some conceptual fuzziness on the relationship between populism and nationalism.

The difficulty in classifying these movements also stems from the chameleonic nature of populism. The ideational turn to understanding populism has shown us it is remarkably malleable (see Hawkins et al. 2019; Hawkins and Littvay 2019). Many scholars have argued that populism's adaptability stems from its nature as a "thin-centered ideology" (Mudde 2004, 543; Abts and Rummens 2007; Stanley 2008). Populism lacks a complete worldview and set of related policy prescriptions, unlike the more classical "thicker" ideologies of liberalism or socialism (Freeden 1996). Accordingly, populism gains much of its substance from its attachment to other ideologies. This is what allows populism to have left and right variants that can shift according to differing political contexts in developed or developing countries (Taggart 2000, 2002). This is also what allows populism to have both "inclusive" (often left-wing) and "exclusive" (often right-wing) iterations (Mudde and Rovira Kaltwasser 2013). The more exclusionary populist movements tend to be built around a restrictive definition of the people and a political program aimed at sociocultural issues, with the goal of protecting the majority (Mudde and Rovira Kaltwasser 2013, 167). In these movements, ethnic nationalism, anti-immigrant sentiments, and xenophobia are often central themes and rallying points that leaders capitalize on (Goodwin and Milazzo 2017).

Despite the contributions of this ideational turn in understanding populism, it can reinforce the conceptual fuzziness of the relationship between populism and nationalism. A measure of conceptual slippage comes from subsuming nationalist ideas *as a feature of* populism. Approaching populism as a thin-set ideology means attributing much of the substance and structure of a populist movement to its attachment with other ideas, like nationalism. This formulation is central to the work on more exclusionary forms of populism. For example, the preoccupation of European populist movements with sociocultural policy dimensions and exclusionary, anti-immigrant programs reflects the grafting of xenophobic, nationalist ideas onto populist platforms (Mudde and Rovira Kaltwasser 2013). A conceptual tension emerges here, though: Freeden's (1996) ideological formulation casts *nationalism* as a thin-set ideology like populism. Nationalism is singled out by Freeden (1998) as one of the ideologies that gains meaning and structure from its context and attachment to other ideas (a view often replicated in the ideational work on populism; see, for example, Mudde and Rovira Kaltwasser 2013, 150). This produces an opaque relationship between populism and nationalism (Halikiopoulou and Vlandas 2019). Does populism gain its depth from nationalism, or does nationalism gain its depth from populism? Is it that nationalism gains meaning through attachment to things like liberalism, socialism, or even—as Freeden has noted—populism (2017, 3). Or is it that populism gains a richer political program from its attachment to ideologies like socialism—and in its exclusionary form, nationalism? In our view, the conceptual fuzziness here comes from a failure to capture the complexity of nationalism, which in turn can obscure its structuring power over populist movements in varying contexts.

In this book we highlight the structuring power of ethnic nationalism. As we lay out in the subsequent chapter, one of the main ways that ethnic nationalism gains its substance and appeal is through a complex set of myths, symbols, and cultural repertoires. These ideas define the core parameters of dominant ethnic groups—their history, membership, goals, aspirations, and unique characteristics. These ideas are institutionalized and carried through time, often emerging to shape politics during periods of perceived crisis. In this respect, ethnic nationalism is not so much a thin-set ideology as a complex set of ideas about the nature and direction of a political community, which can move from the background to the foreground of political life quickly and with remarkable force. When these ideas are combined with populism, they have proven to be especially good at mobilizing people.

This viewpoint begs consideration of the role that ethnic nationalism—understood as a thicker, richer set of ideas about the nature and direction of a political community—plays in shaping the new nationalism across the West. In our view, we can augment existing accounts of the new nationalism by focusing on the role of ethnic nationalism. This does not mean we are ignoring populism. Rather, we are seeking to foreground nations, nationalism, and national identity in our analysis. We are avoiding an approach that subsumes nationalist ideas as a secondary set of ideas under the rubric of populism. This focus on nationalism better reflects the conceptual core of the new nationalism as, first and foremost, an expression of ethnic nationalism. In short, we think that focusing on ethnic nationalism can help us understand the content of the new nationalism, and why it is reverberating with dominant ethnic majorities in our three cases.

In addition to helping clarify the conceptual relationship between populism and nationalism, our approach can also contribute to the empirical scholarship concerned with the drivers and success of the new nationalism. Empirical work on the new nationalism examines how the "supply" and "demand" of populist ideas is shaped by shifting conditions. Much of this work follows a familiar pattern of treating the puzzling rise of populism as an exception to the norm of liberal politics in the West. The shared logic here is that eroding socioeconomic structures are driving affected populations to seek solace in ethnic nationalism, which is seen as a break from normal political patterns. The commonly cited exogenous factors stimulating this process are rising economic inequality, disillusionment with political elites and institutions, and high levels of immigration (Ivarsflaten 2008). There has traditionally been a split among those that privilege the economy (Judis 2016; Halikiopoulou and Vlandas 2019), shifts in political culture (Inglehart and Norris 2016), or immigration (Ivarsflaten 2008; Goodwin and Milazzo 2017) as the principal driver. However, a consensus is emerging that difficult economic conditions are combining with a backlash to liberal policies to propel support for today's exceptional ethnic nationalism (Norris and Inglehart 2019; Halikiopoulou and Vlandas 2019). Numerous qualitative studies, particularly in the US and the UK, have detailed a pervasive sense of disaffection and grievance among those who have been affected by the loss of low-skilled manufacturing jobs—the "white working class," or the "left behind," as they are often labeled (Hochschild 2016; Calhoun 2017; Wuthnow 2018).

Joining the insights on shifting socioeconomic conditions is the research on communication technology and social media. Studies have shown how developments in the technology and practice of mass media and communication have saturated citizens with increasingly polarized media content, thereby creating new opportunity structures for leaders to exploit (Mazzoleni 2014).

With the advent of social media, supporters of right-wing populism can increasingly find like-minded communities and participate in them with relative anonymity (Gerbaudo 2014; Groshek and Koc-Michalska 2017). By the same token, leaders can use social media to spread their messages unfiltered by conventional media platforms (Engesser et al. 2017). The common point stemming from this work on social media—which has gained traction in academic and popular consciousness—is that there is an elective affinity between the rise of social media and the rise of nationalism and populism (Gerbaudo 2018; Waisbord 2018).

These important lines of scholarship point toward the broader structural shifts that make populations more disposed to support ethnic nationalism. However, these findings do not tell us everything about why these populations are specifically drawn to *ethnic* nationalism rather than another ideology. Why not embrace, for example, socialism, which is arguably a more direct response to socioeconomic dislocation? Why do *particular* ethnic nationalists and populists succeed over others? If social media is a driver of populism, how do we account for the fact that not all of the most successful new nationalists use it in the same way (Moffitt 2018)? The common issue here is that structuralist explanations are largely "contentless" (Abromeit 2017; Halikiopoulou, Mock, and Vasilopoulou 2013, 111). They highlight proximate causes. They pay too little attention to how ethnic nationalists craft their messages and programs, and why this content reverberates with particular constituencies. As Bart Bonikowski (2017) has argued persuasively, we need to pay more attention to why particular nationalist ideas are "resonating" when trying to explain the success of today's movements. To do this, we need to consider the cultural dimensions and patterns of both political leaders and national communities (Bonikowski and DiMaggio 2016; Bonikowski and Gidron 2016).

Scholars investigating the discursive strategies of nationalist and populist political entrepreneurs have more to say about these cultural patterns and specific ideological content. This work has highlighted the importance of performance and political style in the success of today's populists (Moffitt 2016). A core part of this analysis points to the seeming universality of moral binaries in the political communication of leaders that venerate "us" and vilify "them" (Moffitt 2016; Moffitt and Tormey 2014; Jagers and Walgrave 2007; Wodak 2015). However, the findings of this work only go partway to explaining "resonance." In this regard, the explanations on this front tend to be quite "thin." While they shed light on broadly comparable elements of discourse across different movements, they say less about how this discourse can differ across space and time. In other words, these findings downplay the "thick" content of discourse. By layering on a consideration of the origins and evolution of cultural content, and situating the cultural content in this changing context, we can better understand and compare today's ethnic nationalism. Uncovering this "thicker" content can help us understand both the "supply" and "demand" side of the equation—how and why particular ethnic themes are employed and why certain populations are mobilized by this particular ethnic nationalist discourse. Addressing these questions requires a deeper investigation of the historically, and spatially, situated elements of nationalist discourse than we often see today.

Taken together, the structuralist and discursive approaches characterize the new nationalism in the West as arising in an exceptional moment of socioeconomic crisis, which strategic political entrepreneurs have capitalized upon by making ethnic nationalist and populist appeals to the affected population. Our broader criticism of this characterization of the new nationalism is that it is based on an underlying view that this phenomenon is a kind of aberration from "normal" politics. The implication is that if a socioeconomic crisis did not occur, and if we did not have self-interested political entrepreneurs, then we would not have ethnic nationalism. But the fact that ethnic nationalism is pervasive and recurring throughout the West casts some doubt on this view as a sufficient explanation. What is needed therefore is an approach that also takes seriously the "thick" cultural content of ethnic nationalism, by locating it within its spatial and historical context. Such an approach does not run counter to or dispute the main thrust of the dominant tide of work on populism; rather, it seeks to augment and contribute to these accounts by taking the content of what ethnic nationalists and populists are saying seriously and unpacking the foundations and evolution of these ideas. A shift in perspective that sees ethnic nationalism in the West as a deeply embedded social fact, not as an aberration, can help us understand important elements of the new nationalism. Ethno-symbolism provides a useful lens to carry out this type of analysis. Applying it to the leading cases of ethnic nationalism and populism in the West helps show how leaders and parties are tapping into long-established ethnic myths and symbols that both structure their communication and help explain why they are reverberating with majority groups. In short, our perspective helps to uncover the deep roots of the new nationalism.

Structure of the Argument

The remainder of this book is structured to highlight the role of ethnicity, culture, and history in shaping the new nationalism in the West. The logic behind this structure is to illuminate the political and social dynamics at play in the US, UK, and France, but also to demonstrate the promise of ethno-symbolism.

In the next chapter we elaborate upon our theoretical framework. The goal of chapter 2 is to introduce and systematize ethno-symbolism as an explanatory framework that can be applied to the new nationalism. Part of this systematization is clearly explaining how we understand core attributes of nationalism, notably its civic and ethnic variants. But our principal aim is laying out how the core foci of ethno-symbolism—namely the role of ethnicity, culture, and history—can help to augment existing accounts of political dynamics today.

In chapter 3 we build on these theoretical foundations to outline how we will examine the impact of ethnicity, culture, and history in the digital age. We construct a novel analytical tool that applies the ethno-symbolic framework to trace the role of ethnicity and culture in the dynamics of nations and nationalism. This schema can be used to map core ethnic myths and symbols over time: it codifies the establishment, crystallization, and change in a myth-symbol complex across five key categories associated with an ethnic conception of group identity (people, homeland, history, religion, and ethos). This schema can also be used for comparative analysis between cases, as we do in this book. We also discuss how we apply this schema to analyze the social media campaigns of Donald Trump, Marine Le Pen, and the Brexit campaigners. In doing so, we argue that we need to pay greater attention to the message, rather than the medium, when thinking about social media as a driver of the new nationalism.

In chapter 4 we apply our schema to uncover the roots of American ethnic nationalism. The chapter starts by considering the conventional understanding of America as a beacon of civic nationalism, against which a growing body of literature argues that American political culture has long been marked by a competing, ethnic stream of identity. Drawing on a wide range of historical literature, the chapter examines how foundational ethnic myths and symbols were established in the eighteenth and nineteenth centuries. Following this, we trace the development of ethnic nationalism as a persistent undercurrent of American politics in the twentieth and twenty-first centuries. This analysis makes a case for why it is important to pay close attention to the history of ethnic nationalism in America to understand how it is manifesting itself today.

In the next chapter we turn to the contemporary period to examine how Donald Trump tapped into, and reshaped, this long-running ethnic stream of American politics. We show that ethnic nationalism was the central feature of Trump's political strategy. In making this case, we highlight how the white majority was the core of his support base, while also showing how his political program was built upon a moral dichotomy that valorized this group and vilified outsiders. To provide a systematic account of Trump's ethnic nationalism, we present a comprehensive analysis of each of his over 5,000 tweets during the 2016 presidential primaries and campaign. From this analysis, we argue against the prevailing view that sees Trump as an exception. We do not think it is puzzling he won in 2016, that he stayed relatively popular during his presidency despite constantly courting controversy, or that he had a strong showing in 2020.

In our view, Trump's rise was not something that happened despite his ethnic nationalism—it was the key to his success.

The sixth and seventh chapters compare Trump's ethnic nationalism with similar cases in the West. The goal of this comparison is to better understand the particularities of these movements and what is driving their success. These chapters largely replicate our approach for the US. In the sixth chapter we focus on the use of long-standing ethnic conceptions of French identity in the social media campaign of Marine Le Pen's 2017 presidential run. We show that, like Trump, Le Pen's political program taps into a long-standing undercurrent of ethnic nationalism in France.

In the seventh chapter we examine the ethnic roots of English nationalism and trace how the Leave campaigners in the 2016 Brexit referendum tapped into these myths and symbols. Here we argue that to understand Brexit we need to account for the centrality of an ethnic English nationalism in the leave campaign. Together, these two chapters help to show how ethnic nationalists are using similar approaches and mediums (tapping into well-established cultural repertoires and communicating their programs through social media), but that the precise content of their messages have important differences (based upon their unique set of ethnic myths and symbols). We argue it is this combination of techniques and unique content that allows ethnic nationalism to resonate as legitimate with dominant ethnic majorities. As much as the new nationalism is a global-level phenomenon, it is also necessarily local.

We conclude the book by reflecting on our temporal and cross-case comparisons. Our analysis shows the remarkable persistence of ethnic identity over time—something that is constant across the US, UK, and France. While not an unchanging and immovable force, the resiliency of a foundational set of ethnic myths and symbols clearly has a significant impact on contemporary politics. Our analysis also shows that there is considerable similarity in the discursive process of ethnic nationalists across the West. At the same time, the cultural content varies across contexts: content matters a great deal in mobilizing ethnic majorities. The persistence and resiliency of ethnic nationalism across our cases leads us toward the conclusion that the new nationalism is not new, and that we are not necessarily at the end of this period in our politics.

2

Making Sense of Ethnic Nationalism in the West

Nationalism is a notoriously difficult concept to parse. In this chapter, we outline our understanding of the concept. In doing so, we discuss the distinctions between ethnic and civic nationalism, and between hot and banal nationalism. Following this, we outline our theoretical framework for understanding ethnic nationalism in the West. Our framework builds on ethno-symbolism, which focuses on the ethno-cultural dimensions of nationalism. Ethno-symbolism has taken shape through comparative-historical research on a wide variety of cases throughout the globe. Here we draw together insights from this work and apply them to the Western context. As its leading pioneer, Anthony Smith (2009, 1), acknowledges, ethno-symbolism is best seen as an approach rather than an explanatory or causal theory. One of our objectives in this book is to refine ethno-symbolism so that it is more amenable to testing and refinement. Accordingly, in this chapter and the next, we seek to systematize its key insights and integrate a new schema that enables fine-grained, comparative tracing of ethno-cultural processes across time and space.

A more general aim of this chapter is to introduce ethno-symbolism to a broader audience. Although it has a firm footing in nationalism research, ethno-symbolism is less well known outside this field. With the resurgence of nationalism across the globe, many scholars from diverse areas are turning their gaze back to this phenomenon. We think it is important at this moment to highlight the value of ethno-symbolism in explaining the deep roots of today's ethnic nationalism. In line with this objective, we start the chapter with a brief overview of some of the key concepts related to nationalism, particularly its civic and ethnic variants. We then turn to providing a systematic account of the ethno-symbolic framework, focusing on the importance of dominant ethnicity, culture, and history in understanding the dynamics of ethnic nationalism.

Understanding Nationalism

Nationalism is difficult to understand, in part, because it is so prevalent. Nationalism is the preeminent source of legitimacy in the global system of nation-states, and it is central to how many people understand their identities. Nationalism is so pervasive that one leading scholar has likened it to the air we breathe (Bieber 2018, 519). Like the air, nationalism can be difficult to perceive. In the West, nationalism is so dominant that it does not even compete with other political ideologies. Instead, it provides the framework within which "normal" politics occurs. For example, we can be so focused on the disagreements between "progressives" and "conservatives" that it is easy to forget that both sides tend to accept they are members of the same nation, and that on this front there is much agreement between them. Most importantly, both ideological positions have largely reconciled with the main tenet of nationalism—that the "nation" should be the primary focus of our political concerns, above all else. When politicians from either side of the political divide put forward policies, they inevitably embed them within a nationalist framework. Ultimately, what is at stake in modern politics is the *nation*—where it came from, what it is today, and what it could be.

Nationalism's dominance in world politics today is all the more remarkable when we consider that it is a relatively recent phenomenon. Most scholars agree that nationalism is a modern ideology, originating in Europe in earnest in the nineteenth century (although the precise timing and the degree to which nationalism builds on premodern ideas and culture are key topics of debate, as we discuss). The idea that a type of political community called a "nation" should command our allegiance above all else is a fundamentally modern idea. This exaltation of nations was unknown in premodern Europe, when allegiances were defined by one's affiliations to their rulers and to their religion. Moreover, the very idea of a nation as a community whose bonds transcend the social status of its members would have been anathema to premodern Europeans, who generally believed that the rulers and the ruled were fundamentally different categories of human (Greenfeld 2019, 7–9).

What, then, is nationalism? Smith supplies a leading definition: "an ideological movement for attaining and maintaining autonomy, unity and identity for a population which some of its members deem to constitute an actual or potential 'nation'" (Smith 2010, 9). This definition is distinct for several reasons. First, it suggests that nationalism is more than a diffuse form of collective "consciousness" or "sentiment." For Smith, nationalism is an action-oriented ideology that is linked to a clear set of goals. Second, among these goals, Smith focuses on autonomy for the nation, rather than full statehood. This acknowledges that there have been numerous national movements that are satisfied with relative autonomy within an existing state, rather than pushing for outright independence. Third, Smith's definition suggests that nationalism does not necessarily lose its motivation after its goals have been attained. Instead, this definition helps us see that there are often recurring efforts aimed at maintaining the goals of nationalism. This is an important point when examining nationalism among the white majorities of the West: while these populations have largely attained the main goals of nationalism, they have nevertheless been recurrently convulsed by nationalist movements aimed at ensuring those goals are maintained.

More generally, it is also notable that the three goals of nationalism that Smith lists in his definition—autonomy, unity, identity—encompass both the political *and* cultural spheres. This runs counter to much of the research on nationalism, which tends to focus on its political aims to achieve political and territorial autonomy for the nation (see Breuilly 1993; Gellner 1983; Giddens 1986; Tilly 1994). By including the goals of "unity" and "identity," Smith suggests that nationalism is not only a political project; it is also cultural project. This sheds light on the nationalist activities of cultural actors, such as intellectuals or artists, who seek to cultivate the nation as a distinct community. It also enables analysis of how the political and cultural goals of nationalism are often intertwined and mutually reinforcing. Political nationalists cannot help but become involved in cultural nationalism—when they represent the nation in their demands for autonomy, they are implicitly contributing to the cultivation of its identity. Similarly, when poets and writers extol the virtues of some aspect of the nation's identity, they are also implicitly supplying a rationale for defending its autonomy (see Hutchinson 1987; Woods 2015).

Smith's work is especially concerned with the cultural dimensions of nationalism. Surveying the myriad rites, ceremonies, sounds, and iconography that accompany nationalism, and the reverence with which nationalists treat certain myths and symbols, Smith sees in nationalism a pattern of meanings that is strongly redolent of a religion, in which the nation represents the sacred rather than a supernatural god or gods. All of this suggests that nationalism is more than merely a political ideology. Rather, it can be seen as a kind of political religion, which builds on, and borrows from, much older forms of community and worship. This understanding of nationalism informs the ethno-symbolist argument for why nationalism can elicit such strong emotions among its supporters, and why it has proved to be so enduring. Nationalism, in this reading, is so powerful because of its capacity to provide meaning in our ostensibly secular age (Smith 2010, 36–39; 2003).

The power of nationalism is most obvious when it runs "hot." "Hot nationalism" describes a context when nationalism is at the very center of the political arena as a self-conscious ideological movement. It usually emerges in periods of great social ferment, with ordinary people, community activists, journalists, intellectuals, religious leaders, politicians, and many others coalescing in defense of the nation. A "politics of the street" is common during hot nationalism, with mass marches and demonstrations. During this time, media and culture are also suffused with nationalist imagery, myths, and symbols. The French Revolution of 1789, as depicted in Eugene Delacroix's famous painting, *Liberty Leading the People*, provides an excellent illustration of hot nationalism that captures how nationalism can take on the characteristics of a mass social movement, with an attendant efflorescence of emotions (see Hutchinson 2005, chap. 4). In this respect, hot nationalism can take on the characteristics of what Émile Durkheim referred to as "collective effervescence" by generating intense feelings of solidarity (2001, 162).

But nationalism is not only expressed during extraordinary periods. It also manifests itself in our everyday routines and practices. Michael Billig's (1995) work on "banal" nationalism has shown us how it is endemic to Western life—how it can be so widely diffused throughout a population that it is no longer a self-conscious political concern. In this context, nationalism is generally a taken-for-granted, background feature of our lives. Billig and a host of others have shown how this type of nationalism is reproduced via a myriad of banal routines and texts, rather than taken up as a self-conscious ideological movement (see Fox and Miller-Idriss 2008; Knott 2015; Skey and Antonsich 2017; Edensor 2002; Nieguth 2020). Among many examples of banal nationalism, Billig rather poetically mentions the "unwaved" national flag that stands outside of public buildings. Rather than a vector of nationalistic fervor, passers-by mostly ignore the flag.

This distinction between "hot" and "banal" nationalism is central to our understanding of how it develops through time. While Billig (1995, 43–51) argues that the original hot nationalism of revolutionary periods cools over time and fades into the background, more recent work has challenged this linear understanding to show that hot nationalism can be episodic and recurrent (Hutchinson 2005; Jones and Merriman 2009). Recurring phases of hot nationalism are generally triggered by some phenomenon being perceived as an existential threat to the nation, such as war, terrorism, famine, mass migration, economic hardship, or pandemics. These phases of hot nationalism are, by definition, periods of upheaval and uncertainty: they are periods when cultural understandings of who "we" are become unhinged and take on a degree of "liminality," in the language of cultural sociology and anthropology (Turner 1986). For this reason, periods of hot nationalism have a potential to trigger new forms of national identification (Hutchinson 2005, chap. 4). Once the perception of a threat has faded, and a period of banal nationalism slowly returns, this new national identity will be institutionalized and largely recede as a conscious political concern—until, that is, the next perceived crisis triggers a new phase of hot nationalism. Thus, the historical development of nationalism can be seen as an oscillation between hot and banal nationalism.

We want to emphasize that there are no *objective* criteria for what gets perceived as a threat during a phase of hot nationalism. What is important is that something is *perceived* as a threat. For example, in this book we are mainly concerned with a variant of hot ethnic nationalism in the West that is directed toward migrant communities. It would be difficult to make the case that migration has objectively posed an existential threat to any of the national states of the West, even at its peak in nineteenth-century America. Nevertheless, there have been recurring phases of hot nationalism in the West, in which nationalists have capitalized on the *perception* that migrants pose an existential threat (for a discussion of threat perception by majority groups, see Orgad 2015). In this regard, the phenomenon of hot nationalism shares much with the concept of a moral panic, which occurs when there is a widespread perception that some group or phenomenon is threatening the moral standards of a community (Cohen 1972).

The role of threat perception also draws our attention to the relational nature of nationalism. We follow the seminal work of Fredrik Barth (1969) that shows how ethnic identities are constructed through a relational process with other ethnic groups. Nationalism is an inherently inward-looking ideology: in large part it rests on identifying and defending the unique characteristics that constitute its nation's identity. But nationalism is also inherently outward-looking. A nation's identity, like all identities, is built through contrast. The nation's identity markers emerge through comparisons with other groups, often presenting the other in a negative light (Armstrong 1982; Barth 1969). From this contrast, powerful cultural boundary markers can form that distinguish "us" from "them." Much of this book is about exploring how today's nationalists are structured by and use historically rooted notions of "us" and "them." As we explain in the next section of this chapter, an ethno-symbolist perspective helps us understand how these ideas about "us" and "them" form and shape our politics. But before we get to this, it is important to discuss one of the principal ways that people understand national identity and differentiate their community from others—as either civic or ethnic.

Civic and Ethnic Nationalism

Since we are mainly concerned with a rise of ethnic nationalism in the West, it is necessary to elaborate on this concept and the well-known distinction between civic and ethnic nationalism. The civic-ethnic dichotomy is an oft-repeated idea. It has had many labels. Smith prefers the terms "territorial-ethnic" or, more broadly, "voluntarist-organic," to refer to these two kinds of nationalism (2010, 38–46). Liah Greenfeld (1992) refers to "individualist" and "collectivist" forms of nationalism. Walker Connor (1994) distinguishes "patriotism" from "ethnonationalism." Hans Kohn (1944) provided the most influential, and debated, formulation. Kohn associated the dichotomy with different territorial populations in Europe, contrasting "Western" and "Eastern" forms of nationalism to refer to the ostensibly different ways the ideology had been taken up on either side of the Rhine River. Despite the variation in names, the fundamental meaning of the civic-ethnic dichotomy has broadly remained constant.

Civic nationalism conceives of the nation as a "voluntarist" community united through adherence to the liberal principles of individual liberty and equality. The origins of civic nationalism can be traced to early modern England (although some historians argue that it occurred first in the Netherlands; see Gorski 2000), which then sees its full expression at the end of the eighteenth century in the revolutionary ideals and constitutions of France and America. An ideology that is simultaneously individualist and collectivist might seem contradictory. However, the way in which civic nationalism arose in England made these ideas inseparable. The "War of the Roses" (1455–1488) precipitated the erosion of a long-held view that the rulers and the ruled constituted different categories of human (Greenfeld 1992, chap. 2). At the war's end, a new aristocracy was ascendant, many of whom had been born into the lower classes. As a result, this newly minted elite was especially amenable to the idea that all propertied men were fundamentally equal (women were generally not yet included in this liberal formulation, nor were people of color). In this context, a conception of English nationality emerged that was premised on a belief in the fundamental liberty and equality of its individual members, irrespective of their social status. Moreover, the intertwining of liberalism with nationalism ensured that a sense of cosmopolitan solidarity with other individuals outside of England did not occur. Instead, liberty was attributed to a special quality of Englishness—to be English was to be "free" (Greenfeld 1992, chap. 2). As we discuss in chapter 7, a similar process took place in the archetypal civic nation of France, where liberal, republican values were grounded in being French citizens and members of the French nation (Brubaker 1992; Bell 2001).

One of the most influential accounts of civic nationalism is from a Frenchman, Ernest Renan, who depicted the nation as a "daily plebiscite," in which its individual members voluntarily choose to belong (Renan 1882). This illustrates the view that, in theory, civic nationalism is open to all, and does not discriminate on the basis of one's cultural background. For this reason, civic nationalism has tended to be seen as an inclusive ideology and, generally, as a positive force in politics. For some, civic nationalism is not even nationalism. As noted earlier, scholars such as Walker Connor prefer the term "patriotism," arguing that it stresses allegiance to the state, rather than the nation. And it is commonplace for many people in everyday life to proudly declare themselves to be patriots, while distancing themselves from the ostensibly less virtuous label of nationalist. We try to avoid such normatively loaded and fuzzy language. Civic nationalism, in practice, is not entirely virtuous. Most national communities are dominated by certain powerful ethnic groups, irrespective of their claims as voluntary associations. Outsiders might be able to join the community, but to do so, they must relegate their culture to the private sphere and conform to the dominant public culture (Smith 2003). More generally, civic nationalism does not seek to create a cosmopolitan ethic; it is a nationalist ideology that prioritizes the national "us" over the foreign "them."

Ethnic nationalism shares with civic nationalism a view of the nation as a "horizontal" community that transcends the social status of its members. However, in its ideal type it rejects civic nationalism's emphasis on liberalism as the basis of solidarity. Ethnic nationalism defines the nation primarily in terms of a perceived common ethnic heritage and culture that developed organically over many generations ("since time immemorial") in its territorial homeland. The intellectual origins of ethnic nationalism can be traced most clearly to eighteenth-century German "proto-Romantic" idealist intellectuals, such as Johann Gottfried Herder and Johann Fichte, who argued that each nation was endowed a unique moral character, or spirit, and that for individuals to properly flourish they needed to unify with that spirit (see Beiner 2018). German Romanticism notably took shape in the shadow of a powerful and expansive French nation-state. With liberalism associated with the French, the Romantics went in search of an alternative basis for unifying Germans. To do so, they looked inward, toward German language and folk practices. Within these forms of culture, the Romantics found a purported authentic German spirit. This spirit was depicted as sentimental, primordial, and inherently solidary. On these grounds, it was held to be superior to the ostensible alienating rationality of (French) liberalism. The Romantics therefore implored Germans to rediscover their "authentic" language and culture, while deploring their tendency to use the French language and "imitate" French culture. In doing so, they sought to elevate the status of German culture from its demotic origins to become equal to French culture (Greenfeld 1992, chap. 4; Jusdanis 2001, chap. 3).

As these ideas coalesced into the ideology of ethnic nationalism, and spread outward to other social contexts, the pattern of disapproving foreign influences while urging populations to "rediscover" their perceived authentic local cultures has remained central. This has spurred an enduring demand for professions linked to the discovery and cultivation of an "authentic" national heritage, such as history, philology, and archaeology. It has also made ethnic nationalism a remarkably powerful ideology among "stateless" populations who aspire to political autonomy, such as colonized peoples and ethnic minorities within states. It has also resonated among populations that already have political autonomy. Indeed, as we show in subsequent chapters, elements of this ethnic nationalism have been grafted on to today's populist politics, whereby leaders claim to be the "true" authentic voice of the nation, fighting against foreign influences and their elite allies. As we discussed in chapter 1, this merging of populist and ethnic nationalist ideas has become a defining feature of the new nationalism.

Ethnic nationalism tends to be seen as an exclusive ideology because of its idealization of a nation's perceived ethno-cultural inheritance. Although this strategy can provide a powerful source of solidarity among those who are seen to share that heritage, it excludes those who do not. While it is certainly possible for an outsider to apprehend another community's culture, in the view of an ethnic nationalist, if they were not born and raised within that community, they will never truly belong. To understand why this is the case, we need to return to the Romantic roots of ethnic nationalism, which linked cultural practices with the "innate" spirit of the nation. For an ethnic nationalist, an individual needs to be born into that national community to be able to embody its spirit. Thus, it is not surprising that Fichte once wrote of the risk that Jews posed to the Germans (Abizadeh 2005). Nor is it surprising that, a century later, the Nazi Party found in Fichte a suitable basis for its political ideology.

This exclusivist view has ensured that ethnic nationalism is often intertwined with outright racism. Race and perceived physical differences have continually been powerful symbolic border guards for ethnic nationalists. As Sivamohan Valluvan (2019) and others have shown, a deep hostility and aversion to racialized groups is pervasive in the nationalist ideas of the West. As we trace in this book, this hostility and division has tended to manifest most clearly as a distinction between whiteness and other groups based on perceived physical traits. As we discuss later in this chapter and in the book, we focus on how these racist ideas are integrated into a broader ethnic nationalism.

While ethnic nationalism provides a logic to excludes outsiders, it often also makes common cause with other ethnic nationalisms. This is because ethnic nationalism at its core reflects a pluralist view of humanity, which is believed to be composed of a finite number of unique nations, each of which is worthy of cultivation and autonomy on the basis of that uniqueness (Jusdanis 2001, chap. 3). The symbolic power of ethnic nationalism partly derives from this pluralist worldview. Ethnic nationalists claim that "we" as a nation are worth defending, because "we" are the bearers of a unique culture in this world. The ideal world for an ethnic nationalist is one in which each nation can pursue its own modes of social, economic, and political life within its territorial homeland, free from external influence.

At first blush, the ethnic nationalist worldview might seem to present a rather benign vision for world peace. However, it contains serious problems—so much so that since its emergence, ethnic nationalism has been at the heart of many of the world's most intractable and violent disputes. The ideology creates a powerful motivation for communities to claim nationhood. Following the logic of ethnic nationalism, if a community is not perceived to constitute a nation, then it does not have a legitimate basis for autonomy. This logic risks setting off conflict among rival groups vying for territorial and political autonomy on the basis of the presumed authenticity of their claims to nationhood. This problem is compounded by the fact that many of the world's states are a legacy of imperial calculations that had little regard for the diversity of the populations that they contained within their territorial borders. The spread of ethnic nationalism throughout the world has therefore resulted in a recurring pattern of conflict, as communities contest one another for primacy over their perceived historic homeland. In Europe, the emergence of ethnic nationalism has resulted in centuries of recurring war, persecution of minorities, population exchanges, and ever smaller states—as each presumed nation takes up the baton and seeks autonomy. Many observers suggest that this "sorting" of populations is at the heart of much of the civil strife now occurring in the rest of the world. Taken to its most extreme, ethnic nationalism provides the logic for genocide: in order for the nation to properly unify with its authentic spirit and flourish, perceived malign outsiders need to be exiled or eliminated from its homeland (on nationalism and violence, see Hechter 1995; Wimmer 2012; on the logic of nationalism and the problematization of ethnic pluralism, see Schertzer and Woods 2011; Schertzer 2016, chap. 1).

The dichotomy between civic and ethnic nationalism that we have described here has been increasingly criticized. Many scholars have challenged the association of either civic or ethnic nationalism with different territorial populations (i.e., "West" and "East") (Kuzio 2002; Shulman 2002). Other critics have attacked the dichotomy on theoretical grounds, arguing that the distinctions between civic and ethnic nationalism collapse upon close examination given the exclusive nature of both forms of identity (Yack 1996). Anthony Smith has also criticized the dichotomy, observing that most nationalisms are actually a composite of civic and ethnic conceptions of the nation (Smith 2010, 42–46). As a result of all this criticism, several leading scholars, including Rogers Brubaker (1999), have called for the dichotomy to be discarded.

And yet, despite these misgivings, the dichotomy retains value and is widely used in some form by many scholars. In our view, this is because there is a "kernel of truth" in the civic-ethnic dichotomy (Smith 2010, 43). Indeed, some of the more recent and innovative work on the framework turns away from a deterministic view of nations as "ethnic" or "civic," to show how nationalists use symbolic resources to frame their nations in more civic or ethnic terms at different points in time and in response to different types of threats (Zimmer 2003; Hutchinson 2005). Despite all the criticisms levied at the dichotomy, we take the position that it nevertheless continues to have use as an analytic framework, particularly for examining national conflicts that occur *within* nations. As we demonstrate in this book, these internal conflicts, or "cultural wars," as they are now often labeled, display characteristics that suggest an important axis of conflict turns on the question of whether the nation should be conceived along civic or ethnic lines—over whether it should be defined by a commitment to liberal principles or by the culture of the dominant group.

But how can we reconcile criticisms that pure forms of civic and ethnic nationalism do not exist in reality with the fact that these ideas continue to shape politics? Here we take up Geneviève Zubrzycki's (2001, 2002) call for the dichotomy to be employed as a social scientific "ideal type." As described by Max Weber in his original formulation of the concept, an ideal type is constructed through careful observation of multiple manifestations of a social phenomenon. This enables identification of the phenomenon's core characteristics to reconstruct an idealized version. The "ideal" version can then be used by researchers to identify further manifestations of that phenomenon, and to comparatively analyze variations by observing the degree to which they conform to the ideal type. In other words, an ideal type is an interpretative, or "heuristic," device. Like a frame around a painting, it enables researchers to isolate and "see" a social phenomenon, so that it can be analyzed and compared. Therefore, when we employ the civic-ethnic dichotomy in this book, it is to help us identify manifestations of civic and ethnic nationalism (particularly the latter), so that we can analyze how these phenomena differ in time and space. Furthermore, we broadly conceive of the civic-ethnic dichotomy as a continuum, with the ideal versions of "civic" and "ethnic" nationalism at either end. In this way, a given nationalism can therefore be analyzed on the degree to which it sits closer to the ethnic ideal or the civic ideal.

As we show in our analyses in subsequent chapters of ethnic nationalism in the three archetypal civic nations of the United States, England, and France, the lines between civic and ethnic identity within groups can be fuzzy. This fuzziness is evident in the emerging trend whereby ethnic nationalists are adopting, or co-opting, ideas and language traditionally associated with civic nationalism. This practice has been particularly apparent in how European states have adopted strong immigrant integration policies designed to preserve "Western civilization" from perceived illiberal threats—a form of illiberal liberalism (Triadafilopoulos 2011). Similarly, far-right parties and actors have increasingly adopted liberal political discourse as part of a "civic zeitgeist" to present themselves as the defenders of the Western values of their nation (Halikiopoulou,

Mock, and Vasilopoulou 2013). This blurring of lines between the forms of identity—the strategic use of civic discourse to promote exclusive ethnic nationalist ends—speaks to the fluidity of the concepts and the challenges of using the analytical framework. However, as we show in this book, this emerging tendency can also signal to us that those nations we tend to see as leading liberal, civic communities may also have deeper ethnic roots.

Ethno-Symbolism: Dominant Ethnicity, Culture, and History

Ethno-symbolism was developed in response to an ongoing debate on the origins of nationalism. On the one hand, "modernists," whose position is by far the dominant one, argue that nationalism is a wholly modern phenomenon, which arose in the eighteenth century as a result of a constellation of sociostructural changes associated with modernity, such as industrialization, secularization, state formation, and innovations in communication technology (Anderson 2006; Breuilly 1993; Deutsch 1966; Giddens 1986; Gellner 1983). Several "modernists" also focus on the instrumental behaviors of elites, who are depicted as capitalizing on these social changes to "invent" nationalist ideologies to legitimate their power and status (Brass 1991; Brubaker et al. 2006; Hobsbawm and Ranger 1983; Hobsbawm 1990).

The modernist position is critiqued by a smaller but diverse group of "perennialist" scholars who think nationalism has a longer history. Several scholars in this camp argue that nationalism emerged in sixteenth-century England and The Netherlands following the Protestant Reformation (Gorski 2000; Greenfeld 1992; Hastings 1997). Other critics of modernism push the history of nationalism back even further, with some scholars finding ideas resembling nationalism in medieval Europe (Reynolds 1997) and even in Middle Eastern antiquity (Gat 2012; Grosby 2002; Roshwald 2006). This latter position, in turn, veers close to a "primordialist" approach, which suggests that nationalism is, at its core, an expression of a universal human tendency to associate "like with like" (Geertz 1973; van den Berghe 1981).

Ethno-symbolists seek a middle ground between modernism and perennialism. They acknowledge the modernity of nationalism, but nevertheless assert that it cannot simply have been invented *ex nihilo*. Here ethno-symbolists point to the ethno-cultural legacy imparted by powerful, premodern ethnic communities. Through historical research on a wide variety of cases, ethno-symbolists have found that the core myths, symbols, and traditions of many modern nationalisms are derived from dominant ethnic communities. Further, for ethno-symbolists, the persistence of this ethno-cultural content helps explain why nationalism can command such widespread and enduring loyalty. By referring to this long-established ethno-cultural content, nationalist leaders are able to position their messaging as legitimate to help it resonate with people. Here ethno-symbolists take particular issue with the argument that nationalist ideas can simply be "invented" and imposed by elites (see Hobsbawm and Ranger 1983; Gellner 1996).

Thus, we can discern three key related elements to an ethno-symbolist understanding of nationalism: dominant ethnicity, culture, and history. We elaborate on these elements and their significance for our research below as part of our effort to systematize and refine the ethno-symbolic framework.

Dominant Ethnicity

The ethno-symbolist approach to ethnicity is broader than how this concept is conventionally understood in Anglo-American scholarship. In this work, ethnicity tends to be narrowly associated with minority communities arising from migration. However, according to ethno-symbolists, ethnicity can also refer to the communities that dominate nations (Kaufmann 2004a; Kaufmann and Haklai 2008; Lecours and Nootens 2009). These communities are referred to as "core," or "dominant," ethnic communities. We favor the latter term, to foreground the political nature of these groups, but all these labels get to the same point. The concept of dominant ethnicity is also closely related to the concept of *Staatsvolk* (O'Leary 2001, 285). However, *staatsvolk* refers to any dominant group within a national state, which could be an ethnic or national community. Dominant ethnicity, as its name makes clear, refers specifically to dominant *ethnic* communities.

The concept of dominant ethnicity is a powerful tool for unpacking the cultural "black box" of the so-called white majorities of the West. Sociologists have conventionally tended to treat these communities as post-ethnic, loose groupings of individuals with little sense of shared culture—as exemplified by the long-held convention in ethnic studies to refer to them as seemingly neutral "host societies" (Doane 2003, 3–7). The emergence of "whiteness studies" in recent decades has helped to correct this approach by demonstrating how the white majorities behave as distinct cultural entities, particularly in the way that they maintain dominance and protect their cultural boundaries through racism (Doane 2003; Kolchin 2002; Nayak 2007). Although exponents of dominant ethnicity and whiteness studies have previously debated the benefits of one approach over the other (see Roediger 2006), we take the view here that they are complementary: dominant ethnicity can complement whiteness studies by showing how racism works alongside a broader repertoire of ethnic boundary-making strategies, such as the use of religion, language, and other ethno-cultural elements. In short, using the frame of dominant ethnicity helps us see that—despite its centrality—more than racism is at play in shaping the political actions of white majorities. Furthermore, as we explain later, the concept of dominant ethnicity helps illustrate the relationship between the white majorities and *ethnic nationalism* in the West.

Dominant ethnic groups are integral to an ethno-symbolist understanding of nationalism in the West. Despite the apparent predominance of civic nationalism, Smith (1986) observes the continued significance of cultural content that is decidedly ethnic. This cultural content permeates everyday life, through the persistence of vernacular languages, religions, myths, memories, symbols, practices, and traditions. This content tends to derive, in part, from the most powerful ethnic communities during the process of nation-formation. Thus, the ethno-cultural content of the UK came to partly reflect that of southern, Protestant English people. Northern, Catholic Franks played a similar role in France, while white, British-origin Protestants did the same in the US. As the nationalizing state both expanded outward through conquest and downward through the bureaucratic incorporation of middle and lower classes, the cultures of the dominant ethnic groups were imposed as the new national culture. Even when elites initially ascribed to a different culture from the "masses," as in England, the nationalizing impulse was such that elites ultimately incorporated elements of the dominant vernacular culture, which was in turn imposed on the wider population (Smith 1986, chap. 4).

An important consequence of the fusion of dominant ethnic groups with Western national states is that their members often perceive themselves as having privileged autochthonous claims to them. These ideas are often colloquially expressed through ideas that "this is 'our' nation, and that 'we' deserve to be in control of its government and territory" (Kaufmann 2004b, 4). This point is crucial for an ethno-symbolist understanding of the recurrence of "hot" ethnic nationalism among the white majorities of the West. In sum, this kind of ethnic nationalism occurs when dominant ethnic groups perceive their privileged, autochthonous relationship with the nation-state to be threatened. Hot ethnic nationalism on behalf of dominant ethnic communities in the West therefore tends to be expressed as a movement for restoring or maintaining ethnic dominance (see Kaufmann 2004a; for similar depictions, but not from an ethno-symbolist perspective, see also Lecours and Nootens 2009; Wimmer 2004).

Curiously, despite a pattern of recurring efforts to maintain their ethnic dominance, dominant ethnic groups often fail to recognize their particularity. Instead, because of the blurring of boundaries between their communities and "their" nation-states, they tend to disavow identification with the former in favor of identifying with the latter. For example, white, English-speaking Canadians tend to simply see themselves as unhyphenated "Canadians" (Schertzer and Woods 2011; Woods 2012). Similarly, white English people in the UK tend not to distinguish between their Englishness and Britishness (Kumar 2003). In the US, the dominance of white Americans is also such that they often fail to see their distinctiveness vis-à-vis other groups—they simply see themselves as "Americans" (Doane 1997). This eliding of ethnic particularity in favor of a broader national identification means that when ethnic majorities defend their community, it is depicted as a defense of the nation writ large.

It is important to underscore here that the concept of dominant ethnic community does not always refer to groups that have a demographic majority within a nation-state. Prior to the emergence of nationalism and the concomitant veneration of the "people," it was far more common in the polities of the West for the dominant ethnic groups to be demographic minorities representing an aristocratic, imperial class (Kaufmann and Haklai 2008). Even in the nation-states of today's West, internal diversity is such that the dominant ethnic communities do not constitute demographic majorities throughout their territories. For example, Belgium, Canada, Spain, the UK, and the US all have large portions of their territories wherein a minority community, rather than the dominant ethnic group, is the demographic majority, such as Wallonia, Nunavut, Catalonia, Wales, and Puerto Rico, respectively. Furthermore, increasing diversity from migration, and the tendency of recent migrants to favor certain cities, means that in many of those cities, the members of the dominant ethnic groups no longer comprise the demographic majority. Examples abound of these "majority-minority" cities, including Leicester (UK), Marseille (France), Vancouver (Canada), or Los Angeles (US).

However, just because there are many regions and cities throughout the West in which the dominant ethnic communities are not demographic majorities, it does not follow that they are no longer the dominant ethnic groups. The concept of dominant ethnicity, as we have presented it here, is primarily a cultural, rather than structural, category. This means that even if members of a dominant ethnic community reside in a region where they are a demographic minority, they can nevertheless still be counted as members of the dominant ethnic community if they perceive themselves, and are perceived by others, to have a privileged, autochthonous status within the nation-state by virtue of their ethnicity. This will hold true even if they are not only a demographic minority, but also culturally, economically, or politically subordinate to other groups. Indeed, as we show in subsequent chapters, this understanding of dominant ethnicity helps us to understand precisely why ethnic nationalism is finding support among many poorer, disadvantaged members of the white majorities of the West—because of its promise to restore their ethnic dominance and to protect their culture.

Culture

Ethno-symbolism's argument that there is historical continuity between premodern ethnicity and modern nationalism opens it up to criticism that what it offers is little more than a variant of primordialism—that it is implying there is a transhistorical ethnic "essence" to be found at the heart of the national communities of the West. This, for example, was at the heart of the criticism leveled by Ernest Gellner (1996). However, ethno-symbolism explicitly eschews primordialism. To do so, it focuses on *culture*. Culture, for ethno-symbolists, is not an "essence"—it is a sociological concept. The ethno-symbolist view of culture broadly aligns with a Weberian approach, in the sense that culture is understood to be primarily a vehicle for transmitting meaning (Smith 2009, 24–26). But, unlike many Weberians, for ethno-symbolists, culture does not just exist in the mind; it is also expressed as a "real" phenomenon in the world through objects, texts, and practices. Much like anthropologist Clifford Geertz's (1973) famous method of uncovering cultural meanings via "thick description," ethno-symbolists seek to reconstruct the meaning and significance of these various cultural forms by relating them to their historical, social, and political contexts.

Sociologists who focus on macroscopic, societal cultures have long been criticized for their lack of conceptual precision. Ethno-symbolists address this challenge by conceptualizing the cultures of ethnic and national communities as "myth-symbol complexes" (Armstrong 1982; Smith 1998, 181). We define a myth-symbol complex as an intersubjective system of norms, myths, symbols, memories, practices, and values that together provide ethnic and national communities with meaning. In other words, a myth-symbol complex serves to define the collective identity of a community. Like other signifiers of identity, there are two sides to myth-symbol complexes: they simultaneously indicate who "we" are (*i.e* the "in-group"), as well as who "we" are not (*i.e.* the "out-group"). In this respect, myth-symbol complexes should be understood to be constructed through a relational process of distinguishing between in-group and out-group (Barth 1969). From this perspective, myth-symbol complexes are mechanisms for constructing and maintaining cultural boundaries (Smith 2009, 23–24). This process is particularly visible in deeply divided communities such as Northern Ireland, where identification with a religious category, specifically Roman Catholic or Protestant, simultaneously serves to signify the in-group and the out-group.

Myth-symbol complexes also provide nationalism with its cultural content. In this regard, they can be seen as a set of cultural resources—they provide nationalist activists with a "repertoire" of cultural content to draw upon in their efforts to attract and inspire followers (Smith 2009, 31–33). For example, a nationalist actor might refer to some bygone heroic battle, sacred text, or core cultural attribute or practice as a rallying cry. From an ethno-symbolist perspective, the degree to which this cultural content is known, and held to be important, by the target population helps to explain the degree to which it will have symbolic power and resonate as legitimate. In other words, from the perspective of ethno-symbolism, nationalist leaders need to draw upon preexisting cultural content to increase the chances that their messaging is going to succeed. As cultural resources, myth-symbol complexes can therefore be seen as both "enablers" and "constraints"; while they provide elites with cultural resources to garner support, they also delimit the range of available resources that will be perceived as legitimate by the target population.

We do not want to imply that myth-symbol complexes are monolithically institutionalized throughout a population. Quite the opposite: they are often unevenly diffused and highly contested by members of the same nation (Schertzer and Woods 2011). Some individuals might identify strongly with some element of a myth-symbol complex, while others might be indifferent. Others might not even be aware of it, and still others might contest it. This last point is an endemic feature of the national communities of the West, which have long been riven by cultural wars over the nature of their identities. In these cases, multiple, rival interpretations of myth-symbol complexes are put forward—as exemplified in the contestation between civic and ethnic conceptions of national identity (Hutchinson 2005). Finally, in addition to being contested, myth-symbol complexes are also dynamic—they can, and do, change over time.

History

We have argued that ethnic and national cultures should be understood as a sociological, empirical phenomena, called myth-symbol complexes. If culture is a sociological phenomenon, then it follows that to become established within a population, it must undergo a historical process of "social construction." On this point, ethno-symbolists are in broad agreement with modernist scholars. However, ethno-symbolists make the further argument that culture can be difficult to "deconstruct" once it has been constructed. Here is where we part company from many leading modernists. Rogers Brubaker (2004), who is known for a relatively uncompromising variant of social constructionism, depicts culture as being largely dependent on the politics of the day. Similarly, Ernest Gellner (1983, 124) argued that nationalists could use virtually any piece of history to construct a national culture. For his part, Eric Hobsbawm (in Hobsbawm and Ranger 1983) argued that elites could simply "invent" new traditions. In contrast, ethno-symbolist scholars suggests that culture often displays a degree of resistance to the vagaries of politics or the machinations of particular elites in a given period. But more than merely resisting change, ethno-symbolists argue that culture can also *influence* politics. Accordingly, a proper analysis of the historical development of nationalism needs to account for culture, much as it would account for politics, economics, or other social forces.

From a wider social science perspective, ethno-symbolism is most closely aligned with "new institutionalist" approaches that focus on the significance of culture in the unfolding of history (Powell and DiMaggio 1991; Lecours 2005). The key concept in institutionalism is "path dependence." Path dependence posits that history creates "paths," which influence how the present unfolds, or, to put it more succinctly, it is a theory that "history matters." From an institutionalist perspective, we might therefore depict ethno-symbolism's argument as follows: when the myth-symbol complexes of powerful dominant ethnic groups become embedded in the institutions of national states, they create historical "pathways," such that they can persist through time, and ultimately play a role in shaping how nationalism is expressed. This perspective shares much with work on "political development." For scholars of political development, time is an important variable when seeking to explain continuity and change in complex political orders involving culture and institutions (Pierson 2000; Orren and Skowronek 2004). As Lucas and Vipond (2017, 229–30) put it, political development seeks to answer big questions about how political ideas and institutions remain stable and change over large periods of time. This, too, is the focus of ethno-symbolists, as their work unpacks how ideas about the nation have been codified in myth-symbol complexes, and how these complexes develop over time. But, before we elaborate upon *how* this occurs, we need to firstly say more about the origins of myth-symbol complexes.

As we touched on briefly in the previous section, the ethno-symbolist account of the origins of ethnic myth-symbol complexes draws heavily from the seminal insights of anthropologist Fredrik Barth (1969). In sum, Barth argues for the importance of external "Others" in the construction of ethnic identity. Against the prevailing view at the time, that ethnic identities emerge independently through an endogenous process occurring within a population, Barth argued that ethnic identity formation occurs through a relational process occurring between populations. But how does a theory of ethnic identity formation that emphasizes interaction with exogenous Others square with ethno-symbolism's emphasis on the significance of endogenous cultural forces in the persistence of ethnic identity? The answer to this question lies in what happens with the various elements of ethnic identity *internally*, as they take shape *externally*. Here ethno-symbolists focus on how those cultural elements become institutionalized and thereby integrated into a population's myth-symbol complex. Once this happens, they can become relatively resistant to change.

One of the challenges with arguments for cultural persistence is tracing how earlier notions of collective identity are transposed and influence groups over time. As John Breuilly (2005) argues, early modern and premodern ideas of nationhood were fragmented and narrowly held—and, more to the point, historical correlation between group attributes does not equal causal influence. John Hutchinson has sought to address this question through the concept of "institutional carriers." Across a large number of cases, Hutchinson (2005) finds that several key institutions—such as militaries, religions, legal systems, commemorative practices, etc.—act as temporal vehicles, or "carriers," for ethnic myth-symbol complexes. The argument here is that these institutions, and the people that identify with them, often work to ensure they endure through the process of nation-formation.

However, some see this approach as being overly "top-down." The criticism here is that it does not address the extent to which the wider population identifies with those institutions, nor does it account for the wide range social institutions that characterize ordinary life (Fox 2014). Here the recent turn to the investigation of banal and everyday nationalism is useful. As we described earlier, during a phase of banal nationalism, a nation's myth-symbol complex will largely be an apolitical, unremarked-upon feature of social life. Although some scholars of ethno-symbolism and banal nationalism have positioned their work against one another (see debates in Tsang and Woods 2014), we take the view that the two approaches are mutually reinforcing. Taken together, these "top-down" and "bottom-up" approaches provide a compelling multilevel depiction of how ethnic myths, symbols, memories, and practices of nationhood can persist through time.

Media is also an important carrier of cultural content. Indeed, the rise of mass communication technologies is often assigned pride of place in accounts of the history of nationalism (Deutsch 1966). Benedict Anderson's (2006) *Imagined Communities* is well known for arguing that the rise of "print capitalism" played a key role in the dissemination of nationality. Despite the increasingly global reach of communication technology in the twentieth century, much of the now vast body of research on the relationship of nationalism and various forms of media, including print, radio, television, and film, tends to reinforce Anderson's argument by demonstrating how media as medium remains a powerful force in the construction and reproduction of nationalism. There is even strong evidence that nationalism can be reinforced and distributed through newer forms of digital media (Skey 2020). As we discuss in the subsequent chapter, an ethno-symbolic approach can help us move beyond a focus on the *medium* of media to also consider how the *content* of culture and ideas are distributed to the population.

Work to date on the relationship between the media and nationalism provides a powerful case for the media's role in the construction and persistence of nationhood. However, thus far, it has said little about the significance of premodern, *ethnic* cultural content in mediated forms of nationalism. Anderson notably takes a modernist perspective, and minimizes the significance of premodern forms of solidarity. As we discuss in the subsequent chapter, much of the work that follows Anderson's approach takes a similar view. For their part, ethno-symbolists have also said relatively little about the significance of developments in communication technology and mass media. This is perhaps understandable, given their focus on the significance of premodern ethno-cultural content. However, in light of the ever-expanding presence of media in social and political life, it is an area that demands more attention from ethno-symbolism. There is an important role for ethno-symbolism to play in uncovering the historical, ethnic bases for today's mediated expressions of nationalism, as we make clear in subsequent chapters in our analysis of the ethno-nationalist content of several political leaders' Twitter communication.

This overview of core elements of ethno-symbolism explains how we think ethnic myth-symbol complexes persist—largely by becoming widely institutionalized throughout different orders of society. But it does not tell us much about how myth-symbol complexes change. Indeed, a theory of change has been somewhat of a blind spot in ethno-symbolism. This is likely because ethno-symbolists have long argued against the modernist idea that cultural content can simply be invented by elites. But Smith (1998) has laid out some of the groundwork here: he argues that any new cultural content must account for the preexisting cultural landscape if it is going to resonate with that community. As such, Smith finds that "new" cultural content is constructed through a process of "re-invention" rather than "invention," whereby existing content is repurposed to fit new circumstances. We prefer the term "adaptation" to signal that this process involves both continuity *and* change.

In a process of adaptation, both exogenous and endogenous factors are important. On the exogenous front, external Others play an important role in the adaptation of national identity. To put it in the language of social-psychology, interactions with an out-group can trigger changes in the identity of the in-group (Taifel 1982). However, because the in-group already has a myth-symbol complex in place, these changes will not solely be based on interactions with the out-group. Rather, the myth-symbol complex will also shape how changes occur. In short, adaptation occurs as a two-step process: (1) relations with a new out-group triggers the construction of new cultural content, which (2) occurs by adapting existing cultural content to fit the new relational context. The upshot of this process of adaptation is that, despite undergoing change, new ethno-cultural content retains a sense of continuity, and thereby preserves its capacity to resonate with the wider population. Indeed, as we demonstrate in subsequent chapters, the foundational elements of a myth-symbol complex may remain quite fixed, while slight adjustments and adaptations of content help it to fit new contexts and the emergence of new significant Others.

The process of adaptation can be amplified during a phase of hot nationalism. In our description of hot nationalism, we suggested that it can act as a "critical juncture." Among institutionalists, critical junctures describe situations of high uncertainty, which can result in a change of path-dependent processes (Capoccia and Kelemen 2007). Given our focus on culture, theories of cultural sociology are also illustrative here. From this perspective, a phase of hot nationalism can be likened to a "social drama." During a social drama, the myths and symbols of collective identity can undergo such intensive contestation that their previously established meanings take on a degree of "liminality." In a situation of liminality there is high potential for cultural change (Turner 1986). In short, hot nationalism creates the conditions for adaptations to the nation's myth-symbol complex. In the midst of the rapidly unfolding context, existing cultural understandings of the nation will be brought to the fore and adapted to the suit the new perceived threat. After the sense of crisis recedes, and a phase of banal nationalism returns, these newly adapted cultural elements can undergo a process of institutionalization, and thereby become integrated into the existing myth-symbol complex—ready to be drawn upon in future phases of hot nationalism. Of course, the adaptation can only stray so far from the original set of myths and symbols that are foundational to the nation's identity.

Tying Together the Threads of Ethno-Symbolism to Understand Ethnic Nationalism

In this chapter we have brought together some of the key insights from ethno-symbolism and corresponding work in the study of institutions and culture in order to construct a framework for understanding ethnic nationalism among the white majorities of the West. In contrast with many scholars of race and ethnicity, we define the white majority communities as ethnic communities. More specifically, we define them as *dominant ethnic communities*—a type of ethnicity distinguished by a perception among its members that they have a unique and privileged autochthonous claim to the nations in which they reside.

Our framework is primarily concerned with the cultural dimensions of dominant ethnicity. We are interested in how these communities' *cultures*—their myth-symbol complexes—become institutionalized as dominant elements of their respective national political cultures. In our view, this institutionalized ethno-cultural content is an important part of the explanation for *why* ethnic nationalism occurs and *how* it is expressed among white majorities. First, we posit that ethnic nationalism can be triggered by perceived threats to the dominance of this ethno-cultural content. Second, we argue that this content structures the response and provides a set of symbolic resources for ethnic nationalists to draw upon in their efforts to garner support. Thus, in our view, culture is both an object of ethnic nationalism and a means for its expression.

However, we also suggest that ethnic nationalism can be a catalyst for cultural change. This occurs when the existing myth-symbol complex does not readily provide appropriate cultural content to respond to some new perceived threat. In this situation, ethnic nationalists will try to adapt (but not invent) cultural content to fit the new threat. The upshot of adapting existing cultural content, rather than creating new content, is that it helps ensure that the new content retains a sense of continuity and, therefore, legitimacy. If the process of adaptation is successful—in the sense that it resonates with the wider population—we expect that the newly adapted cultural content will undergo a process of institutionalization and thereby be integrated into the myth-symbol complex. As such, it will be available to be drawn upon (and adapted) in subsequent waves of ethnic nationalism.

These arguments provide a theoretical framework for analyzing the significance of ethnicity, culture, and history in the occurrence and expression of ethnic nationalism in the West. At its heart, our framework suggests that the ethno-cultural elements of ethnic nationalism that are specific to time and space matter. In order to properly understand ethnic nationalism, we therefore argue that its ethno-cultural content needs to be historically and spatially situated by examining where it comes from, and how it changes—even if sometimes through subtle shifting codes. Now, in order to properly employ these insights in comparative-historical analysis—and to understand how this cultural content is used by todays ethnic nationalists in their social media communication—we need to assemble them in such a way that makes fine-grained tracing of the development of ethnic myth-symbol complexes possible. To do so, we have created a comparative schema of several core elements of ethnic myth-symbol complexes, which we outline in the subsequent chapter.

3

Mapping Ethnic Nationalism in the Age of Twitter

The previous chapter outlined our theoretical framework, highlighting the role of dominant ethnic groups, culture, and history in the dynamics of ethnic nationalism. Here, we explain our methodology for mapping the foundational ethnic myths and symbols of a nation, both in the past and in the Twitter communication of today's new nationalists.

We start by introducing a new schema designed to trace persistence and change in the historical development of ethnic myth-symbol complexes. As part of this, we elaborate on what we mean by "myths" and "symbols," which are sometimes difficult and opaque concepts that can lead to fuzzy analysis. We then discuss how we apply this schema to code and analyze the Twitter communication of the new nationalists in our three cases. We also consider the role of social media in the rise of the new nationalism, and justify our focus on this medium. We use this schema and the methods outlined here in the next four chapters to explore *how* nationalist leaders in the US, UK, and France use foundational ethnic myths and symbols in their Twitter communication, which is the necessary first step in understanding *why* these messages reverberate with their target populations.

A Schema for Mapping Ethnic Myth-Symbol Complexes

What are myths and symbols, and how are they related? Today, cultural analysis in the humanities and social sciences tends to more commonly refer to the "narratives," "frames," and "discourses" of collectivities than to their *myths*. It is difficult to pin down why this has occurred. Perhaps it is because myths are often associated with a now discarded twentieth-century variant of structuralism put forward by the likes of Claude Lévi-Strauss. Perhaps it is because of the term's lingering pejorative association with fiction, illusion, tradition, and irrationality (Overing 1997). Whatever is behind this development, myths remain a useful concept, particularly when we turn away from the pejorative use of the term and understand them as Durkheim did in his pathbreaking research on the topic. In this respect, a myth refers to a *foundational belief that a community holds about itself* (see Schöpflin 1997). However, we depart from classic Durkheimian works by taking the view that myths are central to all human collectivities, irrespective of whether those collectivities are "premodern" or "modern." This is in keeping with a recent intellectual movement in social sciences—of which ethno-symbolism is a part—which argues that the transition into modernity did not lead to the predicted replacement of meaning with a disenchanted rationality (Rambo and Chan 1990; Sewell 1992; Alexander 2003). Rather, meaning continues to be central to modern life, and myths remain vital components of the meaning-making process (see Bouchard 2013, 2017).

Myths are usually expressed in the form of a historical narrative. However, unlike professional history, myths are not necessarily concerned with recounting historical truths (Kumar 2015, 199–200). But, at the same time, myths often rest upon a "kernel of truth" to give them power (Archard 1995, 474). Myths, above all, provide communities with meaning. They answer existential questions about the basis of the community, such as: Who are we? Why are we here? Where did we come from? Where are we going? What is our place in the world? What is our purpose? In addressing these kinds of meaning-centered questions, myths are more akin to religious stories than historical writing (Overing 1997). In this respect, myths are "morality tales"—they seek to convey to the community what is right and what is wrong. Relatedly, myths can also act as ciphers for collective emotions (Morden 2016). For example, the recollection of myths describing how a community persevered through the struggles of the past can provide inspiration and relief when faced with the uncertainty and hardship of the present. And while myths recount a community's past, they do so with an eye to the present and the future. Thus, it is by recalling myths of a community's "glorious past"—an imagined time when the community is believed to have most closely conformed to its ideals—that it can find a sense of direction for what it could, and should, be (Smith 1997). Myths also make boundaries: by depicting who "we" are, they indicate who "we" are not. This will generally be expressed as a moral boundary, with "our" community's virtues contrasted against another community's vices (Schöpflin 1997, 19). Finally, myths have a legitimating function. By recounting how and why a community exists, they provide it with the legitimacy to exist (Armstrong 1982, 9).

To fulfill these various social functions, ethnic myths need to be externalized so that they can be communicated. This occurs through symbols. Symbols can be linguistic, material, or gestural. They can be used in everyday life or during extraordinary events. It is through interaction with symbols that the meaning of the collectivity is communicated. Notably, as Durkheim (2001) made clear, symbolic communication occurs via an affective process (see also Alexander 2003). We do not apprehend the meaning of symbols through reason, but through emotions. For example, we *feel* the importance of symbols that are sacred to the group, such as a monument to some particularly tragic event that occurred in the past. Furthermore, the process of symbolic communication is not necessarily a conscious one. Often, symbols will be employed and interpreted without our being consciously aware of it. For instance, we can think here of the many unconscious symbolic cues that are employed in everyday life, from gestures to sartorial fashion, that are used to communicate collective identity. Notably, symbols will also often simultaneously have a dual communicative function: they can be directed internally at fellow members of the group, or externally to outsiders. In this regard, the most durable symbols tend to be the ones whose main purpose is to demarcate boundaries between "us" and "them"—"symbolic border guards," as Armstrong refers to them (1982, 9; see also Barth 1969).

Symbols also play a key role in communicating meaning through time. It is often said that the dead communicate with the living through symbols (Armstrong 1982, 8). Indeed, some symbols persist for many generations. In this way, they provide the "through line" that connects present-day members of the group with their predecessors, thereby ensuring that the collectivity endures (Kumar 2015, 202). But while the *form* of symbols can be remarkable persistent over time, their mythic *content* can change. Finally, if symbols are the mechanism for communicating myths, by the same token we can also say that myths provide the structure for symbols (Lévi-Strauss 1963, 210). In other words, myths connect otherwise disparate symbols into an interrelated system of meaning. The relationship between myths and symbols is therefore mutually reinforcing and difficult to untangle. Myths are communicated via symbols, but we can only interpret the mythic meaning of symbols if we already know the myth—hence our use of the term "myth-symbol complex," and our tendency to focus on *foundational ethnic myths and symbols* in our analysis of the past and the Twitter communication of nationalists today.

Before we discuss how we map the constituent elements of a myth-symbol complex, we should address a potential critique that the concept does not fully capture how culture manifests. Focusing exclusively on myths and symbols can elide the role of ritual and performance as key cultural expressions. Despite omitting ritual from the term "myth-symbol complex," the ways in which culture is ritualized and performed has been central to ethno-symbolism, from

Armstrong's (1982) original formulation onward (Tsang and Woods 2014). In truth, the ethno-symbolist conception of culture would have been better labeled a "myth-symbol-ritual complex." Nevertheless, in this book we have retained the original term. In part, this signals continuity between our work and the ethno-symbolist tradition. More practically, we are more concerned here with the foundational ethnic myths and symbols than with rituals and performances.

To trace persistence and change in the historical development of ethnic myth-symbol complexes, we have created a new coding schema based on five mytho-symbolic categories of ethnic identity. We have chosen these five categories by drawing on a wide reading of research on ethnicity, particularly the foundational work of Armstrong (1982) and Smith (1986). While these works provide inspiration, our schema reflects our specific aims. Smith (1986, 22–30) was concerned with discerning the foundational "dimensions" of ethnicity in order to produce a working definition of the concept. By contrast, our chief concern is to uncover the foundational components of a group's identity *as an ethnic group*, and how these markers of ethnic identity persist and change over time. In choosing the categories that make up our schema, we therefore need them to be sufficiently specific to delineate the distinct ways that ethnicity is expressed through culture, but also broad enough to avoid getting lost in particular manifestations. Ultimately, we have settled upon five categories: people, homeland, religion, history, and ethos. In Table 3.1 we elaborate on each of these categories, providing some *indicative* (i.e., generic) ethnic myths and symbols for each category distinguishing an ethnic group's identity markers. The specific cultural content will obviously vary for each nation, but this schema can facilitate comparative analysis of the foundational ethnic myths and symbols over time and across cases.

Together, these categories define the key components of an ethnic myth-symbol complex. We readily acknowledge that they are not necessarily discrete; many myths and symbols will overlap several categories. Our expectation is that "people" will be the primary category and referent of political communication: all other categories contribute in some way to defining who are members of the nation and who are not members. References to "people" and "history" will be particularly intertwined because questions of "who we are" are inevitably linked to questions of "where we came from." We also notably included a separate category for religion, rather than subsume it within the category "people," because of its near universality in ethnic conceptions of identity. "Ethos" is a somewhat ambiguous category. It is true that all of these categories partly speak to an ethnic community's uniqueness and superiority. However, there are often ways in which an ethnic community represents its uniqueness as a set of ideals and principles that do not easily fit within the other categories. For example, as we demonstrate in our case studies of ethnic nationalism in America, France, and England, the ethea of the dominant ethnic communities of the West are

Table 3.1 **Schema to Map Ethnic Myth-Symbol Complex**

Categories of Ethnic Myths and Symbols	Indicative Ethnic Myths and Symbols
People: *how membership to the national community is perceived*	Myths: • The nation is an ancestral and cultural community whose members are united by their shared ethno-cultural inheritance. • The nation excludes people based upon their ethno-cultural attributes—biology and culture determine who does and does not belong. • The state is legitimate insofar as it safeguards the nation's ethno-cultural inheritance. Symbols: • Repositories of ethno-cultural characteristics—including biological symbols (e.g., phenotype, ancestry), vernacular culture (e.g., language, folk practices), and "high culture" (e.g., literature, arts). • Individuals, groups, and movements that are perceived to embody the nation's ethno-cultural ancestry and inheritance.
Homeland: *how the nation perceives its territory*	Myths: • The territory of the nation is its "homeland" (i.e., it is the site where the nation was born and where it has existed since "time immemorial"). • The unique ecological features of the homeland (e.g., whether it is an island, mountainous, agricultural, cold, hot, etc.) played a central role in shaping the cultural characteristics of the nation. • The nation's legitimate claim to territorial sovereignty is premised upon the idea that the territory is its homeland. Symbols: • References to ecology and geography (e.g., oceans, forests, prairies, mountains, islands) and their role in shaping the culture of the nation. These features will often be represented though art, literature, music, and cinema. • Territorial symbols are often linked to the nation's "traditional" culture, usually through symbols of rural/agrarian life.

(continued)

Table 3.1 **Continued**

Categories of Ethnic Myths and Symbols	Indicative Ethnic Myths and Symbols
Religion: *how the nation perceives its relationship to religion*	Myths: • The national community is defined, in part, by the dominant religion of its members. • Religion helped give "birth" to the nation and has often provided it with succor and support in challenging times. • The nation is often depicted as a "chosen" community—it is a sacred community that has a unique relationship with its deity/deities. • The deity/deities will often also be perceived to have "chosen" the nation to carry out a special mission in this world (e.g., to defend the religion against its perceived enemies). • In some situations, how the state has incorporated or excluded the dominant nation's religion will form elements of an ethnic identity. Symbols: • Religious symbolism that is intertwined with the symbols of the nation (e.g., a national flag will include religious emblems; national places of worship; religious iconography on political buildings).
History: *how the nation perceives its past, and its future*	Myths: • The nation has existed since "time immemorial" and its precise origins are obscured by the distance of time. • The nation's greatness is proved by its long history and its ability to endure across the ages. • The most important event in the nation's history was the time of its "glorious past," when the nation was at its very best. • There may be a narrative that the nation has presently declined, but its destiny is to re-establish its glorious past. • The nation may have suffered great tragedies in its past, but nevertheless endured. Symbols: • Key symbols refer to the nation's longevity and especially its glorious past. • Key events and references to the nation's historic triumphs and traumas.

Table 3.1 **Continued**

Categories of Ethnic Myths and Symbols	Indicative Ethnic Myths and Symbols
Ethos: *how the nation perceives its uniqueness and place in the world*	Myths: • The nation's creed—its unique way of life and values—reflects the attributes of its dominant ethnic group. • The nation's unique ethno-cultural inheritance makes it superior to other nations—it is exceptional, and thus especially well-suited to taking on certain roles in the world. • If the nation is perceived to be "chosen" (see "Religion" category), then it will have a special mission to play in the world in defending or spreading this religion or the values of its national creed. • The nation's unique ethno-cultural inheritance justifies autonomy from encroachment and influence of other nations. Symbols: • People, places and objects that embody the unique values, creed, or superiority of the nation (constitutions, national sites, monuments to victory, etc.). • Events (e.g., wars and rebellions) that exemplify the nation's defense of its specific culture or on behalf of other nations that share its culture.

often expressed through the ideals of liberalism and democracy. What makes these principles *ethnic*, rather than abstract political ideas associated with more civic identity, is the way in which they are often imagined to be uniquely derived from their cultures. Thus, liberalism in England (and also among Anglo-Americans) was once imagined to be a unique property of "Anglo-Saxondom." These types of myths, in turn, are linked to myths that the community has a unique destiny in the world to be a beacon of liberalism and democracy, or, in the case of America, to be a "city on a hill." While we have compiled a list of five categories here, we are also aware that at times certain ones will become more or less salient. Shifting political and social contexts can drive the rise and fall of ethnic categories as mobilizers of the public and perceptions of who is perceived as an insider and an outsider of the group. In short, we can expect to see variation in the use of these categories over time and between cases, depending on changing context.

In the following chapters we apply this schema to the United States, France, and England. In each of these cases, we use the schema to trace the origins and development of ethnic myth-symbol complexes, before analyzing how this content has been employed and adapted by today's ethnic nationalist movements, focusing particularly on the Twitter communication of Donald Trump, Marine Le Pen, and the influential Twitter accounts Vote Leave and Leave.EU. We therefore use the schema to conduct "within case" comparisons of how the myth-symbol complexes of each of the three cases develop over time, as well as "cross-case" comparisons of their similarities and differences.

Finally, a note about how we apply the schema in each of the three cases. Given the importance of out-groups in the construction of ethnic identity, we use the schema to code the representation of in-groups and out-groups. This enables us to track the persistence of an in-group's myth-symbol complex, and how it is variously renewed and adapted over time in response to different perceived out-groups. Paying attention to how the out-groups are represented is especially important to our analyses of more recent expressions of ethnic nationalism. In recent decades, liberal dominance of the public sphere in the US, France, and the UK has been such that outright expressions of ethnic nationalism have been somewhat muted. To circumvent liberal norms, ethnic nationalists have sought to avoid directly referring to who "we" are in overtly racial or ethnic terms. Instead, they tend to emphasize who "we" are *not*. However, by paying attention to how those out-groups are represented, we can reconstruct the implied in-group—indeed, the implied in-group is readily apparent by its very omission.

Applying the Schema: Mapping Ethnic Nationalism through Social Media

Tracing continuity and change in the foundational ethnic myths and symbols of the US, France, and UK has value in its own right. However, we are primarily carrying out this analysis to examine how leaders and movements use these foundational ideas today, with a particular focus on their social media campaigns. Our study thus engages with a tradition exploring the links between media, technology, and nationalism. Media has long been recognized as a core driver of nationalism (Skey 2020). Karl Deutsch (1966) was among the first to draw our attention to how early advances in communication technology allowed leaders to spread their nationalist messages to wide swaths of the population. Similar ideas about advancements in the modes of communication, like the advent of print capitalism (Anderson 2006) or the routinization of nationalist ideas through various mediated channels (Billig 1995), are central to some of the most influential accounts of the rise and permanence of national identity. These works echo a broader focus on the role of communication in politics, a theme that has become even more prominent with the emergence of newer social media technologies. Indeed, work on the role of social media (e.g., Twitter, Facebook, and Instagram) in contemporary political movements and campaigning is vast and growing at an exponential rate (for an overview, see Bruns et al. 2015).

At the forefront of this expanding field are theories about the role of social media in the rise of populist and nationalist politics. Much of this work builds on the idea that the shifting media landscape is structuring politics today and that the new medium of social media benefits populist and nationalist leaders (see, Aalberg et al. 2016; Engesser et al. 2017; Zulianello, Albertini, and Ceccobelli 2018; Gerbaudo 2018; Maurer and Diehl 2020; Krämer 2017). This view holds that platforms like Twitter and Facebook give leaders unmediated access to "the people," while the relative anonymity of the Internet allows people to express more extreme positions (Gerbaudo 2014; Groshek and Koc-Michalska 2017). In this respect, these platforms facilitate populist and nationalist claims that they can bypass traditional filters to bring sender and receiver together, even if they are not synchronously connecting (Engesser et al. 2017; Hameleers 2018). Paolo Gerbaudo has tied these threads together with his idea that there is an "elective affinity" between a "populism 2.0" and social media, arguing that the structural features of this medium play into the discursive tendencies of leaders to set the people against elites (Gerbaudo 2012, 2014, 2018).

The empirical study of the relationship between social media and populism largely follows this theoretical perspective to examine the discursive style of leaders using platforms like Twitter and Facebook, along with the actions of the consumers of this media. The main approach here, particularly when looking at Twitter and populist politics, is to paint a broad picture by looking at a relatively large numbers of posts from multiple accounts. These studies adopt a range of quantitative and qualitative methods, but are trending toward a mixed-methods approach (for a broader discussion of the split between big-data approaches to the study of Twitter and politics and smaller qualitative studies, see Gonawela et al. 2018). Scholars working in this area identify hashtags, word strings, and sentiments that correlate with populist themes, often comparing the discourse of candidates within and across cases to identify different forms of populism or categorize leaders as less or more populist (e.g., Ernst et al. 2017; Waisbord and Amado 2017; Maurer and Diehl 2020; Breeze 2020). At times, scholars will also look at how these themes are picked up on by followers through "retweets" or "likes" as a proxy to measure the acceptance of populist ideas in the wider public (e.g., Pancer and Poole 2016; Bucy et al. 2020; Curiel 2020). Complementing these broader studies are those that take a narrower view by looking at smaller collections of tweets. Often this work focuses on one individual or political party over a relatively short period of time to provide a rich description of the populist or nationalist content sensitive to the related political and social context (e.g., Lacatus 2021; Kreis 2017; Saul 2017).

Both approaches are well represented in the emerging work on the role of social media in the resurgence of ethnic nationalism and populism in the US, France, and UK. For example, Hänska and Bauchowitz (2017) examined over 7.5 million tweets to show us that Leave supporters were much more active on Twitter than Remain supporters during the Brexit campaign. Usherwood and Wright (2017) added to this analysis by demonstrating how Leave campaigners were more focused on immigration in their tweets and were more negative than Remain campaigners. A further study of over 1.4 million messages on Facebook shows how different notions of British heritage were drawn upon by those supporting Leave and Remain in the referendum (Bonacchi, Altaweel, and Krzyzanska 2018). At the smaller scale, an analysis of just over one hundred of Marine Le Pen's tweets outlines how she constructed a Muslim threat (Maksić and Ahmić 2020). Others have compared Le Pen to her contemporaries, showing she is a strong ethnic nationalist and populist (Curiel 2020). Among these studies are interesting comparisons between Le Pen and Trump, showing similarities in their rhetoric targeting elites and immigrants (Maurer and Diehl 2020, 7).

Studies of Donald Trump's use of Twitter are the most prevalent, given his stated affinity for the medium and his emblematic status as the harbinger of the new nationalism. As noted above, much of this work situates Trump among other populist and nationalist leaders by categorizing his rhetorical and discursive style on Twitter and other mediums (e.g., Maurer and Diehl 2020; Bucy et al. 2020; Lacatus 2019). But this work goes beyond just describing Trump's brand of ethnic nationalism. It has also shown us how he used Twitter to intentionally bypass conventional news media (Enli 2017). We have also learned about his tendency toward grandiosity (Ahmadian, Azarshahi, and Paulhus 2017) paired with simple and uncivil language (Ott 2017). There has been interesting and important work on the gendered nature of his political style, particularly how he used masculine language in contrast to Hilary Clinton in 2016 (Lee and Lim 2016). Some of these studies have explored themes close to the ones in this book. Kreis (2017) shows how Trump's tweets had an informal style that reinforces an image of a homogeneous people threatened by a dangerous Other. Similarly, Saul (2017) explores how Trump's speeches and tweets often employed "racial fig leaves," a linguistic strategy that uses normatively acceptable utterances to imply racialized ideas. Mercieca (2020) has shown that this strategy expands well beyond Trump's Twitter communication: he relies heavily on a rhetorical technique of "paralipsis" to say two things at once, promoting an idea through the rhetorical device of "I'm not saying—I'm just saying."

The broader work on Twitter and populism, and the more specific focus on Trump, Le Pen, and Brexit, has significantly advanced our understanding of the new nationalism and the role of social media. This literature provides a conceptual roadmap to think about the relationship between social media and the new nationalism, outlines broad trends in the use of the medium by leaders and movements, and provides insights into the communication style and techniques of today's nationalists. But there are still some issues with this work and gaps in our knowledge. The central problems here reflect both conceptual and theoretical issues, along with some limitations in the methodological approach of these studies.

The conceptual starting point for much of the work on the relationship between social media and the new nationalism puts too much emphasis on the structuring power of the medium. Like other explanations of the rise of the new nationalism that focus on external drivers (e.g., economic inequality), blaming social media for the success of nationalist political movements is too thin. As Michael Skey (2020) argues, emphasizing the structuring power of a communication medium takes our analytical focus away from the content of messages and the context within which they are received. The now famous axiom that the "medium is the message" (McLuhan 1964) sometimes needs to be offset with a focus on the message itself to understand why it resonates. Of course, we have to recognize that social media has become a key part of modern campaigning and politics for virtually all candidates in liberal democracies. It also does have attributes that favor nationalist politics. Like other earlier advances in mass communication technology, platforms like Twitter and Facebook assist movements in getting their messages out to their intended audiences at greater numbers and with greater saturation, while also removing some of the social stigma of promoting racist and nationalist ideas through a veil of anonymity. But, even here, we need to be critical of the claim that this medium allows leaders to directly connect with their supporters: we should not just accept the claims of nationalists that these platforms allow them to truly connect with the people, bypassing liberal institutions and conventional media. As Benjamin Moffit argues, this underlying assumption of much of the work on Twitter and politics today does not hold up to close scrutiny: it conflates the *purported* "directness" with actually "being in touch" with the people (2018, 31). There is still a significant gap between the sender and the receiver on Twitter. Despite claiming to facilitate reciprocal communication, social media is mainly used by political actors as another broadcast platform—not a dialogical venue.

In a similar vein, we need to move beyond generalizing from a few cases. There are important examples where social media is central to a leader or movement's success. But we should not overestimate from these cases the medium's impact on the political trajectory of the new nationalism *in general*. In practice, there is a broad spectrum in how nationalist and populist leaders use Twitter—from those with weak and moderate reliance (like Silvio Berlusconi and Jean-Marie Le Pen) to those with stronger and very strong reliance on the medium (like Pauline Hanson, Geert Wilders, and Donald Trump) (Moffitt 2018, 39).

These conceptual problems are replicated in the empirical work. Larger studies relying on cutting-edge techniques of analyzing big data provide remarkable insights into the broader trends and usage of social media; but they can also be *too broad* and lack consideration of how the context and content of messages mobilize people. In this respect, a careful reading of the content of posts and messages from a human reader who is sensitive to the political and cultural context is sometimes needed to unpack the complex ideas being communicated. At the same time, some studies that adopt this more focused approach and provide narrative assessments of single leaders or topics over a short period of time through a limited number of posts can be *too narrow*. In these studies, too much emphasis can be placed on single messages or themes. Without the broader political and historical context, it is difficult to generalize about the role of social media or even the meaning behind the content in messages. In short, the empirical work has tended to either underplay the content of message and context, or overplay the impact of the medium and particular narratives from narrow case studies. The approach we take in this book is designed to address some of these issues and to fill gaps in our knowledge of how the new nationalists are using social media.

Our Approach: Balancing Breadth and Depth

Our empirical research in this book is guided by a set of principles. The overarching principle is to balance the breadth and depth of our analytical focus. We adopt a relatively standard approach of qualitative content analysis to unpack how ideas are communicated through the text of tweets. At the same time, we have purposefully expanded the number of tweets examined to ensure that we can account for the breadth of themes broached in our case studies. All told, we look at over 15,000 tweets in this book from Donald Trump, Marine Le Pen, and the two main Leave campaigns in the UK. But we do not simply provide a high-level overview of this data—we balance this breadth with a depth that situates each tweet in context. Rather than relying on machine reading or automated coding to identify trends, we have used human readers and coders. At least two people *personally read each of the 15,000 tweets*—carrying out analysis sensitive to the historical and contemporary political context of the messages.

The importance of historical and comparative context is the second principle guiding our research. We have sought to historically situate our analysis of the Twitter communication of today's new nationalists. We do this by taking seriously the historical context within which the campaigns are operating. We focus on how they ground their messages in long-standing ideas about the ethnic foundations of their nations. At the same time, we also situate our analysis in a comparative context. We examine how each of our cases employ similar techniques and themes and how they vary in terms of the content of their messaging.

We complement this historical and comparative focus with a principle of balancing both inductive and deductive analysis. One of our main aims in this book is to explore how the new nationalists are using ethnic myths and symbols in their social media communication. Accordingly, we focus on identifying when and how our targets are evoking foundational ethnic myths and symbols in their tweets. But, to avoid "tunnel vision" in our assessment and confirming any biases about the likelihood of seeing ethnic messaging, we have offset this more deductive approach with an inductive method that identifies recurrent and important themes and topics that emerge in the communication of our case studies (for example, positions on policy issues, responses to the media, attacking political opponents, among many other topics).

To carry out this analysis, we collected the Twitter data from the leading examples of the new nationalism across the West: Donald Trump, Marine Le Pen, and the two most prominent Leave campaigns during the UK's Brexit referendum (the official Vote Leave and the highly influential Leave.EU campaigns). As discussed previously, these three cases exemplify the resurgence of ethnic nationalism in the West that emerged in 2016 and 2017. For Donald Trump we collected tweets for his entire primary and presidential campaign between June 15, 2015 (the day prior to announcing his presidential bid) and January 20, 2017 (the day of his inauguration). Trump sent 5,516 tweets from "@realDonaldTrump" in this period, which we captured from a widely cited and reliable public archive.[1] For Marine Le Pen, we collected tweets for the six-month period before the final vote in the 2017 presidential campaign (November 7, 2016, to May 7, 2017). Le Pen sent 2,851 tweets from "@MLP_officiel" during this period, which we captured directly from the Twitter API.[2] For the two Leave campaigns we collected tweets for the six-month period before the referendum vote (December 23, 2015 to June 23, 2016). Vote Leave sent 2,957 tweets from "@vote_leave" and Leave.EU sent 4,416 tweets from "@LeaveEUOfficial" during this period, which we captured directly from the Twitter API. We excluded retweets from our data for two reasons: (1) we are interested in examining the *direct* messaging of these leaders and movements, and particularly how they employ ethnic myths and symbols in their political strategy and communication, rather than how these messages echo or amplify other's views; and (2) we are not focusing here on the ensuing discussions that take place among those following or commenting on the tweets from these accounts, particularly given indications that large portions of these discussions are driven by bots (Bessi and Ferrara 2016).

To analyze this data, we applied tailored versions of the schema introduced earlier in this chapter. As we explain in the subsequent chapters, for each of our cases we have populated the schema to map the foundational ethnic myths and symbols that have emerged, become institutionalized, and shifted over time in the US, France, and UK. For each case, we were thus able to construct a coding framework that indicates when messages evoke foundational ethnic myths and symbols relating to the people, homeland, religion, history, and ethos of each nation.[3] To identify correspondence between a tweet and these categories, we searched for words and phrases, sensitive to their context, that drew upon historically situated ideas. We identified the use of ethnic myths and symbols both through a top-down approach of searching for specific key words in the corpus of tweets and a bottom-up process of reading each tweet in sequence and manually applying codes. Members from our research team,[4] along with ourselves, coded the tweets using a computer software package (NVivo). All coded tweets were reviewed by at least two individuals, always including one of the authors, to increase inter-coder reliability. Our interpretive approach does introduce an element of subjectivity. However, the scope of the study, including all tweets over defined campaign periods and the transparency of the coding frameworks, helps address these limitations.

Why Twitter?

Our approach here raises questions that warrant consideration. A number of these questions stem from our focus on Twitter to better understand why ethnic nationalism is gaining currency across the West, and how movements differ across countries and why their programs are reverberating with ethnic majorities.

First and foremost is a question about why we are looking at *this medium* to understand the political communication of new nationalists. Politics is performance, particularly campaigning. In the contemporary media landscape, the public is saturated with messaging through multiple, overlapping, and fragmented mediums. Leaders get their message out through speeches, newspaper stories, television spots, interviews, ads on all kinds of mediums, Internet memes, and through viral social networks, to name only a few outlets. Increasingly, these messages are tailored through highly sophisticated targeting of the interests and behaviors of niche audiences. As has often been argued, the performative nature of political campaigning—the imagery, and the narrative and ritualistic nature of events—can have significant power in creating a connection between a leader and their followers (Tsang and Woods 2014). This all feeds a valid critique that looking at Twitter—a primarily textual medium—may be missing important and rich aspects of the political messaging of today's new nationalists. In addition, the constraints of the 280-character limit mean that the micro-blogging platform could simplify and obscure deep meaning in the content of messages.

These are valid concerns about our focus on Twitter. But they do not diminish the value of our enterprise. Twitter is central to campaigning today and a main element of the new nationalist playbook. It certainly warrants study. The expanding literature we cite is testimony to this claim. The primarily text-based nature of the medium facilitates the kind of analysis we are aiming for here: we can identify how ideas are employed in constellations of words through nuanced analysis that avoids subjectivity by using tried and tested methods. But, critically, Twitter is much more than text. People use many different modes of communication on the platform, including images and videos. In our analysis, when videos and images are included and specifically referenced in a post, we incorporate these to better situate and code the text and the tweet. In this respect, while Facebook is certainly a more visual medium than Twitter—an attribute that opens avenues to consider the performative nature of the new nationalism—our analysis of Twitter does not fully ignore these forms of communication.

More to the point, Twitter has become an aggregator for campaign content. It acts as a central clearinghouse for the many different streams of a political campaign. Leaders and movements post their campaign speeches and stops, clips from television and Internet ads, and memes through Twitter. We consider and include much of this content in our analysis. We do focus primarily on the directly written text on Twitter. But we also treat it as a window into the overall campaign strategy and messaging. Given our scope of analysis—looking at every tweet over the duration of a campaign—we are confident that our account reflects the broader campaign messaging.

This leads to a related question about the scope of our study and whether we can compare our three cases, given that there was variation in the role of Twitter in the respective campaigns. As previously noted, leaders and parties use Twitter differently and have vastly different levels of followers. This is certainly true for our cases. Donald Trump had over 88 million followers and over 55,000 posts before he was permanently suspended from the platform in January 2021. He was among the most followed and active *people* on Twitter—let alone *politicians*. In contrast, Marine Le Pen has fewer followers, approximately 2.6 million, and has just over 23,000 posts. The two Leave campaigns for Brexit—as issue-specific accounts focused on a single campaign—have even fewer followers: Leave. EU has just under 300,000 followers with nearly 25,000 posts and Vote Leave has just under 60,000 followers with over 6,000 posts at the time of writing. The difference in absolute numbers here speaks to potential variation in terms of the role of Twitter in the campaigns. However, this variation does not negate the value of comparing these campaigns. Despite the difference in absolute numbers, the *relative* reliance on Twitter throughout the campaigns as a central broadcast medium is consistent across the cases. Trump's reliance on the platform is well documented, and this shows in his rates of daily tweeting during the 2016 campaign: in the six-month period prior to the November 8 vote, he was quite active, averaging 10.3 tweets per day from his account. Marine Le Pen was similarly active: in the six months prior to the 2017 French presidential election, she averaged 15.7 tweets per day. The two Leave accounts were even more active during the Brexit referendum campaign: in the six months leading up to June 23, 2016, Vote Leave averaged 16 tweets per day and Leave.EU averaged 24 tweets per day. In short, each of these campaigns was highly active on Twitter—indeed Marine Le Pen and the Leave campaigners were, on average, more active than the archetypal Twitter politician, Donald Trump.

This leads to another related set of questions about the importance of Twitter to a campaign. How many people, really, are following these leaders and reading their tweets closely? On this front, there are two important considerations that justify our focus on Twitter.

The first consideration is the reach of Twitter *beyond the followers* of an account. Donald Trump's use of Twitter exemplified the potential for Twitter as a political agenda setter and attention-grabbing medium. A study in 2018 showed that while, at the time, only 8 percent of Americans actually followed him directly, 76 percent of Americans reported regularly seeing, reading, or hearing about his tweets (Newport 2018). Trump recognized the power of this medium and its reach—he regularly spoke about its ability to shift the media narrative. As he boasted: "Boom. I press it," (sending a tweet) "and, within two seconds, 'we have breaking news'" (as quoted in Shear et al. 2019). In this respect, the reach of Twitter is not so much in bypassing the media as setting its agenda. As a *New York Times* profile showed, Trump built Twitter into the functioning of his entire administration, and increasingly relied on it over the course of his time in office (Shear et al. 2019). His engagement with the platform grew his direct reach—before he was banned from the platform he had more than six times as many followers as when he was elected in 2016 (Lerman 2020)—only augmenting the secondary attention paid to his posts. The centrality of Twitter to Trump's political brand has become even more apparent following his ban. His ability to interject his perspective into the daily news cycle and shape the coverage of events has been significantly curtailed.

Even if we set aside the exceptional attention paid to Trump's tweeting, the centrality of Twitter to modern campaigning provides a powerful justification for our focus in this book. In this respect, we are treating Twitter as a window into a wider campaign and political program. This means that we are less concerned with the actual followers of accounts, and more focused on the messages as indicative of the broader political strategy of a leader and movement. While there is some targeting and differentiation in the form of messaging on Twitter, cross-platform posting and the use of the site as a central broadcast venue give us confidence that our analysis is reflective of the general campaign strategy and messaging. Indeed, a great deal of work goes into the strategic use of social media as a core element of today's political campaign machinery. This strategy is again evident with Donald Trump. Despite his brand as a reactionary and impulsive politician—in many respects a well-earned reputation—Trump also reportedly spent significant periods of time (hours, days, even weeks) sitting and reflecting on single tweets to refine them and find the most opportune moment to deliver them (Shear et al. 2019). Of course, he did not always run his own Twitter account (Draper 2018). Like many politicians today, he had a sophisticated social media operation. He spent a reported $94 million on his 2016 digital campaign—and his 2016 digital campaign director (Brad Parscale) was named as his 2020 re-election campaign manager, before he was replaced for a series of early missteps (BBC News 2018). During his time in office, he relied heavily on his White House social media director, Dan Scavino. Scavino reportedly occupied "a closet-sized room just off the Oval Office" while managing Trump's Twitter account, and suggested tweets categorized in terms of their outrageousness—from hot to medium to mild (Shear et al. 2019). While some of these attributes are likely unique to Trump and his unconventional approach to politics, the broader point about the strategic calculations and investment in time and resources to social media speak to the importance of the medium to campaigning today. All of this is to say that the tweets we analyze here, even for a leader who is not widely seen as an exemplar of strategic calculation, are part of a broader, concerted, and planned communication strategy.

In the chapters that follow, we work to uncover how ethnic nationalism is a central plank of these campaign strategies. Our aim is to show how these campaigns are drawing from foundational, historically rooted, ethnic myths and symbols to define "us" and "them." To further this objective, in the subsequent chapters we provide an overview of the emergence and institutionalization of the foundational ethnic myths and symbols. We then consider the contemporary political context, before examining how these myths and symbols were used in the Twitter communication of largely successful campaigns that were emblematic of the new nationalism in the West. Through this analysis, our goal is to move beyond a singular focus on rhetoric or discursive technique to explain the success of the new nationalists: we are examining the role of ethnic myths and symbols in shaping politics by tracking their presence in one of the most prevalent and important forms of political communication today, Twitter.

4

The Foundations and Development of Ethnic Nationalism in America

This chapter traces the origins and development of a long-standing tradition of American political culture that is often overlooked: ethnic nationalism. America is conventionally understood as a civic nation, defined by ideals of liberty, equality, and democracy (Arieli 1964; Hartz 1955; Kohn 1944; Lipset 1996; Greenfeld 1992; Schlesinger 1998). As such, ethnic nationalism tends to be presented as antithetical to a political community that is thought to have transcended the ascribed hierarchies and primordial attachments of the "Old World." This view has been reasserted so often, and is so widely believed throughout American society, that it has long ceased to be merely an academic position. Rather, it is more akin to a religious myth—it is the American "Creed" (Myrdal 1995). We take issue with this view of America—particularly the view that illiberalism and ethnic nationalism are exceptional or somehow "un-American." We argue that they are very much part of what it means to be "American."

In taking this position, we join a fast-growing body of revisionist literature. According to this line of research, the illiberal features of American political culture are not "un-American," but have actually been core to the development of its identity. Many of the most powerful findings of this research have shed light on the ways in which racism has been central to—even constitutive of—American identity (see Allen 1994; Laforest and Dubois 2017; Kendi 2016; Morgan 1975; Painter 2010; Scheckel 1998; Roediger 2001). Others point to similar processes at work in anti-immigrant nativism and religious bigotry (see Higham 2002; Horsman 1986; Jacobson 1999). A related line of research points to the role of patriarchal conceptions of gender in constituting American identity (Marston 1990; Nagel 1998; Smith-Rosenberg 2010).

But how can we make sense of these contradictory interpretations of American political culture? Is America fundamentally liberal or illiberal? One of the more compelling responses is to answer "yes" to both questions. In this regard, a growing number of researchers now suggest that American political culture is a conflicted composite of liberal *and* illiberal traditions, with each one having extensive footholds in beliefs and institutions (see Blum 2015; Foner 1988; Gerstle 2017; Kaufmann 2004b; Lieven 2012; Smith 1997; Grant 2012; Trautsch 2016). While our concern in this chapter is with the anti-liberal (specifically ethnic) tradition of American nationalism, this "multiple streams" perspective is useful for our analysis because it illuminates how American ethnic nationalism has often developed in opposition to the civic nationalist tradition.

Before we begin, we should clarify once again why we focus on ethnic nationalism rather than racism. For most observers, racism is at the heart of America's illiberal traditions. We agree that racism is critical to understanding American political culture, and we are deeply indebted to those working in this area. However, we think that ethnicity better captures the totality of the phenomena we are concerned with in this book. As we outlined in chapter 2, we define ethnicity as a complex of interrelated myths, symbols, and practices that together provide a group of people with a sense of kinship, history, and identity. This "myth-symbol complex" is constructed historically and relationally, through interaction among members of one's group (the in-group) and with perceived outsiders (the out-group). From this perspective, "race" may be an important component of an ethnic group's myth-symbol complex, but there are likely to be other components as well, such as language or religion. The extent to which any of these components becomes an important myth-symbol distinguishing the in-group from the out-group depends on the specificities of a given context of social relations. In the case of America, this perspective helps to shed light on how seemingly disparate phenomena, such as racism or religious bigotry, are related to one another as expressions of the same broad phenomenon: they are manifestations of a dominant ethnic group's efforts to fend off perceived threats to their dominance. In other words, ethnic nationalism.

To trace the development of American ethnic nationalism, we start by exploring its cultural foundations, which emerged in the mid-eighteenth century. To map these foundational elements of American ethnic nationalism, we apply the schema introduced in the previous chapter. We then explore how core aspects of the ethnic conceptions of the American people, religion, history, homeland, and ethos persisted and changed from the nineteenth to the twenty-first century.

The Cultural Foundations of American Ethnic Nationalism

American ethnic nationalism first took shape in the decades before, and after, the American Revolution—from approximately the 1740s until the 1820s. At the time, it was expressed as a defense of the dominant group in the colonies: English Protestant settlers and their progeny. From the seventeenth century onward, the pace of migration from the British Isles (especially from England), alongside the propensity of the settlers to procreate, was so great that by the eighteenth century they had overwhelmed the Indigenous and non-British European communities in the colonies (Kaufmann 2004b, 12). They had also begun to forge a collective identity, which partly transcended regional particularisms and class hierarchies, and which was distinct from metropolitan England. This identity supplied American ethnic nationalism with an enduring set of myths and symbols.

For much of the eighteenth century, the English settler community did not use a stable demonym to refer to themselves. "English," "Anglo-Saxon," and even "British-American" were all common. After the Revolution, the name "American" took hold—a term that metropolitan English had previously used to refer to Indigenous Americans and, to a lesser extent, to depreciatively refer to Anglo-Americans (Breen 1997, 30). However, this term is not very helpful to our analysis, which necessitates that we distinguish among various groups of Americans. For this reason, we follow the convention that uses the name "Anglo-American." The proclivity for Anglo-Americans to perceive themselves simply as Americans, rather than as a distinct "Anglo" community within America, is not unexpected. Like dominant ethnic communities elsewhere, the Anglo-Americans saw America as an extension of their own community—from their perspective, Anglo-America *was* America. For instance, "founding father" John Jay was merely stating a perceived matter of fact when he wrote that America was populated by "one united people—a people descended from the same ancestors, speaking the same language, professing the same religion" (cited in Babb 1998, 32).

The process by which Anglo-American identity took shape was adaptive and relational; the colonists *adapted* their English Protestant identities to new sets of social *relations* in the colonies, resulting in the formation of a new collective identity. These relations occurred with their fellow Anglo-Americans (the in-group) and with various groups of perceived outsiders (the out-groups), including the Indigenous and non-British white settler communities, African Americans, as well as metropolitan British. The most important event driving relations within the in-group was the First Great Awakening, a Protestant evangelical movement that swept through the colonies in the 1730s and 1740s, touching almost every Protestant denomination and social strata. In doing so, it helped to break down regional cultural boundaries among Anglo-Americans (Heimert 1966, 76). In addition, the combination of a burgeoning inter-colonial trade, a vibrant print culture (Warner 2009), and rapid growth of consumer capitalism (Breen 1997) in the decades prior to the Revolution facilitated the mixing of people, ideas, and practices across the colonies, reinforcing the sense that Anglo-Americans constituted a pan-colonial, imagined community.

The most significant out-group prior to the Revolution were Indigenous Americans, with whom frequent conflict reinforced a sense of common difference among the colonists. Conflictual relations with the Spanish and French similarly reinforced the Anglo-Americans' sense of distinctiveness vis-à-vis non-Anglo, particularly Catholic, Europeans—a development that was greatly reinforced in relation to the French during the warfare of the 1750s and 1760s (Kaufmann 2004b, 13). In addition, the rapid growth of slavery throughout the colonies in the eighteenth century reinforced cultural boundaries between Anglo-Americans and African Americans (Painter 2010, 105–30; Babb 1998, 63–88). In the face of a surge of British nationalism in the mid-eighteenth century, the Anglo-Americans also began to see themselves as distinct from metropolitan English. However, in this case, the Anglo-Americans conceived of themselves not as a separate ethno-cultural community *per se*, but rather as a better representative of the community's culture (Breen 1997). As the common adage of the day went, they were "more English than the English."

The Revolution supercharged this process of identity formation. A recent trend in American historiography is to downplay the Revolution's significance for American political culture by calling attention to ways in which it served to expose divisions rather than forge unity. For example, seeing the Revolution as pitting Patriots against Loyalists, and revealing the extent to which the revolutionaries identified more strongly with their respective regions and colonies, than with the pan-colonial, "national" community (Trautsch 2016, 294–95). These are important caveats. Nevertheless, on balance, it is hard not to see the Revolution as a broadly unifying event. The rupture with Britain accelerated the process by which Anglo-Americans imagined themselves as a distinct community in the world. Furthermore, the very experience of war, as well as the use of citizen-militias, made for a common experience across the colonies that subsequently provided a rich set of symbolic resources for sustaining a sense of collective identity. The fact that the Revolution was successful also greatly abetted the process of identity formation. George Washington—who was acutely concerned during the Revolution that the colonists were not sufficiently unified—turned to the task of forging a common identity almost immediately upon securing independence (Grant 2012, 123). In this regard, the creation of new public rituals celebrating Independence Day were particularly important for sustaining a sense of pan-colonial solidarity (Travers 1997).

Through these interactions, Anglo-American identity took shape. In the following subsections, we elaborate upon the foundational mytho-symbolic elements of this identity, focusing on how they defined their peoplehood, religion, history, homeland, and ethos. While we use these categories to help identify the foundations of American ethnic nationalism, we recognize that these elements are intertwined as a dense complex of beliefs that together defined Anglo-American ethnic identity.

People

Anglo-Americans' sense of peoplehood was mainly informed by three intertwined myths, which depicted them as: Anglo-Saxon, agrarian, and, to a lesser extent, white.[1] The most important of these was the myth of Anglo-Saxon ancestry. From the mid-eighteenth century through the first decades of the nineteenth century, Anglo-Saxon scholarship swept through American intellectual life (Kaufmann 2004b, 18). Jefferson was himself a lifelong student of Anglo-Saxon history and culture, even taking it upon himself to learn the language (Horsman 1986, 22). Indeed, most of the leading figures of the revolutionary generation believed that America's cultural bases were Anglo-Saxon, including Josiah Quincy Jr., Sam Adams, Benjamin Franklin, Charles Carroll, Richard Bland, Patrick Henry, and George Washington (Horsman 1986, 18).

The Anglo-Saxon myth provided Anglo-Americans with a sense of their history and an ethos for understanding what made them distinct in the world. It depicted Anglo-Americans as the descendants of ancient Saxon German tribes (often referred to as Teutons), who settled and formed a distinct ethnic group in England, before migrating to America. The principal traits that Anglo-Americans attributed to their Anglo-Saxon heritage was an innate predilection for liberty, equality, and democracy. These traits were seen to set the Anglo-Americans apart from other communities in the world, revealing their inherent superiority over all other human communities. This sense of superiority informed a belief that it was their destiny to populate all of America and lead the world.

The Anglo-Saxon myth first developed in England.[2] It emerged in the eighth century through Bede's *Ecclesiastical History of the English People*, and was used by King Alfred in the tenth century to justify his claim as the first ruler of a unified England (Hastings 1997, 37–39). It was similarly invoked by theologians during the Reformation as a way of legitimizing Henry the Eighth's break from Rome, by demonstrating that there had already been a distinct Anglo-Saxon branch of the Christian church (Horsman 1986). At the end of the eighteenth century, with the emergence of the Romantic belief that each community had a unique, transhistorical "spirit," England's mythic Anglo-Saxon heritage took on renewed significance. At this time, the myth became more self-centered, depicting the English as a more authentic branch of the Anglo-Saxon tribes than their brethren in Germany (Horsman 1986, 15). English Whig historians went on to reinforce the idea that Anglo-Saxons were inherently liberal—that liberalism was an English trait (Kumar 2003, 214). This revised myth was, in turn, repurposed by the Anglo-Americans, who depicted themselves as the preeminent branch of the Anglo-Saxons—more authentic, even, than the English (Horsman 1986, 9,15–24).

The myth that Anglo-Americans were Anglo-Saxon was closely connected to a myth that they were an agrarian people. In keeping with the Romantic belief that rural communities were the crucibles of a community's culture, many Anglo-American intellectuals venerated small-scale agricultural communities (particularly in New England), peopled by hard-working, Anglo-Saxon, "yeoman farmers" (Hofstadter 1955). Jefferson, for example, declared that "those who labor in the earth are the chosen people of God, if ever He had a chosen people, whose breasts he has made His peculiar deposit for substantial and genuine virtue" (cited in Peterson 1990, 13). The ostensible virtues of agrarian life were frequently juxtaposed with the perceived corrupting influence of industrialization and urbanization. As such, agrarian communities were looked upon with nostalgia, as symbols of an American "golden age" that had sadly succumbed to the baleful growth of industrial cities (Kaufmann 1999, 455–56).

Nearer to the end of eighteenth century, the myth-symbols describing Anglo-Americans as an Anglo-Saxon, agrarian people began to combine more frequently with a racial myth that they were "white." According to this myth, Anglo-Americans shared certain physical traits that distinguished them as members of the white race, and which confirmed their intellectual and physical superiority over all other races. This myth-symbol was the most distinctively American component of Anglo-American identity, and in the coming decades it would become its most significant. However, because whiteness was not the primary component of English identity at the time of the first waves of colonization, the settlers did not initially identify themselves in this way. As Theodore Allen (1994) observes, American colonial records did not explicitly use the term "white" as a social category until the end of the seventeenth century.

By the end of the eighteenth century, "white" had become an important social category. Indeed, the category of "free white" was the only explicitly racial designation in the first national census of 1790. Nonwhite people, specifically black Americans (Indigenous Americans were excluded from national censuses until 1860), were implied through the categories of "all other free persons" and "slaves" (Painter 2010, 104; see also Thompson 2016). Despite the significance of whiteness, its meaning and boundaries remained relatively ambiguous. It was not entirely clear who was perceived as part of the in-group, or who belonged to the out-group. For instance, the 1790 census did not differentiate among the diverse origins of European Americans, implying that they were all white. Yet this is not how many Anglo-American intellectuals perceived the category; for them, only Anglo-Saxons were truly white. In this regard, it was commonplace to point to the "swarthy" complexion of other Europeans to place them in the out-group. Benjamin Franklin, for example, declared that "the Spaniards, Italians, French, Russians and Swedes, are generally of what we call a swarthy Complexion; as are the Germans also, the Saxons only excepted, who with the English, make the principal Body of White People on the Face of the Earth" (cited in Babb 1998, 33).

There was also some ambiguity in how Anglo-Americans viewed Indigenous Americans. Following the dominant racial theory of the time—that differences in the physical traits of groups were a result of the environmental conditions in which they lived—many Anglo-Americans believed that Indigenous Americans could be made "white" if they were properly inculcated into Anglo-American "civilization." Jefferson, for example, expressed the hope that, following a period of tutelage, Indigenous Americans would eventually be absorbed into the white population (Horsman 1986, 107). However, not all of Jefferson's contemporaries shared his perception of the permeability of the racial boundary between Anglo and Indigenous Americans. In regions where conflict with Indigenous Americans was ongoing, highly negative depictions of them predominated, such that they were depicted almost as a different species of human, often more closely resembling animals (Babb 1998, 71–74).

The racial boundary between Anglo and African Americans appears to have been more impermeable in the minds of Anglo-Americans. In contrast to his perception of Indigenous Americans, Jefferson, for instance, doubted whether black Americans could ever become white, arguing that they were "inferior to the whites in the endowments both of body and mind" (Onuf 1998, 2). This boundary of whiteness was reflected in the laws and customs of the time, with each of the states of the newly formed union having laws that, to varying degrees, treated African Americans differently than the white population. Nevertheless, even here there was some ambiguity, with the state of Georgia acknowledging that an individual might be partially "white," in the sense of being mixed-race or "mulatto," and thereby be accorded some of the privileges enjoyed by whites (Allen 1994, 13).

Despite these ambiguities over the boundaries of whiteness, Anglo-American intellectuals were unambiguous in the belief that they themselves were part of the white in-group. It was the other groups, whether they were European, Indigenous, black, or even poor Anglo-Americans, who were, to varying degrees, ambiguous. Thus, at the turn of the eighteenth century, while the myth of whiteness was clearly taking hold, it was nevertheless, at best, depicted as a gradient, with Anglo-Americans—as the preeminent representative of the white race—at the center. This racial myth conjoined with the myths that the Anglo-Americans were an Anglo-Saxon, agrarian people—all of which confirmed their innate superiority. Furthermore, the dominance of Anglo-Americans meant that these myths became intertwined with their perception of American identity writ large. In other words, a truly authentic American was perceived to be Anglo-Saxon, agrarian, and white—and Protestant.

Religion

Protestantism was a central component of Anglo-American identity. Indeed, as is well-documented, the first waves of "pilgrims" migrating to America in the seventeenth century were driven by their Protestantism. For these early settlers, Protestantism was the preeminent source of their common identity. This remained true until at least the late eighteenth century, when it became intertwined with the Anglo-Saxon and white identities described above. Nevertheless, as we discuss later in this chapter, even after these other sources of identity came to prominence, the belief that Anglo-Americans were a Protestant people persisted into the nineteenth and twentieth centuries.

The Protestant component of Anglo-American identity originated in England during the Reformation, after which it was sustained through recurring conflict with Catholic Europe, especially France (Colley 1992). Although there was significant disagreement and conflict between the Church of England and various nonconforming Protestant sects (which was serious enough to provoke widespread migration to America), there was nevertheless a mutual understanding that they were closer to one another than they were to Roman Catholics. As Linda Colley (1992, 19–25) has shown, the various factions of Protestant Britain were thus drawn together by their shared antipathy to the Roman Catholic Church. In this way, Catholicism played the role of significant Other in the development of an overarching British Protestant identity.

This Protestant identity provided English people with a set of sacred myths and symbols that described them as a "chosen people," who had a privileged relationship with God (A. Smith 2003). As such, they were depicted as having been charged by God with a divine mission to promulgate and defend the true faith, particularly against Roman Catholics (A. Smith 2006, 444). Protestantism also infused English territory with a sense of sacredness. In this regard, it was depicted as a holy land—a "new Israel" for God's chosen people (Colley 1992, 29–30).

The first waves of nonconformist settlers in the seventeenth century turned to their Protestant identity to explain why they had come to America. Their justifications for migrating continue to reverberate today. As the historian Susan Mary Grant writes: "The arrival of the Mayflower in 1620 may have brought only a hundred or so settlers to America's Atlantic coast, but an entire mythology, which persists to this day, was constructed on the small boulder that is Plymouth Rock" (2012, 50). Much of this mythology is encapsulated in the writings of the Puritan John Winthrop, who arrived at the Massachusetts Bay colony in 1630. While at sea, Winthrop delivered the now famous sermon, which likened the journey to Moses's journey out of Egypt into the Promised Land. For Winthrop, he and his fellow nonconformists were a chosen people, who escaped persecution in England to create a truly Godly society in America. According to Winthrop, this new society was destined to provide an example for the world—it would be a "city on a hill." However, he also warned his fellow passengers that this destiny was conditional on them maintaining their "covenant" with God by living in a godly way. Winthrop's words rang out:

> [W]e shall find that the God of Israel is among us, when ten of us shall be able to resist a thousand of our enemies; when He shall make us a praise and glory that men shall say of succeeding plantations, "may the Lord make it like that of New England." For we must consider that we shall be a city upon a hill. The eyes of all people are upon us. So that if we shall deal falsely with our God in this work we have undertaken, and so Him to withdraw His present help from us, we shall be made a story and a by-word through the world. (cited in Grant 2012, 53)

The myth that the settlers were a chosen people who had been granted America by Providence in order to create a "city on a hill" provided a framework for them to understand their often conflictual relations with other communities in the colonies. With regard to Indigenous Americans, many settlers—including Winthrop—saw an opportunity to fulfill their mission by converting them to the "true" religion (Grant 2012, 56). However, the settlers could be just as quick to justify violence against Indigenous communities through appeals to this foundational Protestant mythology. In 1637, Puritan leaders celebrated the brutal massacre of most of the inhabitants of a Pequot village, observing that it was a "sweet sacrifice," and that it "was Lord's Doings, and it is marvellous in our Eyes!" (Grant 2012, 57). With regard to their relations with Catholics, the belief that America should be Protestant provided justification for a wide variety of anti-Catholic restrictions (R. Smith 1997, 57).

By the middle of the eighteenth century, the myth that the Anglo-Americans were a chosen people was regularly combined with the Anglo-Saxon myth that they were destined to restore ancient Anglo-Saxon liberties in America. This was subsequently further intertwined with the racial myth that the Anglo-Americans were the preeminent representatives of the white race. Together, these myths and their attendant symbols provided a depiction of the Anglo-Americans as an "essentially Anglo-Saxon people, specially chosen by the Protestant God to carry forth the torch of freedom that was the emblem of their race" (R. Smith 1997, 75).

History

The Anglo-Saxon myth provided Anglo-Americans with an account of their origins. This account reached into the distant past, to the ancient Saxon tribes described by first-century Roman historian Tacitus in *Germania* and to the people described by Bede in the eighth century. From this historical narrative, the founding of the United States was not a singular moment of genesis. Rather, it represented the unfolding of a new—albeit significant—chapter in the long history of the Anglo-Saxon people. Furthermore, the broad acceptance at this time of the Romanticist belief that each ethno-cultural community had an inner "spirit" that endures relatively unchanged through the ages meant that Anglo-Americans perceived themselves to be genealogically, culturally, and psychically connected with their historical predecessors. As such, they looked to the past as a framework for understanding the challenges and successes of their present.

Germania circulated widely among the reading public in England (and in America) through the seventeenth, eighteenth, and nineteenth centuries (Horsman 1986, 16). Its characterization of Germans as a "pure" people like "no one but themselves," who had a deep attachment to liberty, individual rights, and democratic decision-making, shaped how English intellectuals understood key events in the historical development of their community (cited in Horsman 1986, 12). In this regard, key events tended to be read as expressions of a long struggle to recapture the freedoms enjoyed by their ancient predecessors. For many eighteenth-century English intellectuals, the period from the migration of German tribes to England in the fifth century until the Norman victory in 1066 was a "golden age," when their Anglo-Saxon freedoms had flourished. The year 1066, from this perspective, inaugurated a period of decline, during which their Anglo-Saxon freedoms had been stymied by the "yoke" of Norman rule. It was not until the establishment of Magna Carta in 1215 and the Glorious Revolution of 1688 that their ancient Anglo-Saxon freedoms were progressively restored (Horsman 1986, 12).

This historical myth was adapted by Anglo-Americans to make sense of their struggle against Britain. An argument that had formerly been a minority view in

England—that Britain had never really managed to completely rid itself of the legacy of Norman tyranny—captured the imaginations of the Anglo-Americans. They came to see America as the ideal place for Anglo-Saxon culture to finally flourish, free from the deleterious Norman legacy (Horsman 1986, 19). In this way, the Anglo-Saxon myth provided the American Revolution with a powerful source of legitimacy. It suggested that Anglo-American revolutionaries were fighting for more than the recognition of their universal "natural rights"—they were fighting for the re-establishment of ancient Anglo-Saxon liberties that had been lost after the Norman invasion of 1066 (Kaufmann 2004b, 18). Jefferson, for example, made this claim explicit. In discussions over the design of a new American Seal following the Revolution, he reportedly wanted it to contain images of Hengist and Horsa, who, in his words, were "the Saxon chiefs from whom we claim the honor of being descended, and whose political principles and form of government we have assumed" (cited in Horsman 1986, 22). Thus, when Jefferson spoke of liberties that had been usurped in the Declaration of Independence, he was likely not just appealing to universalistic principles of natural rights, but also to the idea that these liberties were specifically due to Anglo-Americans as the inheritors of the Anglo-Saxon tradition (Horsman 1986, 22).

Homeland

An ethnic community's homeland is typically mythologized as the territory in which it has existed since "time immemorial." Over the course of this long history, the territory's ecological features are depicted in this myth as shaping the ethnic community's unique identity through an organic process. As a result, an ethnic community's loss of its territory is usually represented as a blow to its identity. This typical mythology posed a problem for Anglo-Americans, who were a settler community in a new territory. The mythic territorial crucible of their identity was not America, but rather it lay across the Atlantic, in England and, before that, in Germany. Despite this problem, Anglo-Americans were able to draw upon, and adapt, the Anglo-Saxon and Protestant myths to provide a framework for conceiving of America as their "homeland."

We have already outlined how Anglo-Americans came to see themselves as a "chosen people," who had been granted the American territories through divine providence. This myth lent legitimacy to Anglo-Americans' claim over the American territory by infusing it with sacredness. In effect, it replaced the legitimacy that was normally provided by a historicist claim that a community had always existed in a territory with a religious claim that God had gifted the territory.

This sense of legitimacy was further reinforced by the Anglo-Saxon myth, which, as discussed previously, depicted Anglo-Americans as a superior people at the vanguard of civilization, with a destiny to populate the continent. From these beliefs, a myth took shape that the American territory was the rightful homeland of the Anglo-Americans.

Anglo-Americans' self-perception that they were both "chosen" and "superior" enabled them to sidestep the thorny issue that other communities, particularly Indigenous Americans, could potentially lodge a more compelling claim that America was their rightful homeland. Anglo-Americans headed off such claims by representing Indigenous Americans as "savages" and "heathens," who could not legitimately claim the American territory because they lacked civilization and Christianity. For some Anglo-Americans this justified the outright killing of Indigenous Americans to make way for territorial expansion of a superior, chosen people (Grant 2012, 45–46). Others took this idea further by, for example, interpreting Indigenous Americans' high mortality in the face of European diseases as a sign that God was "making room" for them in America (R. Smith 1993, 61). Still others adopted a paternalistic view that Indigenous Americans needed to be "saved" through conversion. In doing so, Anglo-Americans repaid their debts to God and thereby reinforced their claim to America (Woods 2016, 27).

The belief that America was the rightful homeland of the Anglo-Americans was further added substance by the myth that the Anglo-Americans were an agrarian people. This myth conjured up the symbol of "yeoman farmers" who were transforming the American wilderness into a "garden of Eden" (Kaufmann 1999, 669). In this view, Anglo-Americans had a rightful claim to America because they were bringing "light" and "civilization" to a dark and wild place—a "devil's den," in New England poet Michael Winglesworth's words (cited in Kaufmann 1999, 669). This idea also had the effect of delegitimizing Indigenous American claims to American territory. Because Indigenous Americans were not seen to be using the land for agricultural purposes (as defined by Anglo-Americans), they did not have a legitimate claim to the land.

Ethos

The Anglo-Saxon myth also provided Anglo-Americans with an ethos that spoke to their uniqueness and their superiority. This ethos centered on the idea that Anglo-Americans had an innate affinity for liberty, equality, and democracy. Belief in these traits was greatly influenced by Tacitus's description of ancient Saxon tribes, which, as we have discussed, emphasized that these characteristics were unique to them.

Kaufmann (2004b, 37–57) suggests that the pairing of liberal ideas with Anglo-American identity, and the debates that it provoked, was suggestive of a "double-consciousness" within Anglo-American collective identity. This idea helps to explain why the ethnic side of American liberalism has often seemed so hidden. For instance, we have already provided several examples of how Jefferson, one of the great exponents of American civic nationalism, also ascribed to a seeming contradictory, ethnic vision of American identity. For the most part, this contradiction did not provoke outright cognitive dissonance, because these two traditions, at least at the time, were not necessarily mutually exclusive. According to the Anglo-Saxon myth, to which Jefferson ascribed, the liberal tradition *was* an ethnic tradition. Hence, as Rogers Smith (1997) has shown, citizenship law in the fledgling state appears, at first blush, to follow the liberal tradition, but upon closer examination it also demonstrates support for a more ascriptive tradition.

The Anglo-American ethos—that, as Anglo-Saxons, they were innately liberal and democratic—provided them a sense of mission and destiny in America. In doing so, it mirrored, and became entwined with, the religious myth that the Anglo-Americans were a "chosen people." In the decades following the Revolution, Anglo-American intellectuals depicted their new political community as the vanguard of world civilization. This demonstrated to them that they were destined to rule over the whole of the continent. On the surface, this sentiment was usually expressed in civic nationalist terms—in the sense that it was framed as a mission for Anglo-Americans to spread liberty and democracy across the American continent—to be an "empire of liberty," as Jefferson famously put it. However, this civic nationalist language was often combined with Anglo-Saxon myths that belied an underlying ethnic nationalist ideology.

In this regard, the mission to spread liberty and democracy across the continent was linked to a belief that it was the destiny of (Anglo-)Americans to spread westward, to eventually populate the whole of the American continent (Horsman 1986, 92). The movement of liberal ideas and the Anglo-American people, in this view, were one and the same—one was not possible without the other. For some Anglo-Americans, the presence of large numbers of people on the continent who were not Anglo-Saxon represented a potential barrier to the establishment of liberal ideals—hence Jefferson's opposition to black Americans being permitted in the West (Horsman 1986, 92). In the nineteenth century, this ethnic nationalist vision of American expansion would become ever more pronounced, ultimately providing legitimacy for the forced removal of Indigenous Americans from the South, as well as the annexation of Mexican territories in the Southwest (Gómez 2018).

Table 4.1 **Ethnic Anglo-American Myth-Symbol Complex, Approximately 1750–1820**

	People	Religion	Homeland	History	Ethos
Myths	Anglo-Americans are Anglo-Saxon. Anglo-Americans are agrarian. Anglo-Americans are white.	Anglo-Americans are "chosen" by God. America was a gift of divine providence. Anglo-Americans have a covenant with God to ensure Protestantism flourishes in America. America's defeats and triumphs are the result of God's intervention.	America is the rightful homeland of the Anglo-Americans because it was gifted to them by divine providence. America is the rightful homeland of the Anglo-Americans because of their innate superiority. The crucible of Anglo-American identity is in small rural communities of America.	Anglo-Americans' ancestors are ancient Saxon tribes who settled England, before migrating to America. The American Revolution was a fight to restore ancient Anglo-Saxon liberties that were lost in the Norman invasion of 1066.	Anglo-Americans are superior to all other peoples. Liberty and democracy are innate Anglo-American traits.

Tracing the development of ethnic nationalism across these five categories brings to light the foundational myths and symbols of an ethnic, Anglo-American identity. This ethnic identity crystalized in the late eighteenth and early nineteenth centuries as a relatively stable myth-symbol complex. Table 4.1 summarizes the foundational myths and symbols of this ethnic Anglo-American identity using our schema.

These myths are complemented and supported by a collection of symbols. Of course, there are many symbols of ethnic Anglo-American identity. Some of the most significant include the following:

- Symbols of English/Anglo-Saxon heritage (e.g., English names, the English language, dress, etc.)—signaling continuity with the Anglo-Saxon people.
- Agrarian symbols like the yeoman farmer, farmstead, and agricultural land—as a link to the true nature and way of life of the Anglo-Saxons.
- Perceived physical traits, particularly whiteness—as a boundary between the descendants of the Anglo-Saxons and inferior racial others.
- Markers of Protestantism (e.g., vicar, churches, cross, Bible, etc.)—as unifying symbols that set Anglo-Americans apart from Catholics.
- American wilderness (e.g., forests, lakes, etc.)—signifying the open, free, and unoccupied nature of the territory.
- Small, rural agricultural communities (e.g., farms, tilled fields, community churches)—as the heart of the real Anglo-America.
- Great victories and events (e.g., the Revolution, colonial expansion, defeat of Indigenous Americans, etc.)—signifying the successes and triumphs of Anglo-Americans.
- Pillars of liberal democracy (e.g., The US Constitution, founding fathers, Independence Day)—as reflections of the innate superiority and liberalism of Anglo-Americans.

The Development of Ethnic Nationalism in America

In this part of the chapter, we trace the dynamics of persistence and change in the development of ethnic nationalism in America from the early nineteenth until the early twenty-first century. Admittedly, this is a lot of historical ground to cover. However, our aim is not to fully reconstruct the minutiae of ethnic nationalism during this period. Our objective is more limited. We want to highlight—in broad brush strokes—some of the key developments in the content of American ethnic nationalism.

We are mindful of two related dynamics as we trace the development of ethnic nationalism over a series of periods in American history. First and foremost, we highlight how Anglo-American identity transitions from its foundation in a particular set of Anglo-Saxon myths and symbols to a broader, but equally powerful, white American identity. To trace this transformation, we examine how ethnic nationalism was expressed in relation to different out-groups that the Anglo-*cum*-white in-group perceived as a threat, particularly at times of crisis. Here scientific racism and immigration played key roles as drivers of threat perception. The second dynamic we trace is the enduring ideological division *within* the dominant, white majority. This division initially manifested itself through struggles between northerners and southerners, but it was also expressed through a long-running tension between the civic and ethnic conceptions of American identity.

The Ascendance of Whiteness

In the first decades of the nineteenth century, the white racial myth rapidly ascended in the consciousness of Anglo-Americans. This development was partly driven by the emergence of "scientific racism." Following Johann Friedrich Blumenbach's influential typology, scientific racists generally believed that humanity comprised five racial types—usually some combination of European, African, (Indigenous) American, South Asian, and East Asian (Painter 2010, 78–80). These "races" were ranked against one another according to a wide range of "innate" racial characteristics, such as intelligence, physical prowess, and beauty. Underlying this hierarchy was a social Darwinist understanding of interracial dynamics. The dominance of the white race (or "Caucasian," as Blumenbach labeled it) in America and beyond was considered to be the "natural" outcome of their innate racial superiority. Similarly, the subjugation and exploitation of African and Indigenous Americans was thought to be a "natural" reflection of their innate racial inferiority (Horsman 1986, 37).

Many Anglo-Americans embraced this ideology. Ideas and practices inspired by scientific racism, such as phrenology, were hugely popular among the reading public in America (Horsman 1986, 142–43). This is not surprising: the ideas legitimated their dominance over people considered to be racially inferior. However, this new racism did not fully supplant existing ethnic myths and symbols. Rather, scientific racism became intertwined with the Anglo-Saxon myth, infusing it with new racialized meanings that presented Anglo-Saxons as the greatest, and most pure, of the white "races" (Horsman 1986, 198). In addition, the Anglo-American homeland myth—that their innate superiority made them the rightful possessors of the American territory—was boosted by the seeming confirmation of this belief by science. By the same token, the scientific confirmation that other "races," such as Indigenous Americans, were innately inferior further discredited their counterclaims to the American territory.

It is difficult to overstate how much scientific racism and the elevation of whiteness impacted the cultural boundaries of Anglo-Americans. This was especially true of Anglo-Americans in the southern states, where the rapid growth of slavery and ongoing expansion into territories inhabited by Indigenous communities proved to be fertile ground for a racist conception of their cultural boundaries (Horsman 1986, 151). People who were not deemed to be white found themselves on the other side of a seemingly impassable gulf between fundamentally different categories of human. This was especially the case for black people, who, in the slave states of the South, constituted Anglo-Americans' most significant Other. This was not just because African Americans constituted the largest minority population in those states. It was also because they were looked upon by whites as a potential threat. This view was stoked by the memory of the Haitian Revolution, which southern Anglo-Americans recalled as an example of what might occur in America if they were not vigilant (Hunt 2006, 85–107).

For southern Anglo-Americans, the notion of African Americans as a foil was a powerful symbol of belonging. A vast range of formal and informal institutions were established to structure relations between white and black people. These "symbolic border guards" created such powerful barriers that whites and blacks lived large portions of their lives completely separately. Breaching these institutions could result in severe censure. The well-documented history of white terrorism demonstrates how dangerous this could be for black people. Nevertheless, breaches often occurred. Even sexual relations between whites and blacks were relatively commonplace, as indicated by the great number of people whose parentage was white and black (Painter 2010, 116–17). This provoked anxiety among many Anglo-Americans that they would become "tainted" with blackness, leading to the "one drop rule"—a belief that a person was black even if only one of their ancestors, no matter how remote, had been black. This belief was infused with the new race science, which argued that the white race would be degraded if it mixed with the black race (Horsman 1986, 154–55). Black Americans were thereby perceived not only as a cultural and political threat, but also as a biological threat.

With respect to Indigenous Americans, the new racism built upon, and reinforced, existing Anglo-American myths. Scientific racism amplified the long-running suspicion among some Anglo-Americans that Indigenous Americans would never have a place in American society. Again, this view had traction in the South, where Anglo-Americans were actively, and violently, expanding into Indigenous settlements. Through the course of their encounters, many Anglo-Americans rejected the seemingly more beneficent beliefs that Indigenous Americans could either be "civilized" or "Christianized." Instead, they argued that the innate racial inferiority of Indigenous Americans made this impossible. Kentucky congressman Henry Clay, for instance, put this argument to President John Quincy Adams, who apparently readily agreed (Cave 2003, 1347). Adams's successor, Andrew Jackson, the populist president from Tennessee, took the argument further. In defense of his signing of the Indian Removal Act in 1830, which led to the infamous "Trail of Tears," Jackson declared that the only hope for the survival of Indigenous Americans was for them to be deported far from Anglo-American settlements (Cave 2003).

This line of thought was even more stridently expressed among those who argued for America's expansion into Mexican territories (which led to the Mexican-American War of 1846–1848). In this case, the myth of Anglo-American racial superiority was adapted to existing Anglo-Saxon and Protestant myths that the American territory was the rightful homeland of the Anglo-Americans by virtue of their cultural superiority and divine providence. This expansive form of ethnic nationalism, based upon a heady combination of race, culture, and religion, was captured by the term "Manifest Destiny," which was coined in 1845, shortly before the onset of war. For their part, Mexicans were depicted as a racially degraded, "mongrel race," who, because of their presumed mixing with Indigenous people, were incapable of higher civilization (Horsman 1986, 231; Saxton 1990, 53–57).

The new emphasis on whiteness in relations with these out-groups also shaped perceptions of the in-group. In the southern states in particular, whiteness served to partially override social class boundaries between rich Anglo-Americans and their poorer brethren. In other words, poor Anglo-Americans increasingly found that they belonged to the in-group by virtue of their perceived whiteness (R. Smith 1997, 173). In a similar fashion, white Catholics, who had long been excluded from the in-group by virtue of their religion, also found themselves somewhat closer to belonging, at least in relation to groups who were not perceived to be "white" (R. Smith 1997, 202). Thus, while the myth-symbol of whiteness reinforced boundaries with several racialized out-groups, it also provided a mechanism for expanding the in-group.

The biography and politics of Andrew Jackson—a Tennessean from humble roots—exemplified the emergence of an expanding "white" in-group in the South. Jackson swept to the presidency in 1828 on the back of a populist campaign to expand the electorate by removing laws restricting voting to property-owning men. In doing so, Jackson inaugurated what has often been called the "Age of the Common Man." However, Jackson notably did not seek to remove restrictions on racialized minorities voting. In his politics, the "common" man was a "white" man. Indeed, just as Jackson was working to bring poor whites into the political community, he was also working to deport Indigenous Americans. Furthermore, Jackson made his fortune from the enslavement of black people. On the other hand, Jackson was relatively inclusive of white Catholics, writing that, "we ought therefor to consider all good Christians, whose walk corresponds with their professions, be him Presbyterian, Episcopalian, Baptist, Methodist or Roman Catholics" (cited in McClarey 2009).

Thus, whiteness was both reconfigured and made more salient for Anglo-American identity, particularly in the South. This occurred through the rise of scientific racism, rapidly growing numbers of enslaved black people, expansion into territories occupied by Indigenous Americans, and war with Mexico.

However, the symbol of whiteness was not wholly invented through this process; it was already a part of the Anglo-American myth-symbol complex. Whiteness was adapted to fit the new relational context. A similar process also took place in the northern states. However, in the North, the relational context was different, in the sense that Catholics rather than African Americans were the most significant out-group. As a result, Protestantism, rather than whiteness, became the most salient element of their identity.

The Persistence of Protestantism

In the first decades of the nineteenth century, the number of Irish Catholics migrating to the US increased rapidly. This trend further accelerated in the 1840s in the wake of the potato famine (Connor 2019). A majority of these Irish Catholics settled in the large industrial cities of the Northeast and Midwest (Kaufmann 2004b, 24). At around the same time, significant numbers of Catholic Germans were also migrating and settling in the large cities of the Northeast and Midwest (Kaufmann 2004b, 24). Anglo-Americans widely perceived these new migrants as a "threat," resulting in a surge of nativist ethnic nationalism.

In 1854, a new political party presenting itself as the defender of America's Anglo-Protestant identity was formed (Silbey 1985, 111–12). The party was formally referred to as the "Native American Party." But it was more widely called the "Know-Nothing Party," because of its origins as a secret society. The Know-Nothings found immediate electoral success, particularly in the northern states. They might even have captured the presidency if not for the onset of the Civil War, which redirected support to the Republican Party (Kaufmann 2004b, 24–26). In a seeming contradiction, at least to present-day sensibilities, the party was opposed to slavery. This reflected the fact that its support base was in the North, where the most significant perceived out-group was Catholic immigrants, not enslaved black people. Thus, unlike their brethren in the South, for northern Anglo-Americans in the mid-nineteenth century, Protestantism became a more salient symbol of identity than whiteness. However, this is not to say that appeals to whiteness and racism disappeared in the North. Anti-black racism was endemic during this time. Racism was also not entirely absent from how northern Anglo-Americans represented Catholics. Irish Catholics, especially, were frequently depicted as an inferior "race," who threatened to degrade America's "white" character, which was narrowly defined in this case as Anglo-Saxon and Protestant (Jacobson 1999, 40–51).

In a similar vein, the prominence of whiteness among southern Anglo-Americans did not erase the Protestant component of their identity. Anti-Catholic appeals to Protestantism could, and did, become salient, depending on the relational context. For example, the anti-immigrant, anti-Catholic message of the Know-Nothings found significant support in Alabama and South Carolina, both of which attracted relatively high numbers of Catholic immigrants at the time (Farrell 2019). Likewise, anti-Catholicism became prominent among southern Anglo-Americans after the Louisiana Purchase (Kastor 2008), as it did during the Mexican-American War (Pinheiro 2014). In short, in both the North and the South, Protestantism persisted as a powerful myth and symbol for the in-group set against a Catholic out-group in the nineteenth century.

The Civil War and the Endurance of Anglo-American Identity

Despite the fact that Anglo-Americans in the southern and northern states continued to broadly identify with the same complex of ethnic myths and symbols, it was not enough to prevent them from going to war with one another in 1861. History is replete with ethnic groups that are wracked by internal conflict, and Anglo-Americans were no different. The consensus among historians today is that the Civil War was primarily precipitated by irreconcilable differences between North and South over slavery. As such, the violent conflict laid bare the contradiction at the heart of the Anglo-American ethos.

As previously discussed, the Anglo-American ethos was based upon a myth that they had a unique and innate predisposition to liberty, equality, and democracy. According to this myth, liberal principles were therefore understood to be ethnic traits. This seemingly contradictory fusion helps to explain why many Anglo-Americans were able to embrace the civic nationalist creed, while at the same time supporting an ethnic nationalist vision of America. However, this was clearly an inherently unstable construction. The liberal ideas that Anglo-Americans depicted as their birthright also provided a basis for excluded groups to hold them to account and demand inclusion. Former enslaved person and famed abolitionist Frederick Douglass made this argument on Independence Day in 1852, when he demanded of his audience what the celebrations meant to an African American:

> Fellow-citizens, pardon me, allow me to ask, why am I called upon to speak here to-day? What have I, or those I represent, to do with your national independence? Are the great principles of political freedom and of natural justice, embodied in that Declaration of Independence, extended to us? and am I, therefore, called upon to bring our humble offering to the national altar, and to confess the benefits and express devout gratitude for the blessings resulting from your independence to us?" (Douglass 2000, 194)

In this speech, Douglas exposed the inherent contradiction in Anglo-American identity. In doing so, he also pointed to the source of the wider cultural struggle between civic and ethnic nationalist conceptions of American identity. In many respects, this struggle pits Anglo-Americans against one another. On one hand, some Anglo-Americans argued that American identity should be made more inclusive by adhering to the civic nationalist principles of the Constitution. Essentially, the argument here was that the privileged ties between their ethnic community and American citizenship needed to be loosened to bring about a more inclusive political order. On the other hand, many argued for the continuation of Anglo-American domination. This dispute came to a violent head with the onset of the Civil War. Such was the intractability of the conflict over the place of slavery in America—over whether black Americans could be excluded from the rights of American citizenship by virtue of their "race"—that the slave states of the South ultimately opted to secede from the nation to protect a socio-economic and political system that was premised upon white dominance.

Much has been written about the divisions created by the Civil War. Some have even argued that a process of "othering" occurred prior to, and during, the war, whereby northerners and southerners came to view themselves as distinct peoples. Edward Blum (2015, 5–6), for example, observes that southerners distinguished themselves from northerners by referring to themselves as Anglo-Normans (as opposed to Anglo-Saxons) and by embracing a new historical myth that traced their origins to the "Cavaliers" of the English Civil War in the mid-seventeenth century. Northerners, by contrast, were depicted as the descendants of the "roundheads." According to this myth, the conflict between North and South was therefore but the most recent iteration of a longer-running struggle between distinct "nationalities" (Blum 2015, 5).

Yet, despite the terrible violence of the war, the perception that the partisans of North and South were broadly of the same ethnic "stock" largely held. In our view, the war did not trigger a wholesale ethno-cultural rupture between North and South. Rather, at the end of the war, several core elements of the Anglo-American myth-symbol complex remained intact on both sides. To paraphrase Abraham Lincoln, both sides continued to be bound by the same "mystic chords of memory." Blum's work actually provides evidence in favor of our argument. In this regard, Blum (2015) demonstrates the important role that religion played in reuniting northerners and southerners after the war. In our view, it is the persistence of this shared element of their ethnic identity that enabled them to, at least partly, reconcile after the war.

The other core ethno-cultural element of Anglo-American identity that persisted in the North and in the South was whiteness. After the war, the mutual understanding that northerners and southerners were both white remained intact. Indeed, more than any other symbol, it is this perception that ultimately enabled northerners to accept southerners back into the national "we" (even if stereotypes about their inferiority endured). That whiteness persisted as a shared symbol among Anglo-Americans is a truly awful irony of history. For it meant that in spite of all the blood that had been spilled in the name of abolition—and despite the fact that a great deal of this blood was that of African Americans fighting for their freedom—following the war, African Americans nevertheless remained a much maligned Other. In other words, they remained a symbolic foil for Anglo-American identity in the South *and* in the North. As David Blight (2009) demonstrates, the desire for reconciliation among white northerners and white southerners was, in the end, greater than their desire to reconcile with blacks. As a result, many of the promises made to freed blacks were broken, and the federal government looked the other way as the southern states reconstructed their societies as white supremacies. The consequences for the collective well-being of African Americans was devastating (Du Bois 1935; Foner 1988).

While we have made the case that a broadly shared Anglo-American identity was reconstituted in the North and South after the Civil War, we should make clear that we are not arguing that conflict simply vanished. A sense of shared identity does not preclude conflict. In the case of the northerners and southerners, the outright violence of the Civil War may have ended, but mutual resentment and suspicion between the two sides remained deep-seated. As a consequence, the North-South divide continued to be—indeed, continues to be—one of the most significant drivers of cultural and political conflict in America.

The "New" Immigrants and Anglo-American Identity

From the 1870s onward, the number of immigrants from southern and eastern Europe grew rapidly. To a lesser extent, the immigrant population from Asia also increased, especially in the western states. As with Irish Catholics and Germans, many Anglo-Americans perceived these immigrant communities as a threat, driving a new wave of nativist ethnic nationalism.

In their opposition to southern and eastern Europeans, Anglo-Americans sought to defend the Anglophone, Protestant, and white bases of their identity. Even though these migrants were European, Anglo-American nationalists resurrected a narrow definition of whiteness that restricted it to northern Europeans (Jacobson 1999). Intellectuals, religious figures, politicians, and media commentators argued that they these migrants were culturally and racially incompatible with America. Violence was not uncommon. A particularly shocking instance occurred in Los Angeles in 1871, when an estimated seventeen Chinese Americans were mutilated and killed in a grisly mob attack (Zesch 2008, 137–42). A similarly violent attack occurred in New Orleans in 1891, when a mob broke into a jail and murdered eleven Italian Americans (Jacobson 1999, 52–62). The Ku Klux Klan also surged during this time, expanding its membership throughout the Midwest and the North, where its mission to ensure "one hundred percent Americanism" focused primarily on the perceived threat posed by Catholic and Jewish communities (Pegram 2011). The rising tide of nativist sentiment eventually reached the highest levels of government; Congress passed a succession of Immigration Acts (1917, 1918, 1921, 1924) that were increasingly restrictive of immigrants from southern and eastern Europe, and which banned Asian immigration outright.

Several developments converged during this period to fan the flames of antipathy toward the new streams of immigration. The entry of the United States into the First World War led many Americans to question the loyalty of immigrants from countries that were now America's enemies. The 1917 Russian Revolution amplified the vilification of eastern and southern European immigrants, particularly Jews, who were depicted as carriers of the communist "virus." Meanwhile, scientific racism found new life through the rise of the eugenicist movement, which warned against eastern and southern European immigration on the grounds that it would lead to the degeneration of the "native" whites. Interestingly, the scientific racists often depicted Asian (especially Japanese) immigrants differently, in the sense that they tended to be depicted as superior to Anglo-Americans. The argument for their exclusion was therefore inverted: Asians needed to be excluded from the US, lest they overtake the Anglo-Americans (Gerstle 2017, 94–115).

In the face of these new out-groups, some Anglo-Americans began to perceive longer-standing immigrant communities differently. In this regard, there was increased acceptance of Germans, Scandinavians, and other northern Europeans. The perceived virtues of these "older" immigrant groups (increasingly referred to as the "Nordics") were often contrasted with the unfavorable characteristics of the new immigrant communities. For example, a 1907 congressional report on immigration opined that the "new" immigrants were "far less intelligent than the old," and that "[r]acially they are for the most part essentially unlike the British, German, and other peoples who came during the period prior to 1880" (cited in Goldstein 2018, 521). Thus, the rise of the new immigrant out-groups triggered a recalibration of the in-group, with northern Europeans now perceived as allied groups, or at least no longer as a threat.

Not all Anglo-Americans were wholly opposed to the new immigration streams. President Theodore Roosevelt (TR), for example, extolled a vision of American identity that was broadly inclusive of all European nationalities, including the "new" immigrants. Around the same time, in 1908, *The Melting Pot*, a play by Israel Zangwill that celebrated the fusion of diverse communities in America, was premiered to rave reviews. TR, who was in attendance, apparently shouted his approval (Gerstle 1999, 1298). Of course, the envisioning of American identity as a composite of differing communities was not new—as early as 1782, Hector St. John was promoting these ideas through his idealization of the "new man" of America. Notably, however, neither TR's nor Zangwill's hybridized conception of American identity represented a wholesale endorsement of civic nationalist principles. Like St. John before them, their visions of America were restricted to people with European backgrounds.

Zangwill can perhaps be excused for not including people of color in his conception of American identity; his parents' families had migrated to England from eastern Europe to escape anti-Semitism, and his play can be read as a medium for imagining a world where the persecution of Jews did not exist. TR was a different matter. It is true that TR often spoke approvingly of black and Indigenous contributions to America. Fundamentally, however, he saw these racialized minorities as innately inferior to European Americans, and incapable of contributing meaningfully to America's success (Gerstle 1999, 1300–1301). Roosevelt was even more disparaging of Asians, particularly the Chinese, whom he despised (Gerstle 1999, 1301). TR's conception of American identity therefore continued to reflect the contradictory pairing of civic nationalism and ethnic nationalism that had long been at the heart of the Anglo-American ethos—with the key difference being that he took a more expansive view of the in-group by including non-Anglo, European Americans. In this regard, TR's vision presaged the pan-European, white American identity that would come to replace Anglo-American identity in the second half of the twentieth century.

At the time, even TR's limited expansion of the boundaries of the in-group was a step too far for many Anglo-Americans. In the years following TR's presidency, anti-immigrant sentiment continued to grow, culminating in the immigration quotas of the 1920s. In the final analysis, the main thrust of this era was therefore a restoration of the dominance of Anglo-American identity. By putting limits on immigration from eastern and southern Europe, and by banning immigration from Asia, the immigration quotas spelled out clearly the cultural parameters of who was perceived to be compatible with America—those of English origin, who were Protestant, and white.

From Anglo-American to White American

Perhaps as a result of its remarkable success earlier in the century, an explicit ethnic Anglo-American nationalism attenuated in the 1930s. In its place, civic nationalism arose, fueled in large part by the presidency of TR's nephew, Franklin D. Roosevelt (FDR). FDR infused American civic nationalism with left-wing ideas. His administration's "New Deal"—a suite of programs and policies aimed at combatting the economic upheaval of the 1930s—was inspired by TR's "new nationalism." As such, it was guided by the idea that economic succor and national cohesion were mutually constitutive. In many respects, this idea bore fruit. Several initiatives associated with the New Deal, such as the National Recovery Agency, as well as FDR's support of unions, were important mechanisms for the political integration of non-British/non-Protestant European Americans—the "white ethnics"—who were then concentrated in blue-collar work (Gerstle 2017, 168–69).

However, like his uncle earlier in the century, FDR's version of civic nationalism did not generally seek to challenge Anglo-American dominance. Rather, he expected the "white ethnics" to assimilate into the dominant culture. For their part, many among these communities supported this assimilationist vision. For example, it became common to adopt "American" (i.e., British) names. Similarly, many Jews hid their religion. Critically, FDR's civic nationalism was largely limited to Europeans, much to the dismay of many black Americans who had supported him (Gerstle 2017, 167). In these respects, FDR's policies and actions continued to reflect the long-standing ambivalence at the heart of Anglo-American identity between civic and ethnic nationalism.

This ambivalence persisted through the Second World War. On the one hand, the war fueled civic nationalism by reinforcing the myth of America as a force for freedom and democracy—a "beacon" of light in the world. In this sense, the war pitted America's virtuous liberalism against Germany's villainous racism (Myrdal 1995). Yet whiteness continued to be a core boundary symbol distinguishing who truly belonged in America. For instance, while the American military helped unify Americans from diverse European backgrounds, it segregated black Americans and largely treated them as inferior (Gerstle 2017, 210–17). At the same time, the war stoked intense suspicion and fear of the potential domestic threat posed by Japanese Americans—many of whom were rounded up and interned, irrespective of any relationship to Japan (Gerstle 2017, 201–2).

In the 1960s, the conflict between civic and ethnic nationalism came to a head. Civic nationalists increasingly turned their gaze inward, questioning America's record of living up to its ideals. A nationwide social movement demanding equality for African Americans rapidly gathered force. This inspired movements for equality on behalf of Indigenous Americans, Asian Americans, and even "white ethnics." Many Anglo-Americans were sympathetic of these movements, particularly at elite universities. Faced with the horrors perpetrated by Nazi Germany, they questioned the discriminatory practices that had long been associated with the dominance of Anglo-Americans, who were now pejoratively referred to as "WASPs"—White, Anglo-Saxon, Protestants (on this process, see Torpey 2006).

The shifts during this period of American history are well known. There were several major legislative victories. The 1964 Civil Rights Act prohibited discrimination on the basis of "race, color, religion, and national origin." The 1965 Immigration Act abolished national origins restrictions that had been put in place in the 1920s. In the realm of media and cultural production, the celebration of America's white, Anglo-Saxon identity was increasingly perceived as bad taste, as were overt expressions of bigotry and racism. For several approving observers of these trends, America looked to be finally fulfilling its liberal destiny. Writing in 1964, the historian Yehoshua Arieli boldly declared that the "history of the American nation is the history of the successive integration of individuals of ethnic groups and of the group itself into the general body of American society and the American polity" (1964, 858–59). It is now clear that Arieli's proclamation came too early.

Despite the ascendance of civic nationalism, several trends speak to the enduring power of ethnic nationalism throughout the twentieth century. Most obvious here is the dominance of whiteness as a symbolic border guard for belonging to the "real" American nation. The integration of black Americans was fiercely opposed, especially in the South. Despite the passing of the 1964 Civil Rights Act, they continued to face discrimination in education, housing, employment, criminal justice, healthcare, and voting, among many other institutions. "White flight" from major American cities in response to the "Great Migration" of black Americans resulted in *de facto* segregation (Crowder, Hall, and Tolnay 2011). The prevalence of "redlining" further entrenched poverty in the now predominantly black neighborhoods (Squires and Woodruff 2019). Similarly, socioeconomic inequality between Indigenous Americans and the rest of America remained persistently high. In the 1990s, immigration also returned as a major political issue, particularly in California, where anxieties over immigrants from Latin America—especially from Mexico—led some observers to suggest that America had entered a new era of nativist ethnic nationalism (Alvarez and Butterfield 2000).

Over this period the changing relational context affected the content of American ethnic nationalism. Most significantly, the increasing integration of European Americans with Anglo-Americans (Kaufmann 2004b, 192) led to the diminution of myths and symbols that were specifically tied to Anglo-American and Anglo-Saxon identity. In its place, a broader "white American identity" emerged. Whiteness, in this context, was broadened to encompass all European-origin, Christian Americans (Ignatiev 1995; Roediger 1991). Even Jews were increasingly perceived to belong to the white in-group (Brodkin 1998). Yet while whiteness may have been broadened to include non-Anglo, European Americans, it did not lose its edge as a boundary symbol excluding racialized out-groups. In fact, the very pathway for non-Anglo, European Americans to join the white in-group was to distinguish themselves from these out-groups.

Like whiteness, the symbol of religion was also adapted in light of the incorporation of non-Anglo, European-origin Americans. References to the Protestant bases of American identity tended to be replaced with references to its "Christian" roots, in order to reflect the integration of Catholic Americans. To a lesser extent, some commentators also began to speak of America's "Judeo-Christian" heritage in recognition of the integration of Jews (Alexander 2002, 16). While the symbol of religion was broadened, it nevertheless retained its mobilizing power as a boundary marker when it was perceived to be threatened, as was made especially apparent in the rise of anti-Muslim hate crimes after the terrorist attacks of September 11, 2001 (Jamal 2008, 116).

In short, throughout the twentieth century, the content of American ethnic nationalism came to be grounded in a hybrid white identity whose cultural parameters were similar to the one that had been celebrated at the beginning of the century by the likes of Theodore Roosevelt. The symbolic boundaries of this identity may have been wider than Anglo-American identity, but it nevertheless continued to provide powerful cultural resources for excluding out-groups who were perceived as threats.

The Resurgence of Ethnic Nationalism in Conservative America

A series of institutions associated with the contemporary conservative movement in the US have been key carriers for this broader white, European, and Christian basis for ethnic identity. From the mid-twentieth century to today, conservative political, religious, and media institutions have drawn from, and spurned on, this resurgent form of ethnic American nationalism.

In the political realm, the Republican Party (GOP) has increasingly embraced ethnic nationalism. The origins of this development begin with the Democratic Party's decision to support the Civil Rights Act of 1964. This triggered a widespread sense of betrayal in the white South, which had been the base of support for the party since its founding in 1828 by Andrew Jackson. In the ensuing presidential election, Republican Party candidate Barry Goldwater sought to capitalize upon this sense of betrayal by adopting the so-called "southern strategy." The southern strategy was grounded in ethnic nationalist myths and symbols. In sum, it aimed to lure southern whites away from the Democratic Party by opposing federally mandated racial integration (a key component of the Civil Rights Act) and social welfare programs (which were seen by many whites to be primarily aimed at helping black Americans). Goldwater lost the election to Lyndon Johnson, but he did capture five states in the "Deep" South—the best-ever result for a Republican candidate in these states. His Republican successor Richard Nixon embraced this "southern strategy" in his successful runs for the presidency in 1968 and 1972. From this point forward, the GOP increasingly positioned itself as the defender of the myths and symbols of white American identity, while an increasingly ethnically and racially diverse Democratic Party became the defender of an anti-racist and progressive civic nationalism (see Abramowitz 2018).

At the same time, the "southern strategy" did not transform the Republican Party into an exclusively *southern* party. From the 1960s onward, the GOP progressively broadened its support among working-class whites throughout the country, and by the 1980s a majority of white Americans identified with the party (Abramowitz 2018, 47–49). This was in large part due to the party's growing success among the former "white ethnics," who tended to be longtime Democratic supporters as a result of FDR's New Deal. The fact that many of them were now switching to an increasingly ethnic nationalist Republican Party suggests that, by that time, they had truly become part of the "white American" in-group. Commenting on these trends, Anatol Lieven (2012, 110–12) suggests that the white South should now be regarded as a much larger cultural region— a "Greater South," as he puts it—which encompasses blue-collar regions of the Midwest, Southwest, and inland areas of the West. Similarly, Heather Cox Richardson (2020) suggests that historians should revise their interpretation of the Civil War by acknowledging that the South actually won the war, at least from a cultural perspective.

Despite its cultivation of white American identity, the GOP did not fully embrace overtly xenophobic or racist language. The predominance of anti-racist, civic nationalist norms in the American public sphere meant that the party was careful to avoid directly pitching itself as a defender of white Americans against the threat posed by ethnic and racial others. Instead, Republican candidates (like many Democrats) used coded symbols, or "dog whistles," to tap into ethnic myths and symbols. For instance, Goldwater was careful to avoid directly stating his opposition to racial integration. Rather, he expressed his support of "state's rights," which signaled his rejection of federally mandated integration. Further, when Goldwater spoke about the need for "law and order" to "keep the streets safe from bullies and marauders," it was clear to his audiences that he was referring to black Americans. Nixon built on these codes, while also adding new ones, such as the "silent majority" (to refer to white Americans), and by emphasizing his opposition to social welfare, which played on a perception among many whites that black Americans were taking advantage of welfare programs. In the 1980s, Ronald Reagan employed many of the same myths and symbols, notably adding imagery like the "welfare queen," a mythic black woman who ostensibly enriched herself by taking advantage of social welfare programs (Hancock 2004). Memorably, his primary campaign slogan was "let's make American great again"—clearly implying that it was white America he was seeking to protect and return to power.

Conservative religious institutions—notably the "Christian Right," a constellation of evangelicals and fundamentalists—were also significant carriers of this adapted ethnic identity. The Christian Right rapidly spread its base of support outward from the South in the late 1970s. This religious movement's aim was not, strictly speaking, to defend white identity. However, the relationship of evangelicalism with whiteness, particularly in the South, meant the promotion of white identity was an unavoidable byproduct (Maxwell and Shields 2019, 220–22). Efforts to defend Christian values and practices in America tapped into the long-standing religious myths we outlined earlier, particularly those depicting a special relationship between (Anglo-*cum*-white) Americans and God. The Christian Right's promotion of ethnic American identity was solidified by evangelical organizations, like the Southern Baptist Convention, entering the political arena and throwing their support behind the GOP. The merging of conservative Christianity with the GOP crystallized in Reagan's presidency, who himself identified as a "born again" Protestant.

Conservative media also stoked the resurgence of ethnic nationalism in America. In the 1940s and 1950s, several prominent conservatives associated with the nationalist "American First Committee" pushed into broadcasting and publishing to counter what they saw to be a liberal bias in American media. Although their main concern at the time was the threat of communism, ethnic nationalist themes often surfaced. For example, Clarence Manion, a dean of the Notre Dame Law School, hosted a popular radio show called the *Manion Forum*. The show, which later became a television program, was grounded in American nationalism and conservative Christianity (Hemmer 2016, 250). From the mid-1980s, a close relationship developed between conservative media and the GOP. Rush Limbaugh, a radio talk show host who was widely popular among right-wing Americans, was integral in this process. After the Republican Party took control of the House of Representatives in 1994, Limbaugh was dubbed an honorary member in recognition of his support (Jamieson and Cappella 2008, xi). Limbaugh represented a new brand of conservative media activism, which was primarily animated by the "culture wars" over American identity. He would frequently depict immigrants, particularly from Mexico, as a threat to (white) American culture because they did not assimilate like previous generations of immigrants: "Italian-Americans came, and they became Americans. They held on to their traditions... but they were Americans first, not Italians first.... What's happening to immigration now is there is no desire to assimilate . . . they are coming here and demanding that Americans accommodate their culture" (cited in Abramitzky, Boustan, and Eriksson 2020, 139). Limbaugh's juxtaposition of

Italian Americans and "new immigrants" mirrored the way in which the "Nordic" immigrants had once been juxtaposed against "new" Italian immigrants. The difference now was that the latter were perceived to be part of the in-group vis-à-vis new sets of out-groups. Rupert Murdoch's *Wall Street Journal* and *Fox News* further drew from and reinforced these narratives, bringing them into the conservative mainstream at the turn of the twentieth century. Altogether, this "conservative media establishment" increasingly took on the role of taste makers for the American right and as king makers for the Republican Party (Jamieson and Cappella 2008).

While these conservative institutions propelled ethnic nationalism throughout the latter half of the twentieth century, they still faced opposition from those subscribing to more mainstream anti-racist and civic nationalist ideals. This tension meant ethnic nationalism was generally promoted through coded language, and that large portions of the Republican Party still adhered to the civic mythology. These two dynamics were evident during the 1992 presidential primaries between Pat Buchanan and George H. W. Bush. Bush ran on a platform seeking a "kinder, gentler nation." Buchanan argued that Bush represented the interests of liberal elites, infusing his platform with white American myths and symbols that sought to put "America First."[3] Buchanan lost to Bush, but he made a second attempt in the 1996 presidential primaries, running on the mantra that he was the "voice for the voiceless" white majority. Losing again—this time to Bob Dole—Buchanan subsequently tried his luck outside of the party by running, and losing, as a third-party candidate in the presidential election of 2000. Despite these losses, Buchanan lent visibility to an increasingly strident ethnic nationalist wing of American conservatism—a role that he continued to play after he left electoral politics as a media pundit and author (see Buchanan 2011).

In the meantime, the national Republican Party continued to reflect the ambivalence of its membership, between a "grassroots" motivated by ethnocultural concerns and a more liberal, business-friendly "establishment." This tension emerged during the presidency of George W. Bush. Bush won the 2000 presidential primaries under the banner of "compassionate conservatism"—a variant of civic nationalism that blended support for some socially conservative values (such as religion and family) with a relative openness to ethnic diversity and immigration (Gerstle 2017, 380–81). But this agenda was quickly overtaken by the terrorist attacks of September 11, 2001. Bush subsequently embraced a neoconservative agenda (which is itself an aggressive variant of civic nationalism) and undertook to forcibly bring about democratic "regime change" in the Middle East. This response and the ensuing wars in Afghanistan and Iraq have defined Bush's presidency. Nevertheless, domestically, at least in his discourse, he continued to support the modified civic nationalism that had won him the presidency. For instance, in an effort to defuse anti-Islamic sentiment following the terrorist attacks, he declared: "The face of terror is not the true faith of Islam ... Islam is peace ... those who feel like they can intimidate our fellow citizens to take out their anger don't represent the best of America" (Bush, September 17, 2001).

Despite these efforts, it is clear that following 9/11, in the view of many Americans, Islam represented a grave threat. It became a new significant Other. Amid the wave of anti-Muslim sentiment that rippled through the country (Love 2017, 89–97), the myth-symbols of white American identity returned to prominence. Unsurprisingly, the all-important racial symbols defining who is a "real" American (and who is not) were mobilized. However, because Islam is a global religion, it is impossible to identify who is Muslim by their appearance. As a result, attacks against people who were not Muslim, but who were perceived to be Muslim because of their Mediterranean or South Asian appearance, were not uncommon. On September 15, 2001, for example, Balbir Singh Sodhi, a Sikh man, was murdered by a white man who was intent on "shooting some towel-heads" to avenge the terrorist attacks (Love 2017, 1). Religious boundary symbols defining America as a Christian country were also repurposed for the new context. Thus, when Keith Ellison, who is African American and Muslim, chose to use a Koran when he was sworn in as a Democratic member of the House of Representatives in 2006, he was condemned by Republican representative Virgil Goode. In a letter to his constituents, Goode wrote: "[W]e need to stop illegal immigration totally and reduce legal immigration and end the diversity visas policy. . . . I fear that in the next century we will have many more Muslims in the United States if we do not adopt strict immigration policies that I believe are necessary to preserve the values and beliefs traditional to the United States of America" (cited in Goldfarb 2006). Not only did Goode use religion as a boundary symbol in his letter, but he also conflated Islam with "foreignness" by associating it with immigration—despite the fact that Ellison was not an immigrant.

The GOP leadership under Bush did not overtly embrace the surge of anti-Muslim sentiment. However, at the grassroots level and in the conservative media, the perceived "threat" of Islam contributed to the growing assertiveness of white American nationalism. In hindsight, it seems that another perceived crisis was all that was needed to spark a full-scale change of power within the GOP and to prompt it to choose a presidential hopeful in the mold of Pat Buchanan. That spark was provided by the election of Barack Obama to the presidency in 2008.

For many Americans, the election of an African American man to the highest political office represented a severe threat to the dominance of white American identity. It was a crisis that demanded a response. In the ensuing cascade of attacks on Obama, his antagonists drew upon myths and symbols of white identity to demonstrate that he did not belong to the in-group (and was, therefore, an illegitimate president). Critics promoted the "birther" conspiracy theory (with Donald Trump among its leading proponents), which questioned—against all evidence to the contrary—whether Obama was born in America. The movement continued to gain traction after Obama was elected. By 2009, only a minority of Republicans (42%) believed that Obama was born in the US (Daily Kos 2009). Another conspiracy theory falsely suggested that Obama was not a Christian, as he claimed, but rather that he was secretly a Muslim (again, promoted by Donald Trump). This conspiracy theory was also widely believed; in 2009 fully one-third of Americans, and nearly half of Republicans, agreed (Gerstle 2017, 401). The success of these conspiracy theories was no doubt helped by the fact that Obama was the first president to not have a British-origin name, not to mention that his father was a black, Muslim man from Kenya—all of which suggested that he was not part of the white American in-group (Jardina and Traugott 2019). More directly, Obama's blackness was also used as a symbol to demonstrate that he was an illegitimate outsider. For example, racist images and texts circulated among Obama's opponents, including among GOP members, that variously depicted Obama as an ape and as a "witch doctor," while also demanding that he "go back to Africa" (Gerstle 2017, 404–5).

The "Tea Party," which coalesced in 2008 as a grassroots movement, provided an organizational locus for Americans who were opposed to Obama. Initially, Tea Party organizers positioned it as a fiscally conservative movement that was mainly concerned with protecting America against Obama's perceived socialist policies. However, ethnic nationalist themes also simmered below the surface among the primarily white membership of the movement. In the Tea Party's 2008 march on Washington to oppose Obama's inauguration, racist imagery circulated widely, as it did on Tea Party websites (Gerstle 2017, 402–3). Furthermore, although the Tea Party was formally an independent movement, the vast majority of its members were Republican (Abramowitz 2011). In 2010 the twinning of the Tea Party with the GOP was formalized by Republican House Representative Michele Bachman, who formed the Tea Party Caucus within the House. Bachman herself drew upon ethnic nationalist symbolism to attack Obama, arguing in 2008 that he held "anti-American" views, without elaborating precisely on what those views were (cited in Wheaton 2008). As with the denouncements of perceived "un-American" activities of Jewish Americans in the early twentieth century, the strength of this claim was grounded in large part on the perception that Obama was not part of the white American in-group.

How Does This Help Us Understand the New Nationalism in America Today?

Our goal in this chapter was to trace the foundations and development of a complex of myths and symbols that provide the cultural content for ethnic nationalism in America. We have shown America's ethnic myth-symbol complex largely developed in relation to various out-groups who were perceived as threats, particularly at times of crisis. From its initial incarnation as a defense of Anglo-American identity, we teased out the persistent ways that the American people, religion, homeland, history, and ethos were defined in ethnic terms. Our analysis shows that these ideas were remarkably resilient, largely staying intact after experiencing a seemingly terminal defeat in the face of an outpouring of civic nationalism in the Civil War and, more recently, in the civil rights movement. Rather than dissolving following these events, the myths and symbols of American ethnic nationalism endured. In short, ethnic nationalism was embedded in the institutions and beliefs of many Americans even when it was not a self-conscious, prominent component of politics.

The durability of American ethnic nationalism is due, in large part, to its adaptability. We showed how different myth-symbols came to the fore in response to shifts in who was perceived as a threat. These changes in the relational context—in the perception of the Other—shifted elements of the underlying mytho-symbolic content. Among the many changes, we focused in particular on how whiteness became *the* central myth-symbol of American ethnic nationalism. The religious content of American ethnic nationalism also underwent a significant change, with Christian myth-symbols largely replacing Protestant ones. These changes reflected both the incorporation of new ideas (such as scientific racism) and longer-term shifts in social relations, wherein non-British/non-Protestant, European-origin Americans integrated with the white in-group in opposition to several racialized out-groups. As a result of these changes, we suggested that the Anglo-American myth-symbol complex was transformed into a white American myth-symbol complex. But these changes did not represent a rupture with the past. Instead, we found that the development of the white American myth-symbol complex occurred through a process of *adaptation*, whereby new cultural content was integrated with existing cultural content.

This is the historical, cultural, and political context in which Donald Trump rose to the forefront of American politics. It is a context in which an ethnic nationalism that is grounded in the myths and symbols of white American identity was already mounting an increasingly potent resistance to anti-racist, civic nationalist ideas. Furthermore, these myths and symbols of white American identity are themselves adapted from an Anglo-American identity, whose origins reach back into the eighteenth century. In short, Trump's brand of ethnic nationalism is not new. In the next chapter, we turn to examine how Trump successfully drew upon, and adapted, myths and symbols of white American identity to attract an ardent base of followers.

5

Donald Trump and the New Nationalism in America

Donald Trump capitalized on—and has contributed to—the tradition of ethnic nationalism in America that we traced in the last chapter. It was clear from the outset of his political career that he was eager to tap into the power of ethnic nationalism. He entered the political fray by pushing the "birther" conspiracy against President Obama. He announced his intention to run for office by declaring that Mexican migrants were rapists. These actions were not aberrations. As we show in this chapter, ethnic nationalism has anchored Donald Trump's political strategy. He regularly drew from the ethnic myth-symbol complex we outlined in the last chapter, building on the more recent developments of his predecessors. In many respects, he amplified the usage of ethnic myths and symbols and centered them in his politics to a greater extent than we have seen in recent times. But what really sets Trump apart is that he won the Republican nomination, and the presidency, with this brand of ethnic nationalism.

How did this happen? How did Trump win the Republican nomination spewing ethnic nationalist ideas, given the prominence of civic ideals in America and the success of more moderate candidates who adhered to these ideals in the recent past? How did he manage to attract enough votes to carry him to victory in the 2016 general election? How did he maintain relatively stable approval ratings throughout his erratic presidency? How did he get 74 million votes in 2020? Here we seek to shed some light on these questions. To do so, we think it is important to go back and look at Trump's primary and 2016 presidential campaign.

As we discussed in chapter 1, common wisdom attributes Trump's success in 2016 to shifting structural conditions. For many observers, the worsening economic situation facing Americans helps explain why a populist like Trump won: the shadow of the 2008 financial crisis, the declining manufacturing sector in key battleground states, and rising economic inequality all fed anxiety over the economy (see Judis 2016). This played into the hands of a candidate promoting economic protectionism and a populism that blamed international trade deals for the woes of middle-class and blue-collar American workers. But Trump was much more than just an economic protectionist. As we show here, his campaign also tapped into a stream of resentment and anxiety among white Americans who fear that traditional American values are in jeopardy. This "cultural backlash" against an increasingly progressive America has been long in the making. Growing support for liberal and post-materialist values favoring LGBTQ rights, environmental protections, immigration, and racial and gender equality has led to a countervailing resentment among a significant segment of Americans (Norris and Inglehart 2019). Trump did not create these sentiments; rather, he was able to count on support from the vanguard of this backlash—older white men without a college education who feared their traditional values and vision for America were being eroded.

In addition to these large cultural and economic shifts, America's unique political landscape is often seen as central to Trump's victory. The main line here is that even though Hillary Clinton won the popular vote by nearly three million people, Trump won the Electoral College (with 306 votes to Clinton's 232). This disjuncture between popular support and Electoral College votes is a regular and established function of how the US system is designed to increase regional representation and offset the influence of populous urban centers in presidential elections (Krieg 2016). Indeed, there is a case that the Electoral College favors the Republican Party today, particularly in close elections where this disjuncture between popular and Electoral College votes are probable (Geruso, Spears, and Talesara 2019). As is often pointed out, as few as 80,000 people in Michigan, Pennsylvania, and Wisconsin—along with a few other key counties across the US—were the key deciding voters allowing Trump to win the necessary Electoral College votes in 2016 (Nguyen 2016; Mahtesian 2016).

The dynamic of the contest between Trump and his opponent was also significant. Clinton was the first woman running as the headliner for one of the two major parties—and sexism among voters clearly shaped the outcome (Valentino, Wayne, and Oceno 2018). While inherently bound up with this sexism, Clinton also had a long political past, which opened her up to various avenues of criticism. She faced a myriad of political attacks: "stamina," "Benghazi," and "crooked" are just a few of the keywords that exemplify how she was depicted by Trump and his supporters. But perhaps the most important factor here was Clinton's use of a personal email server during her time as secretary of state. The on-again, off-again FBI investigation into Clinton's emails—and particularly the dramatic announcement from FBI director James Comey just a few days before the election that the FBI was reopening the investigation into possible new emails—was a major story of the 2016 election. As has been shown, the "Comey effect" likely influenced the outcome in Trump's favor (Halcoussis, Lowenberg, and Phillips 2019).

The collective wisdom creates a narrative that it was largely a convergence of disparate factors that allowed Trump to squeak through to victory. Statements like "if not for Comey" or "if not for the outdated Electoral College" then Clinton would be president exemplify this logic. Underlying these logics is the notion that the outrageousness of Trump—the fact that he is so far from the expected candidate who should win the nomination of a major party, and certainly never a general election—requires exceptional external conditions and happenstance to explain his victory. We have not even broached the prevalent view that foreign interference in the election favored Trump. In short, the dominant narrative is that Trump did not so much succeed in 2016 as luck his way into the oval office (Bouie 2020). In some respects, the argument here is that Trump won despite himself, not because of any great political strategy or skill.

We fully accept that many of these factors played a role in the 2016 presidential election. They are particularly helpful in understanding why a candidate like Trump was able to gain support *at the time*. But, in our view, pointing to structural shifts or institutional and political opportunities only provides a *partial* explanation. The 2020 election only reinforces the partial nature of this account: Trump lost his bid for re-election, but he still managed to convince a staggering 74 million people to vote for him. In our view, explaining 2016 as a unique combination of factors and external conditions does not hold as much weight given how many people still voted for Trump four years later. In other words, most analyses of 2016 downplay—or even seek to explain away—the role of ethnic nationalism in Trump's campaign and victory. Much of the work on Trump and his new nationalist contemporaries view ethnic nationalism as inimical to the West. These accounts see ethnic nationalism as an aberration that arises only under exceptional circumstances. But as we showed in the previous chapter, ethnic nationalism has deep roots in American political culture and its institutions. In our view, Trump did not win in 2016 in spite of his ethnic nationalism—he won, in large part, because of it: he tapped into a powerful set of ethnic myths and symbols to legitimize his political program and to mobilize the white majority. The power of this majority was still apparent in 2020: despite a disastrous response to the COVID-19 pandemic and a massive economic downturn, he still mobilized a record number of voters. Rather than an exception to the norm, Trump's rise and success signals the ongoing resilience and power of a long-standing element of American political culture—ethnic nationalism.

We start this chapter by looking at the role of white voters in Trump's 2016 win. We then provide an overview of how Trump uses ethnic nationalism to garner support from white Americans, arguing that his entire political program is structured around valorizing the white majority and vilifying outsiders. To systematically demonstrate how Trump uses ethnic nationalism to build his in- and out-groups, we then present our analysis of his Twitter usage in the 2016 election. By going back to the beginning and looking at how Trump won in 2016, we can better understand the role of ethnic nationalism in this period of American politics, how it was linked to what came before, its role in what followed in 2020, and how ethnic nationalism may continue to shape the future.

The Role of Ethnic Nationalism and the White Majority in 2016 (and 2020)

Centering Trump's ethnic nationalism adds depth to the existing accounts of his victory in 2016. It allows us to see *how* he mobilized emerging economic and cultural grievances, and *why* his messaging reverberated with those holding these grievances. It allows us to see how his success rested on more than just rhetorical strategy, divisive campaigning, and demagoguery. These things mattered. But the content of his messaging also mattered. It spoke to and mobilized a particular group—the dominant white majority and those who associate with their culture. By recognizing the deep roots of ethnic nationalism in American political culture, we can better understand why Trump's campaign was able to attract significant levels of support among white voters—why his campaign messaging reverberated with this group as both legitimate and compelling, even though it ran counter to the dominant civic conception of American identity.

It is well known that white voters were central to Trump's victory in 2016, and that they remained his base of support throughout his presidency. Approximately 70 percent of the votes cast in the election were by white Americans: 57 percent of these voters sided with Trump (20 points higher than their support for Clinton), with Trump winning both white men (62%) and white women (52%) (Edison Research/CNN 2016). White, non-college-educated voters were particularly important for Trump, preferring him by a margin of 39 points (Tyson and Maniam 2016; Silver 2016). While white voters have long been the core support base for Republican candidates, Trump capitalized on their grievances and growing turn toward the Republican Party, carrying the non-college-educated segment to a larger degree than previous candidates (Tyson and Maniam 2016; Jones 2019a; Skelley and Wiederkehr 2020). And, as others have shown, he relied heavily on older white men (Inglehart and Norris 2016).

The importance of the white majority to Trump's victory comes into relief when looking at how other ethnic groups voted. Trump had comparatively low levels of support from African Americans (8%), Hispanics (28%), Asians (27%), and other groups (36%) (Edison Research/CNN 2016). Among his supporters, his ethnic nationalism clearly reverberated: 64 percent of those who ranked immigration as the most important issue facing the country voted for him (31 points higher than for Clinton), and, similarly, 57 percent of those who ranked terrorism as the most important issue favored Trump (17 points higher than Clinton) (Edison Research/CNN 2016).

Support from white Americans largely held throughout Trump's presidency. His job approval ratings remained remarkably consistent during his tenure when compared against past presidential swings, even with his erratic behavior and multiple scandals, investigations, and impeachment proceedings (FiveThirtyEight 2021). On average, 41 percent of Americans supported him throughout his presidency, with lows of 35 percent and highs of 49 percent (Gallup, n.d.). Of course, party affiliation is the most important factor in shaping support (Jones 2019b). But we also know that white voters were the core of Trump's continuing support—particularly non-college-educated men (Jones 2017).

The upshot here is that Trump's campaign and political program reverberated with many people in the US, built on a white majority. Nearly 63 million people voted for him in 2016. Perhaps more tellingly, after knowing everything there was to know about the man, over 74 million people voted for him in 2020. One of the interesting turns of the 2020 election was that Trump's support among Latino and black voters rose (Skelley and Wiederkehr 2020). Much was made about this increase in support (Blyer 2020). But we also need to remember that white voters remained Trump's main voting bloc in 2020, by far and away: 58 percent of white voters sided with him according to the exit polls (Cineas and North 2020; Edison Research/CNN, 2020). While his support slipped among white men, particularly those with a college degree, Trump's support among white women actually went up by about two points (Wolf, Merrill, and Wolfe 2020). Across both elections, the core of Trump's support was his ability to attract—and retain—a majority of white voters. So, how did he do this? Why did large swaths of the American population not outright reject his often racist, misogynistic, and divisive messages? Why, even after a damaging pandemic and economic downturn, did so many people stick with him? We think that this is where focusing on how Trump drew upon long-standing ethnic myths and symbols in his political communication can help us understand his relative success.

Donald Trump's Ethnic Nationalism

Donald Trump's brand of ethnic nationalism regularly and unambiguously evokes the foundational ethnic myths and symbols associated with the dominant white conception of American identity. There are many well documented and widely discussed examples of Trump promoting these ideas, reinvigorating them as part of America's contemporary political lexicon. In the first few lines of his Inaugural Address, Trump spoke to what he sees as the "real" America, declaring that "the forgotten men and women of our country will be forgotten no longer ... [that] ... everyone is listening to you now" (Trump 2017). Later that year, in his 2017 Columbus Day proclamation, he stressed the importance of historic European migration as the driver for America's greatness: "[T]he permanent arrival of Europeans to the Americas was a transformative event ... and set the stage for the development of our great Nation." He regularly relies on myths that cast the Anglo-American settlers and white Americans as a virtuous, but embattled, protagonist of American history: "[T]he story of America is the story of good defeating evil.... Americans are the patriots who threw off an empire, won an independence, settled the Wild West, ended slavery, secured civil rights, pushed the boundaries of science, vanquished the Nazis, brought communism to its knees, and put a man on the moon many, many years ago, right?" (Trump 2019). In doing so, he often emphasizes rural Americans as the catalysts of America's golden age—they are the "founders" of the nation, who won independence, and "tamed" the continent (@realDonaldTrump, March 20, 2018).[1] Trump represents himself as a member and leader of the white majority, outright stating he is a "nationalist" (Trump 2018a), while pointing to his Protestant roots (@realDonaldTrump, July 18, 2015), and regularly retweeting when people call him a "real" or "true" American (January, 7, 2015; May 17, 2016).

While we could draw from countless examples to highlight Trump's use of ethnic nationalism, among the most infamous instances was his response to the August 2017 "Unite the Right" rally in Charlottesville and the tragic murder of Heather Heyer. The rally was ostensibly held to protest the removal of a statue of Confederate General Robert E. Lee. In February 2017, the Charlottesville City Council voted to remove the statue, responding to the growing public pressure to remove Confederate symbols from the public sphere with the rise of Black Lives Matter (BLM) and mobilization against systemic racism and white supremacy. These calls were met with resistance from those who felt removing these symbols minimized and imperiled their history and culture. In May 2017, white nationalists held a demonstration against the removal of the statue. These groups increased their actions following the city's decision in June to rename Robert E. Lee Park as Emancipation Park (Fortin 2017). On the evening of August 11, 2017, the night before the planned rally, a collection of about two hundred people from various far-right and white supremacy groups marched through the streets, carrying torches, making the Nazi salute, and shouting slogans like "white lives matter" and "blood and soil" (Coaston 2019). The next day, the Unite the Right rally was met by counter-protests and violence quickly broke out. The governor declared a state of emergency. A documented white nationalist, James Fields, drove his car into a crowd of counter-protestors, injuring nineteen people and killing Heyer (Vera 2019). Following these events, Trump made a series of statements.

On August 12, 2017, Trump tweeted about Charlottesville seven times. These tweets called for unity, condemned hate and violence (August 12, 2017, 12:19 p.m.), sought a swift restoration of law and order (3:23 p.m.), and sent condolences to officers who lost their lives (5:50 p.m.), and some thirty minutes later "to the family of the young woman killed" (6:25 p.m.). During the day, Trump made a statement that he condemned "in the strongest possible terms" the "violence on many sides, on many sides." These comments were quickly criticized for failing to fully denounce the white nationalists and the act of terrorism (Merica 2017a). Trump then followed up with a second statement on Monday, August 14, that more clearly stated "racism is evil. And those who cause violence in its name are criminals and thugs, including the KKK, neo-Nazis, white supremacists and other hate groups that are repugnant to everything we hold dear as American" (Merica 2017b). However, only one day later, when Trump was questioned about the incident, he defended and echoed his initial reaction. When challenged by a reporter on his "many sides" comment, with the reporter stating that "the neo-Nazis started this," Trump replied, "you also had people that were very fine people, on both sides" (Holan 2019). The crux of Trump's comment here is that he sees a rally with avowed white supremacists and far-right nationalists as including "very fine people."

This series of events demonstrated how far Trump was willing to go to court white racial grievances. Clearly, those who marched in the Unite the Right rally hold extreme views about the need to protect white identity. They do not speak for or represent all white Americans. But Trump's words signaled to these groups, and the wider white majority, that their views and members are defensible. Indeed, Trump overtly linked the Unite the Right rally to the broader debate over the removal of Confederate statues from public spaces—an issue that engages a much wider swath of Americans. In his August 15 statement, Trump argued that removing Confederate war monuments was "changing history . . . changing culture" (Holan 2019). He has subsequently repeated this line of argument and sought to reframe his "very fine people" comment as referring to those who defend Confederate war monuments, rather than the white supremacists in the Unite the Right rally (Coaston 2019). But, even here, we can see that Trump is seeking to tap into a grievance that the white majority's culture is under threat, and that defending these symbols is about defending the culture of the "real" America.

The Unite the Right rally, and Trump's response, was an inflection point in the resurgence of ethnic nationalism in the United States today. As Cynthia Miller-Idriss (2020) shows, Charlottesville was not an exception, but rather part of a broader trend of rising extremism and the exponential growth of white nationalist groups in recent years. Trump's moves here clearly indicate how he tapped into these movements and their grievances—amplifying them from the pulpit of the American presidency. After his initial statements on Charlottesville, for example, the neo-Nazi website the Daily Stormer triumphantly declared that his "comments were good" because they implicitly supported the white nationalist cause (Phillips 2017). As we show in this chapter, this is something he has done before and since. His similarly inflammatory remarks during the presidential debate on September 29, 2020, asking the Proud Boys to "stand back and stand by," exemplifies his continued use of this strategy. The seemingly prominent role of the Proud Boys and other extremist groups like the Oath Keepers in the January 2021 Capitol insurrection speaks to the influence and potency of Trump's words here (Polantz 2021). Indeed, Trump's speech on January 6, 2021, where he urged the crowd to "walk down to the Capitol" and exclaimed that "if you don't fight like hell you're not going to have a country anymore," along with his refusal to concede and his inflammatory tweets during the insurrection (January 6, 2021, 12:43 a.m., 8:22 a.m., 2:24 p.m., 6:01 p.m.) speak to his willingness to play to these extreme elements of the white majority. These moves are all part of his political program by which he seeks to position himself as the defender of an ethnic conception of American political culture and white identity.

While many are shocked at these seemingly un-American and un-presidential statements, many also find solace in these signals and codes that reinforce a more ethnic interpretation of America. After Charlottesville, for example, Trump's approval ratings did dip: some polls noted as much as a five-point drop (Shepard 2017), while others showed a slight downtick from previous months (Gallup, n.d.). However, it is also important to note that among Republicans, Trump's approval rating in the weeks that followed Charlottesville was still at 79 percent, and that among those asked specifically about Trump's statements, some 37 percent of respondents said his reaction was appropriate, compared with only 46 percent who said it was inappropriate (Shepard 2017). In short, there was clear pushback against Trump's response to Charlottesville, but it was not a *widespread* and *unanimous* rejection of his ethnic nationalism. Among white Americans, there is a significant constituency for these ideas.

The Charlottesville rally and response were closely bound up with the growing BLM movement, and wider calls to address systemic racism in America. Predictably, Trump has regularly and forcefully attacked BLM. In his statements on Charlottesville this was evident in how he equated the violence and moral standing of white nationalists with BLM protestors—that there was violence perpetrated from "many sides" and "fine people" on "both sides" (Urback 2017; Bump 2020b). He has long painted BLM as a violent movement, labeling them rioters and thugs, while grouping them in with anarchists and "Antifa" as part of the "alt-left" or "radical left" (Bump 2020a). In the aftermath of George Floyd's death in 2020, and the significant mobilization of BLM protests across the US, Trump repeatedly framed the protests as out-of-control riots, arguing that the country needed to restore law and order. He said that "looting leads to shooting" (@realDonaldTrump May 29, 2020), evoking the infamous racist creed of the civil rights era that "when the looting starts the shooting starts." He has repeatedly called for BLM protestors to be "roughed up," while simultaneously arguing that they are violent perpetrators and that white people are their victims (Bump 2020a). He has labeled Black Lives Matter a symbol of hate (Liptak and Holmes 2020). And he has long stood against even the simple and peaceful act of professional sports players kneeling during the national anthem to protest police brutality and anti-black racism—singling out football player Colin Kaepernick (Hill 2019). These are only a few instances in the litany of examples where Trump uses race to help define his in-group as the white majority. In doing so, his favored repertoire is to signal to the white majority that their culture is in danger—particularly by threats like BLM—and that he will be their protector and return them to a place of superiority in the social and political order.

At the same time, Trump is often strategic in how he engages with race in his political messaging. At times, Trump is somewhat ambiguous about who are "real" Americans. It is not always clear that his "in-group" is defined only by symbolic markers of white identity (i.e., born in America, native English speaker, European background, and Christian; see @realDonaldTrump January 18, 2018). For example, despite his anti-BLM rhetoric and his regular derogatory descriptions of cities with large African American populations as "infested" with crime, drugs, and rodents (January 14, 2017; July 27, 2019; July 31, 2019), Trump also explicitly courts African Americans by claiming he is improving their fortunes and has their strong support (September 8, 2015; August 11, 2018; October 26, 2018). He likes to quip that he is the least racist person and that he has done more for African Americans than any other president in history, save, in his view, Abraham Lincoln (who abolished slavery). In part, this ambiguity likely reflects the fact that explicitly racialized political communication remains somewhat outside the bounds of acceptability. Hence, Trump tends to use codes that have emerged in the American discourse on race with the rise of anti-racist and civic ideal that we noted in the last chapter; he uses rhetorical devices that avoid direct attribution (Mercieca 2020) and coded language to speak to white Americans via racial "fig leaves" (Saul 2017). Ambiguity in the definition of the in-group is also a conscious strategy; given the diversity of America's electorate, Trump needs to secure support beyond white America. As he has said on multiple occasions, it is "easy" for him to be politically correct and "presidential," but it is not always in his electoral interests (Trump 2018b). Thus, we can see a degree of ambiguity in how Trump refers to ethnic minorities, particularly African Americans.

Despite ambiguity in how Trump refers to the in-group, it is nevertheless possible to infer from his more overt references to the out-group that Trump's "real" Americans are native-born, European-origin Christians. These themes came together to underpin his first serious forays into politics by leading the "birther movement" against President Obama. Trump was a strong supporter and promoter of the lie that Obama was an illegitimate president because he was purportedly foreign-born, and a secret Muslim (Krieg 2016). These themes anchored much of Trump's political messaging from this point on: he focused on foreigners—often identified by their race, religion, or links to globalization—as invaders threatening the status, way of life, and prosperity of "real" Americans.

Following this same process of identifying who is not a "true" American, he kicked off his presidential campaign by saying Mexican migrants were rapists and drug dealers. As we show later in this chapter, targeting migrants from Mexico and Central and South America was a central theme of his primary and 2016 presidential campaign. These ideas translated into a host of immigration policies following his victory, notably increased construction of a southern border wall and the "zero-tolerance" immigration enforcement policy implemented in 2018. This policy called for border officials to detain all migrants that crossed the border outside regular ports of entry, whether or not they claimed asylum (Kandel 2018). One of the main consequences of this policy was that migrant children were separated from their parents and interred in detention centers. It is estimated that over six thousand families were separated over a four-month period before the policy was suspended (Amnesty International 2018). In the face of outrage over these separations—with images of children held in cages—Trump vigorously defended the policy. In his initial responses he said the policy was necessary to stop the "infestation" of illegal migrants coming into the US by deterring the parents from entering (@realDonaldTrump June 19, 2018). Even in 2020, following reports that those interred faced widespread sexual abuse (Haag 2019) and that some 545 children were still separated from their parents, Trump defended the policy by saying the children were transported by smugglers, and that "they are so well taken care of," that "they're in facilities that were so clean" (Narea 2020).

Along with Hispanics, Trump has targeted Muslims as the archetypal outsider that has invaded America to threaten the way of life and security of the white majority. He has long associated Islam with terrorism—claiming, for example, that Muslims inside America celebrated the terrorist attacks on September 11, 2001 (@realDonaldTrump June 13, 2016). When he speaks about Islam, he invariably uses the phrase "radical Islamic terrorism," opines that "Islam hates us," and raises the specter of Muslims and Syrian refugees as an invading army in waiting—a "Trojan Horse" (Johnson and Hauslohner 2017). When he first introduced a proposed policy to ban Muslims entering the US, he did not differentiate between those who follow the Islamic faith and those who engage in terrorist activity—he explicitly sought "a total and complete shutdown of *Muslims* entering the United States" (@realDonaldTrump December 7, 2015, emphasis added). The actual policy went through numerous iterations following court challenges—with the third version, blocking travel to the US from six predominantly Muslim countries, North Korea, and some Venezuelan officials, being upheld by the US Supreme Court in June 2018. But the initial proposal clearly identified all Muslims as terrorist threats. These pronouncements echo a wider trend whereby Muslims face considerable racism from white, black, Latino, and Asian Americans (Lajevardi and Oskooii 2018). Trump's depiction of Muslims as dangerous outsiders clearly reinforces and capitalizes on these views. He has undertaken a process of racializing people of Islamic faith, marking them as foreigners and enemies of the nation.

Trump's process of boundary setting—where Muslims are outsiders—is also clear in how he regularly conflates race and religion in targeting people as not "real" Americans. For example, he has continually targeted Congresswoman Ilhan Omar—a US citizen who was born in Somalia and immigrated to the US as a child refugee—as not American, as someone who is "telling *us* how to run *our* country ... [h]ow's *your* country doing?" (Choi 2020, emphasis added). He will often link Omar with other women of color in Congress, infamously telling the four members of "the Squad" (Representatives Alexandria Ocasio-Cortez, Ilham Omar, Ayanna Pressley, and Rashida Tlaib) to "go back" to where they came from (@realDonaldTrump July 14, 2019). The signal here is that because these congresswomen are not white, they are not true Americans. Of course, they are all US citizens, three of them were born in the US, and they all serve in the House of Representatives.

These pronouncements are not occasional utterances. They comprise an ethnic nationalist ideology that is built upon long-standing ethnic myths and symbols of (white) American identity. This ethnic nationalism is a defining feature of Trump's political program. However, we cannot make a claim like this by picking from a few high-profile examples. To substantiate this position—and to understand how Trump's ethnic nationalism was central to his electoral victory in 2016—we need a systematic account of his political communication over a sustained period.

Donald Trump's Twitter Nationalism in the 2016 Presidential Campaign

Here we turn to analyze *all* of Donald Trump's tweets in the 2016 primary and presidential campaign. We use the insights from ethno-symbolism to uncover Trump's process of boundary-making, the content of his ethnic nationalism, and its relationship to existing ethnic conceptions of American identity. To help illuminate these linkages to America's foundational ethnic myths and symbols, we apply the framework we introduced in chapter 3. This framework maps how myths and symbols across five categories (the people, religion, homeland, history, and ethos) construct an image of a nation in ethnic terms. Building on the overview of the historical foundation of ethnic myths and symbols of American identity in the previous chapter, we use these five categories adapted to the American context as a framework to code all 5,515 tweets sent from Trump's Twitter account (@realDonaldTrump) between June 15, 2015 (the day prior to announcing his presidential campaign) and January 20, 2017 (the day of his inauguration).[2]

Ethnic nationalism was the most common theme of Donald Trump's tweeting during the 2016 primary and presidential contests. Approximately 1,500 of his tweets (over 27%) used ethno-national myths and symbols. In many of these tweets, Trump would combine myths and symbols to construct an image of an ethnic (white) American identity. In doing so, he would identify who was a member of the nation, and who was not. All told, his tweets employed foundational ethnic myths and symbols nearly 2,000 times during the primary and presidential campaign.[3] His favored topic was to promote an ethnic conception of the American people (over 880 times). As we show later, these tweets focused on migrants and racialized groups (Hispanics, Muslims, and African Americans) contrasted with the "silent majority," the "movement," and the middle class. Trump also regularly tapped into religious myths (almost 260 times), focusing on Islam, Christianity, and evangelicals. In addition, broad historical references steeped in ethnic myths about America's glorious past, and its need to return to its former greatness were a central theme (with over 700 examples, particularly the usage of the slogan "Make America Great Again," or *#MAGA*). Ethnic myths and symbols related to the American homeland and ethos were used less often. However, the overall picture from Trump's tweets is clear: ethnic nationalism was a central—if not the central—theme of his 2016 presidential campaign.

At the same time, Trump covered a lot of other ground on Twitter. Many of his tweets were about mundane campaign matters like announcing events. In line with his populist style, he regularly attacked the establishment and elites. Over 450 of his tweets (8%) had clearly populist themes: allying himself with the ordinary people (using *#ImWithYou* almost 50 times), distancing himself from the elites (e.g., saying he was self-funding his campaign approximately two dozen times) and attacking the establishment in Washington (notably by saying he would *#DrainTheSwamp*, a phrase used nearly 80 times). He adopted a similarly aggressive tone with his political opponents. As others have pointed out, Trump likes to attack people on Twitter (Shear et al. 2019). During his 2016 presidential campaign he attacked his political opponents in over 1,250 tweets

(23% of the time). Predictably, he centered his attention on Hillary Clinton. He attacked her in over 500 tweets. Trump also focused his ire on the media and "fake news." He attacked the press and reporters at least 600 times.

Trump engaged with more substantive policy matters as well on Twitter. As we will discuss in detail, immigration was the most common policy theme. In addition, he focused on foreign policy and the military (just over 250 times), terrorism (about 200 times), the economy and trade (about 200 times), and law and order (about 150 times). Trump's treatment of these issues was quite high-level, as he rarely provided much detail for his plans. Similarly, he was rather circumspect in his treatment of other key policy issues during the 2016 campaign: he discussed healthcare (Obamacare) less than 60 times, he mentioned taxes about 35 times, he talked about the Supreme Court and education policy less than 20 times each, and he was virtually silent on the environment (using the term "climate change" once in his 5,515 tweets, which was to criticize President Obama's view that it was an important issue, see @realDonaldTrump, October 11, 2015).

Even with the considerable breadth in these topics, when stepping back and examining the style and substance of Trump's tweets, we can see how ethnic nationalism underpinned his entire campaign. While he commonly reverted to populist rhetoric, his populism was often imbued with a deep ethnic nationalism. As we discuss later, he sought to define "the people" through an ethnic lens by promoting the idea that he was leading a "movement" of the "silent majority" to rid the country of elites that were working against the interests of "real" Americans. Much like his attacks of the broader establishment, he would often frame his political opponents as enemies of the majority group. For example, Trump would tweet about how opponents were not defending the interests of "true" Americans because they are ostensibly "soft" on illegal immigration or Islamic terrorism (June 28, 2015; November 15, 2015). In the same vein, he tended to present public policy issues through the lens of ethnic nationalism. In over 40 percent of the tweets where Trump discussed a public policy issue, he also relied on ethnic myths and symbols. The use of ethnic conceptions of the American nation was most common when Trump was discussing terrorism (almost 85% of the time) and law and order (almost 65% of the time), along with the economy and trade (about 35% of the time) and foreign policy and the military (over 30% of the time). In short, whether he was attacking elites or discussing substantive policy issues, Trump's campaign was structured by ethnic nationalism.

This overview outlines the main themes of Trump's 2016 social media campaign. But it does not tell us much about the actual content of his messaging, particularly how Trump drew upon established myths and symbols to legitimize his ethnic nationalist ideas. Applying our framework helps further unpack these elements to show the *process* he adopted—and the *specific content* he drew upon. At a foundational level, Trump's campaign focused on creating a moral binary between a virtuous in-group and several villainous out-groups. The in-group was constructed around notions of whiteness, European descent, and Christianity (e.g., his "silent majority," a "movement" of "deplorables" and "forgotten men and women"). Trump contrasted this in-group with a series of threatening outsiders who were depicted as dangerous, immoral, and foreign (particularly illegal Mexican "criminals" and Muslim "terrorists"). Elites and the establishment were also associated with this out-group as threats to the in-group's interests. Unpacking how Trump constructed and reinforced these boundaries between "us" and "them"—drawing from long-established ethnic myths and symbols— can help us better understand why his messaging reverberated with large swaths of the white majority in America.

"Us"

Donald Trump's social media campaign during the Republican primaries and 2016 presidential election was intently focused on constructing a base of support among the white majority. However, this strategy presents an immediate challenge. As we noted earlier, presidential candidates need to avoid *explicitly* racialized messages. Overt racism is largely not acceptable in mainstream American political discourse, particularly given the widespread belief that the nation remains a bastion of civic values in the world. It is for this reason that a great deal of Trump's ethnic nationalist messaging focuses on constructing the villainous out-group, largely defining the "real" America by pointing out who is not a member. Nevertheless, a careful and contextually situated reading of Trump's tweets shows how he did rely upon long-established myths and symbols to construct an image of the American nation through an ethnic frame.

We can see these codes most clearly in how Trump constructed an image of the ethnic character of the American people. Trump never directly referred to "white" Americans, nor to their "European" ancestry, in his tweets. But through his use of myths and symbols he did reinforce that he was speaking to, and seeking to lead, the white majority. A central aspect of his strategy was to mainstream the idea that the dominant ethnic group in the US has been displaced as the rightful heirs of political power (July 17, 2015, 1:32 p.m.). He used coded language to name this ethnic group as the "silent majority," picking up on the phrasing used by Nixon, particularly when speaking to supporters at his rallies (see Figure 5.1). This code speaks to more extreme members of the white majority (e.g., white nationalists), while remaining ambiguous enough to speak to more moderate members of the ethnic group. But the underlying links between the label and the white majority are apparent. Tellingly, his first use of the idea of a silent majority on Twitter was on the same day that his team posted an image that included Waffen-SS soldiers from Nazi Germany (July 14, 2015; Tharoor 2015) These not-so-veiled signals to the white majority in America were continuously paired with calls to mobilize to recapture dominance (December 23, 2015).

Trump's use of the term "silent majority" was paired with other potent symbols designed to position him as the leader of the white majority. He was infamously concerned with the crowd size at his events, tweeting about this well over 120 times during the 2016 campaign. He liked to point out the "record-setting" crowds at his rallies (June 27, 2015), and how he was getting more people than his opponents (October 24, 2015; July 30, 2016). Invariably, in these tweets, he would mention the events were held in rural Middle America, drawing on elements of the myths and symbols that the "true" American homeland was in small, agrarian communities, rather than in the large cities. In these tweets he would exclaim how great the people are in these places, while posting images of crowds that were overwhelmingly white (November 16, 2015; January 20, 2016; February 3, 2016; October 21, 2016). Playing off similar symbolism, Trump would often speak about how he supported law enforcement officers, and how they supported him. This is standard campaigning, particularly for a conservative politician in the US. But Trump would often embrace

(a)

(b)

Figure 5.1 Tweets depicting "the people" as "the silent majority"

the symbolism of these officers as members of the majority group: he would post images and videos of himself posing with large crowds of overwhelmingly white law enforcement officers (January 10, 2016; July 27, 2016). More to the point, he would note how the Immigration and Customs Enforcement officers union endorsed him (October 5, 2016). In short, Trump repeatedly employed law and immigration enforcement officers as symbolic border guards protecting the ethnic majority group.

Throughout the campaign, Trump also layered on religious markers to help identify the membership of his in-group. For example, he sought to exclude Muslims as members of the American nation. He also contrasted this negative depiction with overwhelmingly positive messaging about Christianity and Judaism. He would send well-wishes for Jewish and Christian religious holidays (while not doing so for Islam). He also claimed to have wide support among evangelicals (September 9, 2015). He self-identified as a Protestant—the archetypal religious symbol of the majority group (July 18, 2015). Perhaps most clearly, he argued that Christians and Christian values inside and outside the US were under threat (September 19, 2015). Here, he identified "radical Islam" as the culprit, saying that he alone could protect Christians (March 27, 2016).

Trump underpinned this construction of an ethnic American nation through his use of historical references, particularly by embracing the myth of a lost American golden age. His primary campaign slogan—"Make America Great Again"—encapsulated this myth and its centrality to his strategy. His campaign was structured around the idea that America, and particularly its ethnic majority, was in decline and threatened by enemies domestic and foreign. Much of his campaign revolved around the idea that "our country does not feel 'great already' to the millions of wonderful people living in poverty, violence and despair" (July 27, 2016 10:42 p.m.). He regularly argued he would "rebuild" the "broken" America and make it "strong again" (June 17, 2015; August 21, 2015; December 10, 2015).

Central to Trump's historical narrative was the notion that he could *recapture* the lost glory of the past—and that with his leadership the nation had a bright future. In this respect, the adverb "again" was the critical aspect of his slogan: it implies the decline has already happened, but that a return to past greatness is possible. But the slogan also has ethnic connotations: Trump would speak about the need for the *majority* to recapture or "take back" the state to ensure it was returned to greatness (July 14, 2015). It was this group that had lost its glory and needed a return to prominence. He would single out how specific groups within the majority (e.g., veterans and the middle class) were facing the hardships of America's decline, and that they needed to be returned to greatness (June 24, 2015, 10:16 p.m., 10:17 p.m.). Among his more common refrains in this spirit was to argue that America could not allow foreign migrants to enter the country because those already in America—the ethnic majority—were facing tough times. As he said: "We have many problems in our house (country!), and we need to fix them before we let visitors come over and stay" (December 25, 2015). In total, he employed the general formulation of making American great again (or #MAGA) with these types of ethnic repertoires nearly 700 times in his tweets.

Much of Trump's messaging about restoring American greatness was also bound up with populism and American exceptionalism. His populism was anchored by an ethnic view of the "people" he was seeking to lead back to glory. Trump's populism started early in his campaign, evolving over time. In the fall of 2015, he began a process whereby he represented himself as the only legitimate voice of the anti-establishment movement for the dominant ethnic majority (February 29, 2016). He regularly claimed he was self-funding his campaign and that this enabled him to fight special interests and the establishment (October 30, 2015; March 15, 2016). As part of his attack on the establishment, starting in November 2015, he often referred to his supporters as a "movement" (November 28, 2015). Indeed, during this stage of the campaign he transitioned from identifying his core in-group as the "silent majority" to the slightly more ethnically ambiguous "movement." He represented himself as the leader of this movement, spearheading an attack in their name that was going to recapture America from malign elites (October 27, 2016; October 19, 2016, 8:58 p.m.). To help brand his "people," he often referred to his supporters ironically as "deplorables"—adopting the phrasing used by Hillary Clinton to accentuate that elites held contempt for "real" Americans. As part of this ethno-nationalist populism, he consistently used "#ImWithYou" to signal that he represented the majority against enemies and their elite allies (June 22, 2016; August 1, 2016; August 17, 2016). In a similar vein, he adopted a variant of American exceptionalism that placed the American people as the key referent of his foreign and domestic policy. Trump promised to put "#AmericaFirst"—using this to both signal his realist foreign policy objectives (and their link to restoring American greatness) and the idea that elites were working against the interests of the dominant majority in America (May 23, 2016; November 29, 2016).

"Them"

While Trump used coded and indirect language to define the members of the ethnic majority, he was less subtle when identifying and excluding perceived outsiders. Throughout the Republican primaries and the presidential campaign, Trump consistently used ethnic myths and symbols to identify outsiders and raise symbolic boundaries between "us" and "them."

Among the clearest ways Trump constructed an ethnic American nation was by racializing and criminalizing migrants. A central plank of his campaign was to depict Mexican migrants as dangerous foreigners that threatened the white majority (see Figure 5.2). He started his entire campaign with a speech that, only nine paragraphs in, claimed Mexico was sending rapists and drugs to the United States. This theme was repeated early and often, with claims that drug dealers and rapists were pouring across the southern border (June 19, 2015). As part of this strategy, he leveraged the tragic murder of Kathryn Steinle in July 2015 to reinforce the idea that "illegal" migrants are dangerous criminals, threatening "beautiful" (white) women (July 3, 2015, 6:44 p.m., 11:38 p.m.; July 4, 2015, 6:15 p.m.). Crowning himself as the leading voice for members of the white majority murdered by illegal (Hispanic) immigrants, he regularly pointed out when such crimes took place, reinforcing a threatening image that dangerous outsiders were inside the proverbial wall (July 10, 2015; July 11, 2015; August 10, 2015, 8:29 p.m., 8:58 p.m.). Framing illegal immigrants as threats to the security and way of life of the white majority was a theme Trump relied upon in other areas as well. For example, he embraced welfare chauvinism, claiming that illegal migrants were being treated better by the state and its social and health services than America's own. He often used veterans as the symbolic stand-in for this purported differential treatment (July 18, 2015; October 13, 2015). All

(a)

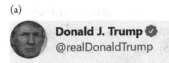

Donald J. Trump
@realDonaldTrump

Druggies, drug dealers, rapists and killers are coming across the southern border. When will the U.S. get smart and stop this travesty?

4:22 AM · Jun 20, 2015 · Twitter for Android

(b)

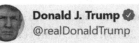

Donald J. Trump
@realDonaldTrump

What about the undocumented immigrant with a record who killed the beautiful young women (in front of her father) in San Fran. Get smart!

12:15 AM · Jul 5, 2015 from New Jersey, USA · Twitter for Android

Figure 5.2 Tweets depicting Mexican migrants as dangerous outsiders

told, Trump tweeted about illegal immigration nearly 350 times—and an overwhelming number of these tweets (over 90%) were negative.

Trump also linked his depiction of the people with territorial symbolism to reinforce the divide between Hispanic migrants and "real" Americans. The southern border was a key symbol in this process of othering. Trump promoted building a wall across the southern border early and throughout the campaign as one of his marquee policy proposals (July 2, 2015; July 13, 2016). He highlighted that immigration and border officers supported the wall (May 30, 2016). He played up its aesthetic as big and beautiful (November 19, 2015, 8:11 a.m.). More tellingly, he directly linked the wall to the very survival of the American nation. He claimed it was necessary to reinforce the border between us and them: "A nation without borders is no nation at all. We must build a wall. Let's Make America Great Again!" (July 14, 2015). In this respect, the wall was a concrete manifestation of Trump's argument that America needed to keep out foreign criminals and terrorists to make the country safe (again) for the white majority.

The symbolism of territory, space, and the homeland was also employed in conjunction with Trump's positioning of the place of African Americans in the nation. In large part, Trump situated African Americans as living in "inner-cities" (August 29, 2016). He repeatedly depicted these inner cities as dangerous and decaying centers: they have been "left behind," and so "crime is out of control and getting worse," and African Americans are being "slaughtered" (July 12, 2016, 7:58 a.m., 8:55 a.m.; August 29, 2016). He claimed these communities had astronomically high rates of unemployment and poverty, using long-established stereotypes and myths (November 14, 2015; August 25, 2016). In short, Trump drew from the deep symbolic boundaries between African Americans and the rest of the white nation. As he said, *their* leaders were letting down *their* communities: "Congressman John Lewis should finally focus on the burning and crime infested inner-cities of the US" (January 14, 2017).

But, as noted earlier, there was also ambiguity in Trump's engagement with race and African Americans on Twitter during the 2016 campaign. While Trump largely framed African Americans and their situation in negative terms, he offset this with some positive messages about their place in America's future under his leadership (July 12, 8:55 a.m.; August 25, 2016). He regularly courted votes from African Americans (September 4, 2016). He would point out that he had support within the community, and that he had prominent African American friends (November 29, 2015; June 11, 2016). In this respect, Trump left open the possibility that African Americans could be included in his definition of the American people—a positioning that likely reflects the centrality of race to American politics, the widespread dominance of the civic mythology of American nationalism, and the electoral calculus at play.

In a similar vein, at points, Trump offset his negative framing of Hispanics with more positive messaging. He courted their votes, noting how members of the community supported him and his policies (July 29, 2015; September 27, 2016). One of his refrains here was to argue that "legal" immigrants and Hispanic law enforcement officers supported his plans for a border wall (July 11, 2015; June 3, 2016).[4] But, as previously noted, Trump's main strategy was to negatively associate Hispanics with the issue of illegal immigration and the southern border. Even in making a more positive case for their support, he seemed to recognize that this was about electoral politics, and it ran counter to the mainstream narrative of the campaign. Trump summed up this pitch as a bit of a flyer for members of these communities to vote for him: "What do African-Americans and Hispanics have to lose by going with me" (August 26, 2016).

There was no ambiguity, however, in how Trump used religion to exclude people from the American nation. During the first few months of the Republican primary, Trump did not tweet that often about Islam or Muslims. That changed in November 2015, following a series of suicide bombings and mass shootings in Paris, France. Trump seized upon this event, shifting how he used religion to reinforce cultural boundaries and notions of foreignness. Between his initial announcement to run and November 13, 2015, Trump only discussed Islam or Muslims six times (with four tweets about a campaign event where he chose to not correct a supporter calling President Obama a Muslim, September 19, 2015). From November 14, 2015, to his inauguration, he tweeted about Islam and Muslims at least 200 times. These tweets were *universally* negative.

Trump presented Islam as a radical religion, and Muslims as terrorists. He *explicitly* linked Islam to terrorism in over 160 tweets (81% of the time when discussing the religion). Put another way, when he raised the topic of Islam, he was doing so to talk about terrorism and to denounce its followers (see Figure 5.3). His favored formula was to point out that other politicians refused to use the label of "radical Islamic terrorism" when discussing terrorist activities or ISIS (December 6, 2015). The claim here was that others were too politically correct and scared to name Islam as a radical religion. He regularly focused on terrorist attacks at home and abroad to amplify this message that Islam was a constant and real threat.

More specifically, Trump sought to present Islam and Muslims as a threat by arguing "they" were "invading" America and "their" values endangered the American way of life. To bring the threat "home," Trump regularly linked the concepts of "terrorism" and "migration" (June 13, 2016). Early in the campaign, he linked the border wall and terrorism, using the symbolism of the wall as a proverbial shield against the threat of ISIS getting into the US through the southern border with Mexico (November 19, 2015, 8:11 a.m., 11:30 a.m.). He continually referred to Syrian refugees as potential ISIS members—as Trojan

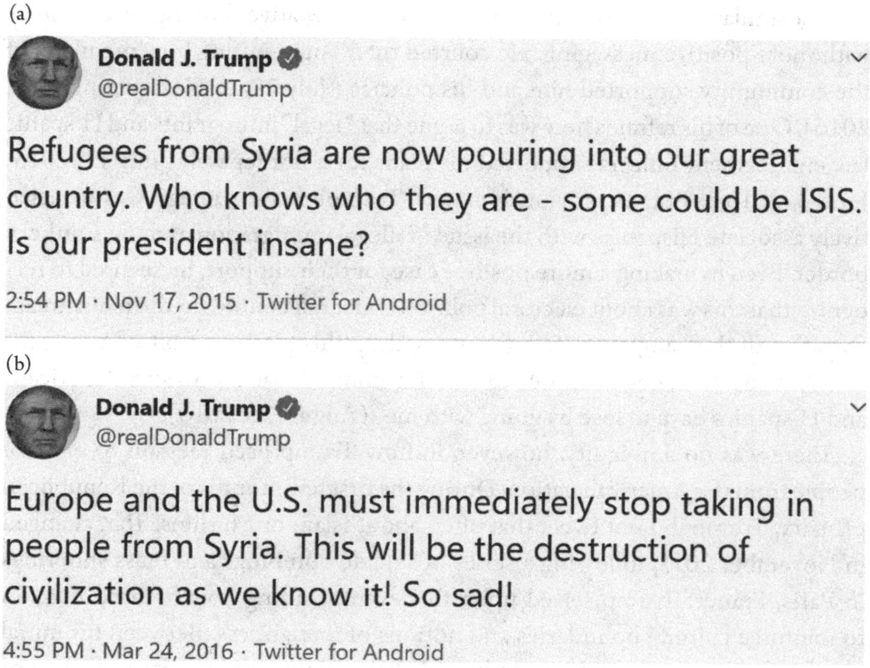

(a)

Donald J. Trump ✓
@realDonaldTrump

Refugees from Syria are now pouring into our great country. Who knows who they are - some could be ISIS. Is our president insane?

2:54 PM · Nov 17, 2015 · Twitter for Android

(b)

Donald J. Trump ✓
@realDonaldTrump

Europe and the U.S. must immediately stop taking in people from Syria. This will be the destruction of civilization as we know it! So sad!

4:55 PM · Mar 24, 2016 · Twitter for Android

Figure 5.3 Tweets depicting Muslims as a dangerous threat to majority group

horses that were pouring into the country, infiltrating the US and other Western countries (November 17, 2015; December 8, 2015; March 24, 2016). It is in this context—stoking fear over the specter of a Muslim invasion—that Trump proposed the ban on Muslim immigration (December 7, 2015). This policy was introduced with an explicit call for "a total and complete shutdown of Muslims entering the United States" because "there is great hatred towards Americans by large segments of the Muslim population," and "until we are able to determine and understand this problem and the dangerous threat it poses, our country cannot be the victims of horrendous attacks by people that believe only in Jihad." As part of his attack on Muslims qua terrorists, he also pushed the narrative that their increased migration to America would endanger the very foundations of American values. He framed his fight against Muslim migration as not just about security, but also as a struggle for the future of the Western world: "Europe and the U.S. must immediately stop taking in people from Syria. This will be the destruction of civilization as we know it!" (March 24, 2016). In this respect, he positioned Muslims as the clearest Other during the campaign.

Trump also used many of these same ideas and themes to identify and attack elites as part of his populist rhetoric. As noted earlier, populism was an early part of Trump's campaign strategy—even during the primaries he took on the

Republican Party as part of the establishment that was blocking real Americans from recapturing power by electing one of their own (March 3, 2016; March 7, 2016). But Trump's anti-establishment rhetoric really ratcheted up during the general election.

During the general, Trump's focus when using populist rhetoric was, unsurprisingly, Hillary Clinton. Trump attacked Clinton as the very embodiment of the establishment, a corrupt politician and an enemy of the dominant white majority's interests (June 26, 2016; August 14, 2016; October 19, 2016). He regularly pointed out how Clinton and the Clinton Foundation had links to foreigners, implying she was an agent working against the interests of the dominant group (see Figure 5.4). He linked these attacks back to his overall theme of "Making American Great Again" by arguing that the people needed to take back the country from self-interested elites like Clinton, who were allied with outsiders and wanted open borders. In this respect, Trump ran on the promise to restore American greatness to a time before enemies like Clinton had captured the state (October 8, 2018; October 19, 2016; October 22, 2016). He tied much of his anti-establishment rhetoric together with his promise to "#DrainTheSwamp" (a phrase he used nearly 80 times in the last three weeks of the election). This pithy slogan—paired with his overall theme of Making America Great Again—encapsulates a strategy that moves beyond a simple populism toward a worldview that tries to mobilize the dominant ethnic group in America to recapture the state from malign elites (November 6, 2016).

(a)

(b)

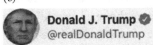

Figure 5.4 Tweets depicting migrants and the establishment as threats to the values and interests of the majority group

The underlying ethnic nationalism of Trump's populist messaging in the campaign is perhaps clearest in how he linked elites and the establishment to his other out-groups, and as direct threats to the in-group. The linkages largely focused on how elites and the establishment were in favor of open borders, which meant increased immigration, trade deals that would jeopardize the white working class, and an influx of Syrian refugees (see Figure 5.4). For example, he often said Clinton would increase the number of immigrants and refugees and jeopardize the safety and interests of Americans (October 19, 2016, 9:22 p.m., 9:34 p.m., 10:31 p.m.; July 28, 2016). He also argued that only he could protect middle-class jobs and the livelihood of Americans working in the manufacturing sector, largely by pulling back on international trade deals he said were pushed by Clinton and her fellow self-interested elites (July 23, 2016; July 30, 2016; October 19, 2016). And, tying these themes together, he often pointed to the existential threats that migration, terrorism, and trade (presented as products of mismanagement by the establishment) posed to the American Dream and American values (June 25, 2016; July 28, 2016; October 19, 2016; October 13, 2016).

Continuity and Change in Donald Trump's Ethnic Nationalism

Ethnic nationalism is a foundational and defining element of Donald Trump's political communication. This becomes evident when we read through his social media, applying our lens sensitive to his use of long-established ethnic myths and symbols. This lens also helps us understand why his political program resonated with large swaths of the white majority: the central theme of his campaign in 2016 and his subsequent actions as president were anchored by an argument that he would return this ethnic group to dominance in American political life.

The core tactic of Trump's strategy was to construct a sense of the white majority as the virtuous protagonists of America, set against a collection of villainous Others by drawing on a wellspring of ethnic myths and symbols (see Table 5.1). He used these myths and symbols to define the real "people" as the "silent majority"—a "movement" of "deplorables." He often situated these people in the rural heartland and Middle America. He positively reinforced that real Americans are Christian and Jewish, not Muslim. And he argued that he alone could lead the white majority back to greatness. In his inauguration speech, he tied these threads of his campaign narrative together, to show how underlying it all was a desire to restore American greatness by enabling the white majority to recapture the state: he promised to make America great again, and to continue the "movement" because "the forgotten men and women of our country will be forgotten no longer" (Trump 2017).

In contrast, he constructed the villainous Other. But these two groups were closely linked: the main way Trump created a sense of "us" was by identifying "them." This approach rests on a long-established process in America of using ethnic markers to identify those who do not fit the mold of "true" Americans. His favored targets were Mexican migrants, Muslims, and political elites, presenting these groups as a threat to the survival and interests of the dominant group. Mexican migrants were presented as dangerous criminals pouring through the southern border, necessitating a wall to protect (white) Americans. Muslims were depicted as radical Islamic terrorists who were infiltrating the state and threatening the foundations of American civilization. Political elites were painted as allies of these groups and in favor of open borders, linking them to nefarious international interests who were destroying the American dream and blocking the "forgotten" Americans from controlling their own state.

Underpinning this process of creating an ethnic connotation of "us" and "them" was Trump's use of positive and negative positioning. As noted earlier, when referencing core aspects of the "in-group" he would largely use positive language and themes. In over 90 percent of the tweets where he spoke about the silent majority, the movement, or other similar codes for the majority group, he used positive messaging. Similarly, when discussing the middle class or Christians, he used positive language over 95 percent of the time. In contrast, 100 percent of his tweets about Muslims and Islam were negative. Over 90 percent of his tweets about immigrants were negative.

Trump's messaging about who is—and who is not—a member of the American nation has deep roots. It is underpinned by ideas that have links back to the ethnic foundations of American political culture that emerged in the

Table 5.1 **Key Distinctions in Donald Trump's Ethnic Conception of the In- and Out-Group in His Twitter Communication in the 2016 Presidential Election**

"Virtuous" In-Group	"Villainous" Out-Group
Silent majority	Migrants (particularly Hispanic)
Middle class	Elites
Veterans and law enforcement	Illegal immigrants and criminals
Rural and Middle America	Inner cities
Judeo-Christians	Muslims and "radical" Islam
Movement	Establishment and global capital

eighteenth and nineteenth centuries. These links can help us understand Trump's rise. Our analysis here indicates the role America's ethnic foundations played in Trump's political program. In short, we think Trump's ethnic nationalism reverberated with the white majority because it tapped into the ethnic stream of American identity. By drawing upon a set of institutionalized ideas about the nature of the American people, its history, and its religion, Trump was able to speak to the white majority in its own codes. These ethnic codes, borrowing a line, hit the right "wavelength" for the majority group (Hobsbawm 1990).

By saying that Trump's ethnic nationalism has deep roots, we are not claiming he simply parroted myths and symbols of eighteenth- and early nineteenth-century America. Railing against Catholics, Italians, Irish, and Germans would not have found support among the dominant majority today. Rather, Trump's Twitter campaign shows how he built upon these foundations and the resurgent tide of ethnic nationalism in the twentieth century by adapting ethnic myths and symbols to the current context. As we have shown here, while elements of his message drew upon longer-standing myths related to religion (Protestantism), homeland (rural America) and history (a glorious past), he also embraced a broader understanding of the dominant ethnic group centered on whiteness. This fits with the developments in ethnic nationalism we outlined in the previous chapter. Trump's core in-group was not limited to Anglo-Saxon Protestants—it was a more diffuse white, Christian, European majority. This shift was noticeable also in the foils Trump selected in his campaign: the threat of Catholicism was replaced by Islam, the perceived invasion of dangerous Italians and "undesirables" from Ireland and Germany were replaced by Mexicans and (Syrian) Muslims. In this respect, while whiteness was a central theme for Trump, our analysis indicates that the content and success of Trump's campaign is about more than just race: his ethnic nationalism drew upon broader *ethnic* conceptions of the American people. He found the content for this ethnic identity deep in America's past. But he managed to simplify and update the coding of these myths and symbols. His social media campaign expressed complicated ideas about the nature of the American people, religion, homeland, history, and ethos in simple and pithy statements. He brought the old signals of America's ethnic identity and the resurgent tide of the twentieth century into the Twitter age.

6

Marine Le Pen and the Ethnic Stream of French Nationalism

In the previous chapter we examined how Donald Trump's ethnic nationalism tapped into long-standing myths and symbols of the white ethnic majority in America. We showed how Trump's campaign messaging was not so "new"; rather, it reflected a long-established strand of American political culture that has recurrently come to the fore during times of heightened anxiety among the white majority. But Trump's messaging did not simply parrot a preexisting ideology. Instead, it was adapted to suit the contemporary context. Such an adaptation in the content of American ethnic nationalism has occurred frequently throughout history. These adaptations resonate with their target population when they retain continuity with existing content. Thus, in our view, Trump was able to garner widespread support, in part, because his campaign messaging built upon existing ethnic myths and symbols of the dominant, white ethnic group. Trump did not invent a new ethnic nationalist ideology. He adapted an existing one.

In this chapter and the next, we look beyond the United States to explore how similar processes played out in France during the 2017 French presidential election and in the United Kingdom during the 2016 referendum on leaving the EU. Like the US, France and the UK are conventionally understood to be bastions of civic nationalism. Indeed, historians of nationalism generally list one or the other as its birthplace, with the preponderance of opinion suggesting that its crucible was the French Revolution of 1789. Here, the classic trope in the literature is to contrast French (civic) nationalism with German (ethnic) nationalism (Brubaker 1992; Meinecke 1919; Renan 1882). Others—most notably Hans Kohn (1944) and Liah Greenfeld (1992)—argue that the liberal variant of nationalism originated in England. Notwithstanding this uncertainty over the location of its origins, there is general agreement that the political cultures of both France and the UK are fundamentally grounded in the ideals of liberalism and civic nationalism. The corollary to this view is that ethnic nationalism, when it occurs in France or the UK, is an aberration that does not truly reflect their political cultures, and so it must be attributable to some external shock. Over the course of the following chapters, we challenge this view by demonstrating how ethnic nationalism has long been central to France and the UK. Furthermore, by examining the Twitter communication of French presidential hopeful Marine Le Pen and the Leave campaigns in the UK, we show how today's new nationalists draw upon these historically constituted ideas to garner support among the white majorities of their nations.

We start in this chapter by exploring the relative success of Marine Le Pen's ethnic nationalism. Focusing on Marine Le Pen and the National Front (Fr. *Front National*) as an exemplar of ethnic nationalism in the West is at once logical and puzzling. Le Pen enjoyed remarkable success in the 2017 French presidential election. She secured the highest ever levels of support for a National Front candidate. While she lost to Emmanuel Macron in the second-round runoff, over 10 million people voted for her. What is remarkable about this, as we show here, is that Le Pen's campaign was structured by, and promoted, a decidedly ethnic nationalism. What is puzzling about both her campaign and its relative success is how her ethnic nationalism managed to garner so much support in the archetypal civic nation.

How did a decidedly ethnic nationalist do so well in the 2017 French presidential election? To help understand this outcome, we look at the foundations of ethnic identity deep in French history. We trace how, over time, a series of foundational ethnic myths and symbols have been institutionalized and become a core—but certainly not the main—element of French political culture. Marine Le Pen tapped into many of these ideas, which helped to propel her to new heights in public support.

This chapter is broken into two broad parts. In the first part, we outline the foundational ethnic myths and symbols of French political culture. In the second part, we carry out an in-depth study of Marine Le Pen's 2017 campaign, examining how her Twitter communication employed these foundational ethnic myths and symbols.

The Ethnic Foundations of French Identity and Political Culture

France's status as the archetypal civic nation rests on two oft-discussed attributes. The first is its role as the harbinger of the modernity. Many see the French Revolution as a catalyst: it is presented as the prime example of how political elites construct a nation, a process that was mimicked by others in Europe and beyond (see, for example, Hobsbawm 1990). This line of thought argues that the French nation was constructed from above by state elites coercively spreading republican ideals, expanding state power emanating out from Paris, and the social re-education of peasants in the hinterlands (Weber 1976). This view has become accepted orthodoxy.

The second purported attribute of French nationalism is that its membership is essentially voluntary. In this view, the French are a heterogeneous block that choose to come together, through a kind of "daily plebiscite," as Ernest Renan famously put it (1882). The nation is the product of state-building within the spatial and territorial frame of the French state (Brubaker 1992, 3). This conception of French nationalism is, in turn, built on the idea that the French Revolution was the point at which rationality and reason began to inform politics.

From the Revolution stems the fervent adherence to secularism in the public sphere, despite the widespread and long history of Catholicism. Even more clearly, the Revolution gives birth to the defining ethos of French civic nationalism—the republican creed of liberty, equality, and fraternity. In short, French nationalism in this view is state-centric and revolves around adherence to a set of political principles (Weber 1976; Brubaker 1992). The implication is that to call France an ethnic nation or to point to its ethnic origins and elements is an oxymoron. This paradigm underpins both common knowledge and academic canon on French history and nationalism.

At the same time, as we argued in chapter 2, and have shown for the US, there are often multiple, competing foundations of national identity. Indeed, as John Hutchinson (2005) has shown, in many cases across the globe, these competing foundations of national identity are expressed through rival interpretations of the nation's character as civic or ethnic. France is no exception. Just as France is central to demonstrating the utility of the civic/ethnic distinction, it can be central to questioning its validity (Yack 1996; Kuzio 2002). Even in one of the constitutive texts for understanding France as a civic nation, Rogers Brubaker acknowledges that nationality has an inherently exclusive streak and that there are clear undercurrents of an ethnic identity in France (Brubaker 1992, 13–14, 45–48, 98, 149).

French historiography reflects these contested, multiple streams of identity. Debates between the many great historians of France have given rise to differing views on the nature of the nation. One of the clearest examples expressing this contested element of French history is Pierre Nora's seminal collection exploring key sites of memory in France (*lieux de mémoire*). As Nora says, "the political myths on which our idea of France is based stem from a relatively limited number of fundamental oppositions, each reflecting and reinforcing the others" (1996, 21). Nora goes on to list these tensions in French history and historiography: the

Revolution and its status as a wellspring of subsequent religious, political, social and national oppositions; immigration, as something that has long shaped the nation; the Vichy regime, as a myth of defeat and occupation; and the struggles between Gaullists and Communists (22).

The works within Nora's collection that revolve around these themes highlight not only the diversity, but also the division, in the nation's set of myths and symbols. They show how French political culture is constructed and reinterpreted over time by popular and academic audiences. David Bell (2001), in a different manner, has also shown how a close and critical reading of French history can raise questions and challenges for the dominant narrative of the Revolution as *the* wellspring for French political and national identity. As Bell shows, there were ongoing and critical debates about the nature of the French nation during the *ancien régime* in the two centuries prior to 1789. These debates shaped subsequent nation-building efforts and reverberate into today's politics (Bell 2001; see also Greenfeld 1992). Perhaps most applicably, Michel Winock (1998) has drawn attention to the "double-edged" sword of French nationalism. As Winock demonstrates, with careful historical analysis, France has both a more open (civic and republican) nationalism, and a more closed (ethnic) nationalism. This more closed nationalism—that of "France for the French"— reoccurs throughout French history, particularly at times of perceived crisis for the ethnic majority group (Winock 1998, 24).

In this section, we draw from selective aspects of French historiography to highlight some of the key, foundational myths and symbols that are the core elements of an ethnic conception of French political culture. Building on Winock's analysis and insights, we can identify examples of the formation, solidification, and modification of ethnic myths and symbols throughout various periods of French history. As with the US, there are important junctures when these ethnic myths and symbols were more overtly drawn upon, institutionalized, and reconceptualized. Often, these moments represented periods of great social and political ferment—where external crises created real and perceived threats for the white, Catholic, ethnic majority and its hold over the French political regime. As in chapter 4, we focus on these periods, paying particular attention to how ethnic conceptions of the nation were employed during the *ancien régime* in the seventeenth and eighteenth centuries, the Revolution, the Dreyfus affair (1890s) and the wider period of Romantic nationalism in the late nineteenth century, and the Vichy regime (1940 to 1944). In line with our method, we map an ethnic conception of French national identity by codifying its ethnic myths and symbols across five key categories. We do this—focusing on these periods—to illuminate a set of foundational ethnic myths and symbols for the French people, homeland, history, religion, and ethos.[1]

People

One of the most prominent and recurrent themes of an ethnic French identity has been the promotion of ethno-cultural conditions for belonging to the nation. Voluntarist and state-based identities certainly dominate French political culture. But ethnic and cultural boundary markers have also been important in defining the in-group and the out-group. A focus on ancestry and blood—and, later, whiteness—as criterions for national membership are among the clearest expressions of these ethnic markers.

The Gauls have long been singled out as the ancestors of the French people. More precisely, the initial ethnic understanding of the French people is bound up in the relationship between three groups: (1) the Gauls, a Celtic people who have occupied territory in present-day France from at least the sixth century BCE; (2) the Romans, who conquered the Gauls in battle in the first century BCE; and, (3) the Franks, a Germanic-speaking people who moved into the territory in the latter days of the Roman Empire and established the Merovingian dynasty (Dietler 1994, 585–87). Accounts of the relationships between these groups paint a complex picture that highlights racial and class hierarchies: the Franks were associated with, and appropriated by, the nobility; the Romans have often been presented as a civilizing influence; and the Gauls were seen as the progenitor of the commoners and body politic (Dietler 1994, 587–88; Pomain 1996, 51–55; Bell 2001, 24–25; Brubaker 1992, 101). Historians have studied the Gauls from at least the fifth century, with a significant uptick in interest in the sixteenth century (Pomain 1996, 45–51). Over time, elites increasingly focused on the Gauls as the main protagonist in the ethnic mythology of France—depicting them as "our ancestors" (Dietler 1994; Pomain 1996). This phrasing emerged in French historical texts dating back to at least the early eighteenth century (with Pezron in 1703 and Pelloutier in 1740), and gained strength with Romantic historians of the mid-nineteenth century, such as: Martin (in 1852), Thierry (in 1866), and Guizot (in 1872) (Dietler 1994).

Elites identified the Gauls as the ethnic core of the French nation in stages, often mobilizing them at key moments in the country's political history. In pre-revolutionary France, historians highlighted the antagonistic relationship between the Gauls and Franks. Henri de Boulainvilliers, for example, was an early proponent of the idea that the Franks were associated with the nobility, defending their right to rule, while claiming that commoners descended from the Gauls (Pomain 1996, 51–52; Bell 2001, 24–25, 57–58). These themes were debated in pre-revolutionary times and became part of the emerging national sentiment that was mobilized in the Revolution. As Liah Greenfeld and others have pointed out, during the Revolution there was a movement to rename the country after the Gauls to push aside the Frankish influence as a symbol of foreign invasion (Greenfeld 1992, 92–93; Dietler 1994, 588). Following the Revolution, in the early nineteenth century, political leaders employed the Gauls as a symbol of French nationality: Napoleon I founded the Académie Celtique in 1805 and focused on the mythology of Roman conquest over the Gauls; Napoleon III regularly invoked the symbolism of Vercingetorix (a leader of the Gauls at the time of their conquest by Julius Caesar) (Dietler 1994, 588–90). The focus on the Gauls and Vercingetorix as a symbol of French identity intensified throughout the mid- to late nineteenth century. Romantic historians centered them as one of the central movers of French history. Monuments were constructed for Vercingetorix and other Gallic themes at a startling pace: between 1850 and 1914 over two hundred sculptures were created. The Gauls became a core theme of literature and a key player in school textbooks on French national history (Dietler 1994, 590–92). Vercingetorix and the Gauls returned as core symbols of the Vichy regime in the 1940s. The regime adopted the two-headed Gallic axe as its symbol and Philippe Pétain promoted an image of himself as the reincarnation of Vercingetorix (Pomain 1996, 29–30). But the French resistance also adopted some of these same symbols and themes, and ultimately Vichy mobilized to melt down statues of Vercingetorix, perceiving the symbol as a threat to the regime (Dietler 1994, 582). Today, the notion of the Gauls as the ethnic origins of the French nation continue in the background of social and political life. The mythology is carried forward in popular culture (like the cartoon *Asterix*), school texts, and in common perceptions of the ancestry of French people. There are certainly racial, class, and cultural implications to centering the Gauls in French history, but there are also more overtly *racial* understandings of French identity.

Blood, common heritage, and whiteness have, at times, powerfully shaped perceptions of who is, and who is not, a member of the French nation. The clearest expression of a racialized, blood-based understanding of French nationality emerged in debates over the long-standing policy of granting citizenship by birth on soil (*jus soli*) (for an overview, see Brubaker 1992). Parliamentarians explicit challenged *jus soli* in the 1880s, for example, critiquing the policy and arguing instead for citizenship by blood descent (*jus sanguinis*). In these debates, politicians spoke uncontested in favor of *jus sanguinis*, claiming "nationality depends on blood," and linking their views to racial hierarchies and national characteristics (Brubaker 1992, 100). One senator summarized the position: "France is not only a race, but especially a *patrie* . . . she possesses that eminently colonial capacity of absorbing in herself the peoples to whom she transports civilization" (as quoted in Brubaker 1992, 102). While *jus soli* ultimately survived these challenges, and elements of these arguments were about class and other political dynamics, this ethnic nationalism was reflective of a growing streak of ethnic identity in France in the mid- to late nineteenth century (98–102). Similar ideas informed later racial understandings of the French people and movements against citizenship and migration policy. For example, the nationalist Action Française promoted the idea that newly naturalized citizens were only French on paper (*française de papier*) (113–43). These ideas were acted upon in Vichy France: during its rule from 1940 to 1944, the regime revoked the citizenship of approximately 15,000 naturalized French, including some 6,000 Jews (215).

This more overtly racialized understanding of nationality also informed other aspects of how the French people have been defined at key points in history. Among the most infamous examples of this conception of French identity occurred during the rise in xenophobic, anti-Semitic, and nationalist sentiment during the Dreyfus affair in the 1890s. The affair revolved around the wrongful conviction of a French captain (Alfred Dreyfus) for treason. Dreyfus, a Jew, was accused of sharing military intelligence with the Germans. Subsequent investigations uncovered that the evidence against Dreyfus was fabricated. The controversy embroiled France. Nearly all aspects of politics and society were split into those who supported Dreyfus and those against him. The anti-Dreyfusard movement held strong anti-Semitic, nationalist, and xenophobic ideals (Winock 1998, chap. 9; Davies 2002, chap. 3). During the affair, a host of ethnic nationalists rose to prominence and gained political currency, notably Paul Déroulède, General Boulanger, Maurice Barrès and Charles Maurras (the founder of Action Française). As others have shown, these Anti-Dreyfusards established an ethnic nationalism based on racist, anti-Semitic viewpoints that has informed far-right politics in France to the present day (Winock 1998, 10–13; Davies 2002, 19, 56, 84). Many of these same themes and ideas—an exclusive, ethnic conception of identity—were the cornerstones of the Vichy regime's political program (Winock 1998, 119–24, 129).

At the same time, an ethnic conception of the French people is not only confined to moments of great social and political upheaval. As David Bell (2001, chap. 3) has shown, early French national sentiment in the eighteenth century was infused with a racialized understanding of difference between peoples. Bell illustrates how the differentiations that were made between the civilized and virtuous nature of the French compared with the "savages" and "barbarians" of England helped build the cult of French national identity (104–6). This racialized ideal of the French as a distinct and superior people manifests most obviously—and adds a clear element of whiteness as a boundary marker— through its colonial legacy in Africa. The racial undertones of French colonialism are laid bare by the *Pieds-Noirs* (black-foots), compared against the treatment of black, Muslim Algerians (Juge and Perez 2006; Brubaker 1992, chap. 7). The *Pieds-Noirs* are *white* French colonists and their descendants who settled in North Africa and returned to France following the independence of Algeria in 1962. When arriving in France, these white Franco-Algerian colonists were widely accepted as "repatriated" French citizens. They were seen as members of the French nation, returning to their home (even though they either settled or were born abroad). In contrast, black, Muslim Algerians who have migrated to France—even those who hold dual citizenship—in many cases have faced a long and systemic legacy of discrimination and racism. The racial and ethno-cultural distinction is clearest in the long-running and recurrent debates about the perceived problems with black Muslims from North Africa as "unassimilable" (Brubaker 1992, 148–51). In short, in the postcolonial period, whiteness, particularly in relation to black North Africans, emerged as a key boundary marker for the definition of the true French people.

This distinction draws attention to how the ethnic identity of the French people is also about defining the out-group. Early on, historians and elites drew distinctions between the natural attributes of the virtuous French and the villainous English. Political actors similarly identified the Gauls as the true core of the French people, set against foreign Franks of Germanic-speaking origin. The anti-Dreyfusards stoked xenophobic sentiment following the Franco-German War of 1870, paired with a strong anti-Semitism. French colonialism was underpinned by racial understandings of identity that reinforced a dichotomy between superior (white) and inferior (black) peoples. This logic has fueled along legacy of systemic anti-black and anti-Muslim sentiment, which is often targeted at African migrants. In this way, French national identity is, in part, built upon distinctions that privilege (white) ethnic identity.

Homeland

The homeland has been a powerful symbol in France. Bell shows us that the *patrie* (fatherland) was a crucial early concept in the formation of French national sentiment. Allegiance to a territory that housed the French nation gained an "awesome symbolic" and "talismanic" power over people and political culture starting in the eighteenth century (Bell 2001, 7, 12). In this way, *patrie* is among the constitutive symbols of the French nation. Of course, in France, *patrie* incorporates civic notions of identity that incorporate devotion and love for the homeland (patriotism)—it can be seen as "a state of mind" (19, 60). But *patrie* also includes notions of a closed community—the fatherland has often been seen as the home of the extended French family that even if foreigners could join through "naturalization," they had to do so by changing their very nature (42).

At the same time, the homeland is *itself* also important in French political culture. The concept of *patrie* reifies the territory upon which the community resides as something that gives it form. This reification is often achieved through sacralizing the homeland to elevate its status in the mythology of French nationalism (Bell 2001, 38). One of the main ways this reification takes place is a vision of the bountiful French territory and its soil as superior to others, and thus its ability to produce superior people (95–96, 144). In this regard, there are both more civic (inclusive) descriptions of the French homeland as a place granting status to those that reside there and a source of common pride, but also more ethnic, exclusive, and ascriptive forms of identity that are tied to the French territory itself as the progenitor of the French nation.

There are many examples of this more ascriptive understanding of the French homeland. Two of the clearest include the aggrandizement of the rural countryside and the more recent concept of *L'Hexigon* as the home of true Frenchmen.[2] The relationship between the metropole and the regions has long been a central dynamic of French nationalism. As Eugene Weber famously argued, a homogeneous French culture was built through a process akin to colonialism: concerted efforts to "civilize" the regions occurred through assimilating local cultures into a dominant Parisian-based monolith (Weber 1976). But this domination also produced counter-narratives and movements to retain and highlight local and regional cultures grounded in the *terroir* (the land). Often these movements depicted the rural space as a more authentic, traditional representation of French life. Themes such as the importance of rural life and folklore were core elements, for example, of the 1937 Paris International Exposition (Peer 1998). These themes were also central to the Vichy regime's notion of French identity. The regime strongly promoted the idea that the real France was in *la France profonde* (deep France)—the rural countryside and villages away from Paris. Between 1940 and 1942 alone it subsidized approximately sixty documentaries on the topic and encouraged regional theater productions and folklore that promoted a vision of a peaceful, fruitful, and real France (Rearick 1997, 253).

In a similar manner, the rise of *L'Hexigon* (the Hexagon) to symbolize France in the 1960s built upon earlier notions of the *terroir* as the fatherland of the real French nation. Educators and leaders only sporadically used this symbol of mainland France as a six-sided polygon in the nineteenth and early twentieth centuries (Weber 1991, chap. 3). But this symbol gained considerable currency in the 1960s: following the collapse of the colonial empire—and particularly after the independence of Algeria—*L'Hexigon* became a common refrain to identify the *true* home of the French nation on the European continent (Weber 1991, 69–70). As noted earlier, the ethnic elements of this symbol are clear in how white settlers from Algeria (*Pieds-Noir*) were "repatriated" as French returning to their homeland of *L'Hexigon*, whereas other migrants were perceived as foreigners who had to undertake a process of naturalization (Juge and Perez 2006, 201; Conklin 2005, 3). *L'Hexigon* is thus a symbolic border guard—it reinforces that the true French are those (white, Catholic) people born in Europe, or those that can trace their roots back to this space, not (black, Muslim) colonists.

Religion

Religion's role in French political culture is complicated. The dominant theme of French nationalism is that the Revolution—despite its horrors—ushered in an age of reason and rationality, replacing divinity as the source of political authority. Republicans fiercely defend a secular public sphere, pushing religion to the private sphere. Nevertheless, French nationalism cannot be understood without accounting for the role of religion and recognizing "just how 'Catholic' the French cult of the nation" truly is at its foundation (Bell 2001, 24). In this respect, religious myths and symbols are central to a more ethnic French nationalism.

Religion has long been used as a heuristic to define who belongs to the French nation, and who is a foreigner. This heuristic sets the "good," Catholic French against threatening non-Catholic foreigners. Among the clearest examples of this dynamic are the antagonism and history of warfare between France and England. Protestantism was a central theme in the vilification of the English, while Catholicism was used to valorize the French—a mythology that has had remarkable endurance (Bell 2001, 43–49, 101–6). The symbol of Joan of Arc as the savior of the French nation is central to this mythology. Throughout history, she has been presented as an agent of God sent to purify the French nation—to rid it of foreign heretics and invaders (Mock 2012, 142–46; Winock 1998, 103–10). Ethnic nationalists and the far right have long framed Joan of Arc as the embodiment of the true French spirit and the symbolic leader of their mission (Davies 1999, 112–16; Bell 2001, 203). The mythology and symbolism of Joan of Arc is also central to the idea of the French as a "chosen people," with a divine right to rule their territory and a nation favored by God.

In a similar vein, there are recurring myths about France as a defender of the Catholic faith against threatening Others. Ethnic nationalists have used the French role in the Crusades as proof of the nation's long civilizational fight against Islam—presenting France as the vanguard of Christendom (Davies 1999, 124). Anti-Muslim sentiment shaped French immigration and citizenship policy throughout the twentieth century, particularly in how North African migrants and colonial subjects were treated (Brubaker 1992, 148–52). And anti-Semitism was the central theme of the Dreyfus affair—it was used to promote a narrative of foreign agents inside the country working against French interests (Winock 1998, 115).

Somewhat paradoxically, France's fierce secularism also reinforces aspects of an ethnic French nationalism. The Revolution was a vehicle for secularism: republicans sought to wrestle power from the clergy and to redefine the people as the constituent power. Separating church and state to achieve equality and unity is a core mythology of republicanism, but secularism in France has a divisive and conflictual past (Gunn 2004, 2005). These conflicts help demonstrate its ethnic roots. Revolutionaries often used secularism to define the membership of the new republic: they originally excluded the Catholic clergy and royals, but over time added Protestants and Jews to the list of foreign enemies of the *patrie* because of their religious affiliations (Gunn 2004, 437).

The myth of secularism gained strength during the Third Republic. From 1870 to 1940, *laïcité* emerged as an organizing principle of French identity (Gunn 2004, 439–42). The 1905 Law on the Separation of Churches and the State exemplifies the increasing institutionalization of the principle. *Laïcité* is an ambiguous and contested concept that has no direct parallel in English—though it is usually translated as "secular" or used as shorthand for the separation of church and state (Poulat 2003; Baubérot 2004). At its core, it promotes a separation of civil and religious society: it holds that the state has no authority over religion and that religion has no authority over political and public matters (Gunn 2004, 420). While often held up as the cornerstone of tolerance and unity in French civic identity, the changing myth of *laïcité* accentuates the ethnic roots of French secularism.

These ethnic roots are evident in the shifting limits of toleration under *laïcité* in the late twentieth and early twenty-first centuries. Starting in the late 1980s, the hijab emerged as a flashpoint in French culture wars. For some observers, it came to symbolize the problematic presence of Muslims in France, pushing the perceived limits of *laïcité*. At the forefront of this conflict was controversy over students wearing the hijab while attending school (Winter 2008; Korteweg and Yurdakul 2014, chap. 2). Political actors seized on court cases and commissions on the principle of *laïcité*, such as the Stasi commission in 2003, to harden the interpretation and implementation of secularism in the public sphere. As part of this episode, in 2003, when proposing a law that banned the wearing of the hijab in schools, then president Jacques Chirac aptly summarized how the seemingly republican ideal of *laïcité* also has ethnic roots. As he said, "*laïcité* is inscribed in our traditions . . . its values are at the core of our uniqueness as a Nation . . . [it is] one of the great accomplishments of the Republic . . . we can never permit it to weaken" (as quoted in Gunn 2004, 428).

These comments exemplify how *laïcité* can be seen as an ethnic symbol. In this regard, seemingly universal, republican values of toleration and equality are conflated with uniquely cultural attributes of French society that stem from its superiority and ingenuity. Chirac's words capture a myth that recasts *laïcité* as a French value and invention—as something that real French are loyal to and something that defines membership to the community. This variant of the myth also defines the outsider: those unwilling to follow Chirac's casting of *laïcité* are no longer welcome members of the French nation. There is also a racialized undertone to this use of *laïcité*: while purportedly applying to all religions, the target of contemporary secularism is invariably racialized Muslims. It is in this way that an ethnicization of secularism has shaped views of Muslims in France—it promotes an idea that those who are not white and those who do not follow a strict secularism are foreigners and unassimilable (on the long-standing foundations of this idea, see Brubaker 1992, 149). In this regard, secularization and *laïcité* are tied to a broader ethnic view of France as an enlightened, white, Catholic nation, which has a *mission civilisatrice* (civilizing mission) to bring rationality to the world and to elevate inferior peoples through conversion.

Ethos

The civilizing mission is a core mythology of an ethnic understanding of France's ethos. It is largely received wisdom that republicans built the French nation through a process of "civilizing" peasants, colonial subjects, and migrants (Weber 1976). Republicans spread the seemingly universal values of liberty, equality, and fraternity after the Revolution with religious zeal—forming the idea of a French nation (Bell 2001). While these points are generally taken as proof of the constructed and civic nature of French national identity, underpinning this process was a decidedly ethnic conception of the French ethos: that the principles of the Revolution stemmed from a unique and superior French political culture. France was, in part, built upon the myth that it had a destiny to spread its distinct, superior culture to its prospective citizens, colonies, Europe, and the world.

The myth of France's civilizing mission has deep roots in its past that continue to shape understandings of French political culture. Romantic historians recast the Roman expansion and victory over the Gauls as a key development in realizing a civilized French nation (Pomain 1996, 67)—a narrative embraced by Napoleon I and III (Dietler 1994, 588–90). The notion of the French as "civilized" fed a sense of superiority in the face of other "savage" nations throughout the pre-revolutionary period and in its colonial enterprise (Bell 2001). Indeed, this mythology was a core rationale for French colonialism: the ideology of the civilizing mission, which "rested upon certain fundamental assumptions about the superiority of French culture and the perfectibility of humankind," was elevated to the level of "imperial doctrine" in France (Conklin 2005, 1). These ideas justified the suppression of cultures among peoples in colonial territories—a legacy that continues to shape policies related to immigration, citizenship, and religious accommodation (Conklin 2005).

These ethnic foundations of a French ethos essentially "nationalize" core elements of republican ideals. Rather than situate these ideals as universal truths, they root them in the French people, its culture, and its history. In this respect, France's true mission is to protect and spread the values of the French nation to those who are receptive (and to embrace them as able to join the French nation) and to shun those who are not (and exclude them from the family). Even the idea of assimilation as a core tenet of French civic nationalism can be reframed to reflect the superiority of French culture. This form of *national republicanism* has been embraced by the far right and ethnic nationalists in France—often presented as consistent with France's civilizing mission in the world (Davies 1999, 93; Bastow 2018).

At times, of course, actors have attacked the values of the Revolution in search of other ethnic ideas that could represent the ethos of France. Most notably and explicitly, the Vichy regime sought to replace the core values of liberty, equality, and fraternity from the Revolution with the trilogy of work, family, and fatherland (*travail, famille, patrie*) (Shields 2007, 16). The regime's political program was largely structured by this objective: Pétain undertook a concerted process of cultivating these ideals as the real attributes of the French nation (Davies 2002, 104–8). Certainly, this counter-revolutionary ethos has been embraced by the far right in France at points, notably by Jean-Marie Le Pen in 2002 (Shields 2007, 2). However, a subtler shifting of the core republican values as reflecting French culture and history is the more recurrent and clear way that the ethos of France is nationalized through an ethnic lens.

History

Many of the above-noted ethnic myths and symbols have been combined over time to craft a history of the French nation that foregrounds its ethnic foundations. To be sure, the Revolution casts a long shadow as the perceived point where a civic, liberal political culture emerged. But, as we just explained, even this most sacred myth and symbol of civic identity can be recast to accentuate an ethnic foundation of Frenchness: as something that stemmed from the superior, distinct French political culture. More common, however, is for ethnic nationalists to conceive of the Revolution as but one moment in France's long history dating back to time of the Gauls. In this respect, ethnic nationalists like Jean-Marie Le Pen have often sought to reframe French history in this longer view, seeing the nation as rooted in an immoral past: "Everyone in the political class is getting ready to celebrate the bicentenary of the revolution of 1789. Why not? France is four thousand years of European culture, twenty centuries of Christianity, forty kings and two centuries of the Republic. The National

Front accepts all of France's past" (quoted in Marcus 1995, 102–3). In short, the examples we have highlighted in this section can be pulled together to recenter one's understanding of French history around ethnic and cultural myths and symbols. The Gauls, Vercingetorix, and Joan of Arc take center stage as heroic symbols, while the English, Germans, Jews, and Muslims are recurrent foils. At least one important understanding of French history that is missing from our analysis so far, however, is that of defeat and resistance.

Like many other nations, the French have a past marked by conflict, warfare, and victory, but also traumatic defeat and resistance in the face of unwinnable odds. These events—and their interpretation and contestation by historians and in public culture—become powerful myths and symbols shaping perceptions of the nation's character (Hutchinson 2005, 2017). Defeat is a particularly important and powerful recurring myth of French history (Mock 2012). The examples are well known: the Roman victory over the Gauls; the English victory at Agincourt; the Seven Years' War and the ceding of New France; historic and humiliating losses to the Germans in 1870, and in the two world wars.

However, these defeats are often paired with a noble tradition of resistance (and ultimately, in the long-run, victory). The most iconic and symbolic totem for this turn in the historical mythology of France is Joan of Arc. As Steven Mock (2012) and others have shown, Joan of Arc represents a history of resisting threats to the French nation (though she has long been a contested symbol, see at 142–46). At various points in history, she has been used as a symbol and rallying point for those who purport to be fighting to protect France from foreign invaders (198–201). This theme of resistance is a common thread in interpretations of French history: the Gauls as resisting the Romans and Franks as foreigners; the French Resistance (in distinction with Vichy) during the Second World War; and, more recently, in movements resisting a perceived erosion of French political culture by increasingly diverse immigration.

This is—by no means—an exhaustive list of the historical foundations of a decidedly ethnic conception of French identity. But these examples can help us understand some of the key myths and symbols—the ideas—of France as an ethnic nation. These myths and symbols can help us see how contemporary themes of ethnic nationalism in France have deep roots in earlier ideas about the nation. Here we have brought together and summarized these aspects of French political culture through our schema (Table 6.1).

Many of these myths incorporate core symbols of the ethnic foundations of French identity. As already noted, these symbols are contested, varied, and have been mobilized throughout different periods of French history. They play key roles in defining both the in- and out-group. Some of the most important include:

Table 6.1 **Foundational Ethnic Myths of French Identity**

People	Religion	Homeland	History	Ethos
The Gauls are the true ancestors of the French people.	The true French nation is deeply Catholic, even if it is secular in the public realm.	The *patrie* is both a state of mind and the home of the French family.	France has a long and storied history that reaches well past the Revolution.	Liberty, Equality and Fraternity are expressions of a distinct, superior French culture and set of values.
The French are defined by their shared blood and their whiteness: *jus sanguinis* not *jus soli* define true Frenchmen.	France is a defender of Christendom, particularly against Islam, and has a duty to carry out its civilizing mission.	The superiority of the French *terroir* feeds the superiority of the French. The real France is found in *la France profonde*.	French history is marked by defeat and sacrifice— but also by resistance to foreign invaders.	France has a *mission civilisatrice* to elevate "savages" and spread French ideals— Western civilization reflects the leadership and values of French civilization.
In its true form the nation is indivisible and homogeneous: while it has long assimilated other groups, there are limits on who can assimilate into the culture, in part because of the superiority of the French people.	Joan of Arc was an instrument of God chosen to defend and purify the French and repel foreign invaders.	*L'Hexigon* is the true home of the real Frenchmen.	In the long-run, resistance leads to glory and vindication of French superiority.	
	Secularism and *laïcité* are unique and superior French ideals: true Frenchmen defend and adhere to a secular public sphere.		The French people and culture have been a prime mover of French, European, Western, and global progress	Along with Liberty, Equality, and Fraternity, France is defined by the values of Work, Family and Fatherland.

- The Gauls and Franks—as the ancestors of the true French people and foreign invaders, respectively.
- Whiteness—as a marker of who is truly French, particularly in relation to migrants from former colonial holdings in Africa.
- Vercingetorix—as the warrior prince of the French resistance to Roman invasion.
- Joan of Arc—as the warrior princess, chosen by God, to rid France of foreign invaders.
- *Patrie*—the fatherland as the home of the true French.
- *France profonde*—deep, rural France as the real home of the French people.
- *L'Hexigon*—mainland France as the true home of the French, in opposition to colonial holdings and the black, Muslim people who come from the colonies.
- Religious symbols, and particularly the hijab—as markers of outsiders who are not able to integrate into French culture.

We do not claim this is a comprehensive overview of the political and cultural foundations of French identity—nor even of its ethnic component. This is not a book on French history, *per se*. Nor is it even a book on the ethnic foundations of French identity. Rather, we are focused on identifying a series of core and recurring myths and symbols that support an idea of France as an ethnic community. There are counter-narratives and elements of this identity we have likely missed. As Mock's (2012) in-depth treatment of the symbol of Joan of Arc shows, even one symbol can feed and reinforce multiple different streams and notions of French identity. But the relative ease with which we can draw from French historiography to identify a series of foundational myths and symbols of an ethnic French identity speaks to both the prevalence and permanence of these ideas through time. They are a strong undercurrent of French political culture.

Marine Le Pen and Ethnic Nationalism in France Today

Before we turn to demonstrating how Marine Le Pen tapped into these ethnic myths and symbols in the 2017 presidential campaign, it is important to provide some context on her party and its rise as the main vehicle for ethnic nationalism in post–World War II France.

The National Front has traditionally been—and in many respects remains—an ethnic nationalist political party. The centrality of ethnic nationalism was most obvious during Jean-Marie Le Pen's long stint as leader, from the party's founding in 1972 until his departure in 2011 (DeClair 1999; Davies 1999;

Shields 2007). From the beginning, Le Pen promoted an exclusionary anti-immigrant and anti-establishment program (Stockemer and Barisione 2017, 103). These themes reflected a deeper "ethnocentric worldview"—a privileging of shared ethnicity, culture, and history that shaped the party's policy and rhetoric (Stockemer and Barisione 2017, 103; Hainsworth 2008, 12).

Jean-Marie's ethnic nationalism drew from many of the myths and symbols we just highlighted. He would often point to the Gauls as the ethnic core of the nation, while also praising Vercingetorix as resisting foreign invaders (Dietler 1994). The party sought to reframe the Revolution as birthing a set of unique French values—national republicanism—that needed to be defended. Here, the National Front often positioned itself as the resistance to the demise of these values (Davies 1999, 86–87). Picking up on a core theme of the Vichy regime, Le Pen would present himself as defending the "real" or "true" France in the rural hinterland (*la France profonde*) (Rearick 1997, 253; Davies 1999, 107–11). The National Front was also a fierce defender of Catholicism as a key element of French identity. This defense was clearest in its long-standing opposition to Muslim immigrants. Jean-Marie and his deputies would regularly use the trope of an impending "Islamic demographic explosion" that threatens French culture, civilization, and identity—linking the perceived struggle against this threat to past battles between Christianity and Islam (Davies 1999, 123–25; Marcus 1995, 105–17). Often in this rhetoric, Le Pen would evoke the symbolism of Joan of Arc, drawing similarities between the two of them. He used Joan of Arc as a totem for the defense of France against invaders; for the National Front in the 1980s and 1990s, she symbolized "the 'true France': the agricultural heritage, the military prowess in the face of foreign enemies, the self-sacrifice in honour of the nation, and the Catholic devotion" (Davies 1999, 114).

This ethnic conception of the French people directly fed Jean-Marie Le Pen's strong anti-foreigner and anti-immigrant positions. Anti-immigration has always been the National Front's *leitmotif*: under Jean-Marie it was the anchor issue through which all other issues were viewed (Stockemer and Barisione 2017, 107). This focus had clear ethnic connotations: communication and policy often focused on defending the white ethnic group in France from foreign invaders ("defend our colours"), who were depicted as infections ("bacteria") jeopardizing the pure French nation and threats to its cultural fabric (Davies 1999, chap. 3). These arguments most forcefully and consistently targeted Muslim immigrants from North Africa (Brubaker 1992, chap. 7). They were also used to take on other perceived threats. Anti-immigrant positions were paired with opposition to "foreigners within," with strong anti-Semitism in the party's positions and communication (Davies 1999, 135; Simmons 1996, chap. 6). In the 1980s and 1990s the party also took a strong stand against the policy of *jus soli*. Jean-Marie Le Pen would speak about the "honor" of being French, that "one is born French or one becomes French, either through received blood (*le sang reçu*) or through blood paid (*le sang versé*)" (Davies 1999, 68). This was a common refrain among Le Pen's deputies—it became a foundational narrative that the party was the defender of the *real* French people (white Catholics); that it was the means to rebuild a "French France" (Davies 1999, 66–80).

The consensus view today is that when Marine Le Pen took over the party in 2011, she shifted away from this *overt* ethnic nationalism. She branded this shift as the *"dédiabolisatoin"* (de-demonization) of the party—a purported pivot away from a racist and anti-Semitic political program and messaging toward more mainstream views consistent with French republicanism (Ivaldi and Lanzone 2016; Betz 2018; Almeida 2017; Stockemer 2017). In doing so, Marine embraced a "national republicanism" (Bastow 2018; Almeida 2017). She has largely dropped overtly racist messaging, while positioning the party as the defenders of "our" way of life against dangerous Others who are not civilized (Hutchins and Halikiopoulou 2018). Under this banner of national republicanism, the party has tended to focus on immigration, Islamic terrorism, and *laïcité*, while also turning toward economic populism and protectionism (Hutchins and Halikiopoulou 2018; Stockemer and Barisione 2017; Bastow 2018). At its core, however, the National Front continues to focus on issues of ethnic and national identity: the nation has been a "fixed point of reference" in the political program and discourse of the party, and immigration remains its central issue (Davies 1999, 66; Stockemer 2017; Bastow 2018).

With these shifts, Marine Le Pen has managed to increase the support for the National Front. Under Jean-Marie the party was generally considered as a fringe, far-right party that was unable to gain substantial seats in the legislature (Davies 2002; DeClair 1999; Hainsworth 2008). Nevertheless, the party has managed to achieve a "progressive entrenchment" into the political system over the last few decades (Halikiopoulou 2018). This entrenchment reflects the party's staying power as a fixture on the political scene. But the key factor is Marine Le Pen's breakthrough in 2017, where she received the highest-ever level of support for the party in the second-round presidential vote. Her success was so surprising that it has been heralded as one of the leading signs of the rise of an exceptional, new nationalism in the West (Brubaker 2017; Halikiopoulou 2018; Bieber 2018). This outcome has spurned a lively debate about whether the party has become part of the mainstream (Bastow 2018).

Explanations of the rise and success of Marine Le Pen mirror those used for other examples of the new nationalism in the West. Shifting structural conditions are often singled out as key drivers behind rising support for the National Front. One of the most influential accounts points to changes in the sociodemographic features of the voting population (Mayer 2013; Shields 2013). But, like the US and UK, changing immigration and economic conditions are also foregrounded

(Della Posta 2013). These explanations are complemented with a focus on the discursive strategies of the party, and particularly the above-noted shift from Jean-Marie to Marine Le Pen. Turning away from overtly racist, xenophobic, and anti-Semitic language toward a more complex, national republicanism has allowed Marine Le Pen to grow her support base, while also retaining voters that followed her father's vision (Stockemer 2017; Bastow 2018). As with other cases, these accounts of the structural drivers and discursive strategies can be augmented with a thicker analysis of how the content of Marine Le Pen's political program draws from, and reshapes, historically rooted ethnic and cultural repertoires of French identity. Underpinning a great deal of the current work on Le Pen is the view that the National Front's progressive entrenchment into the landscape—and particularly her 2017 showing in the presidential election—are counter to the norm of French politics. There is a prevalent view that the rise of an ethnic nationalist party is a puzzling exception to the civic values that define France as the prototypical Western nation. As Bastow (2018) and Mondon (2015) point out, this has been a tendency of the work on Le Pen: claims that Marine Le Pen's politics represent a new type of patriotism are a product of a "lack of historical or theoretical analysis" of the party's ideological trajectory over time. Our analysis shows that many of the ethnic myths and symbols we outlined earlier in this chapter have been present through long periods of French history, and they remain powerful elements of politics even today.

Marine Le Pen's Ethnic Nationalism on Twitter in the 2017 Election

The 2017 French presidential election is a remarkable example of an ethnic nationalist campaign attracting significant support. The results of the first round of voting, held on April 23, 2017, were extremely tight: the top four candidates were separated by less than five percentage points (see Gougou and Perisco 2017). Emmanuel Macron, a young, self-styled centrist liberal who was not aligned with the traditional parties, topped the list in the first vote with 24 percent support. Marine Le Pen was close on his heals at 21.3 percent—the highest level ever recorded in the first round of presidential voting for a National Front candidate. The second-round runoff between these two candidates was held on May 7, 2017. Macron went on to win handily with 66.1 percent of votes to Le Pen's 33.9 percent. This was the second largest margin of victory in a runoff election. Nevertheless, Le Pen's 33.9 percent—representing over 10.5 million voters—is still the best result for a National Front candidate ever, by a considerable degree. While she did not win the presidency, this was a highly successful result for Le Pen and the National Front.

Marine Le Pen largely drew from the traditional base of the National Front in this election. Her geographic centers of support clustered in the Northeast and Southeast of the country. Her voters tended to live in more rural communities, were working-class, and had lower levels of education and income (Aisch et al. 2017). This sociodemographic profile of voters is not surprising. These are the people who have traditionally supported her party. However, Le Pen also continued to expand her voting coalition, building on emerging patterns in the 2012 election (Mayer 2013). She was relatively popular among younger voters, particularly in the 35–49 age group. Women also supported her in relatively high numbers—largely erasing a substantial gender gap in support that has traditionally plagued the National Front (Amengay, Durovic, and Mayer 2017). Of course, the size of Macron's victory means he also attracted significant support from many of these constituencies, while also winning votes from more urban, well-educated, and higher-earning voters at startling levels. Nevertheless, over 10 million people voted for Le Pen. One of the key takeaways from this election is thus that Le Pen's messaging built on a strong base and increased support by reverberating with more rural, less educated, working-class, white French voters, but also increasingly younger people and women.

As with the US, we are not necessarily focusing on these voters, but rather on Le Pen's political discourse and strategy. We are interested in why her messaging reverberated with a substantial number of the ethnic majority, why a clearly ethnic nationalist campaign attracted such high numbers of voters, even if she did not win. We are particularly interested in showing how she drew from, and reconstructed, ethnic myths and symbols in her political campaign. To show this, as in the previous chapter, we analyze Le Pen's Twitter communication through our schema, focusing on her direct tweets for the six months prior to the final runoff vote on May 7, 2017.[3] All told we captured just over 2,800 tweets in this period.[4]

Marine Le Pen's Twitter communication during the 2017 campaign clearly and unambiguously drew from ethnic nationalist themes and ideas. It was her main strategy and most common rhetorical device: Le Pen overtly used ethnic messaging more than one-third of the time—in over 900 of her 2,800 tweets. In short, her entire campaign was structured around, and sought to promote, an ethnic French nationalism.

Le Pen's favorite topics show us how she tapped into the wellspring of foundational ethnic myths and symbols of French identity. In the approximately 900 tweets using ethnic messaging, she evoked different foundational myths and symbols over 1,400 times. Often, she would combine myths from multiple categories to paint a narrative in a tweet about either the virtuous character of the French or the dangers of outsiders. By far and away, her favorite topic was to define the French people and outsiders through an ethnic lens. She did this over

500 times (or in approximately 55% of all tweets using ethnic myths)—focusing mainly on migrants, but also the middle and working class, the silent majority (*la majorité silencieuse*), and what defines someone as a true citizen. She also used ethnic myths relating to religion (mainly discussing Islam, but also secularism and Catholicism), the French ethos (promoting French exceptionalism, along with a defense of republicanism and a civilizing mission), and the homeland (focusing on the rural countryside and agriculture, along with borders and suburbs) in almost equal measure. Each of these categories appeared approximately 250 times. Over 130 times she also used an ethnic framing of French history, highlighting the nation's grand past and tradition of resistance. Taken as a whole, Le Pen's Twitter communication in the 2017 election shows a clear pattern of using foundational myths and symbols of an ethnic understanding of the French nation to propel her political program.

Of course, she also engaged in other topics on Twitter. Like virtually all political candidates today, she used Twitter to announce campaign events, thank supporters, and heap praise on herself by highlighting her accomplishments. She attacked her opponents, focusing on Macron (over 200 times) and François Fillon (almost 150 times). Le Pen also used Twitter to promote her manifesto, discussing public policy proposals in over one-third of her tweets. She primarily discussed immigration, the economy, law and order, terrorism, and the welfare state. The European Union and globalization were also common targets for Le Pen—tweeting about them approximately 200 and 130 times, respectively. And, as others have noted, her campaign had a populist bend in both form and substance (Stockemer and Barisione 2017; Bastow 2018). Her slogan was "In the Name of the People" (*Au Nom Du Peuple*). She used this as a hashtag and phrase approximately 125 times, while also using clearly populist, anti-elite, and anti-establishment language and themes at least an additional 170 times.

These other foci in her Twitter communication only reinforce the centrality of ethnic nationalism to the campaign. On the one hand, the already high proportion of ethnic messaging in all of Le Pen's tweets *underrepresents* their role in the substantive strategy of her political program. Many of her tweets were about mundane matters like announcements and standard fare like attacking opponents. On the other hand, even in her substantive tweets on other topics, ethnic nationalism was the overarching theme that linked them together as a part of a broader campaign strategy. Her public policy pronouncements were often underpinned by ethnic myths and symbols. For example, when discussing immigration, Le Pen would regularly argue that migrants were jeopardizing the economic fortunes of French people and stealing their jobs (@MLP_officiel, March 20, 2017; March 15, 2017), were straining the welfare system (March 13, 2017, 7:42 a.m.; February 17, 2017, 6:03 p.m.), or were making communities unsafe and unrecognizable (March 30, 2017, 6:46 p.m.; January 24, 2017,

3:32 p.m.).[5] This approach of "ethnicizing" a policy topic was a common tactic for Le Pen: she did it over a third of the time for key issues like social services, law and order, the economy, and (unsurprisingly) a vast majority of the time when discussing terrorism. Similarly, when criticizing the European Union or globalization she would tap into ethnic motifs around 35 percent of the time; often she would say how Brussels and global forces were threatening the French way of life, its rural and agricultural basis, and the ability of the French to control their own destiny (April 8, 2017, 2:20 p.m.; May 1, 2017, 11:02 a.m., 11:14 a.m.). In the same vein, when using populist language, she would often evoke conceptions of the people as an *ethnic* group set against foreigners (at least one-quarter of the time). Le Pen's campaign also promoted a women's rights agenda, but generally through the prism of liberating women from the perceived oppression of Islam and protecting their equality through a strict enforcement of *laïcité* (March 20, 2017, 9:18 p.m.; March 8, 2017, 9:07 a.m.). When discussing women's rights, Le Pen used these types of ethnic frames over half the time (on this form of "femonatioanlism," see Farris 2017; Geva 2020). In this respect, even when engaging in wider debates and topics beyond the character of the French and the country's enemies, she would imbue her messaging with a clear ethnic nationalist foundation. Her policy stances were structured by, and sought to tap into, a deep-seated ethnic vision of the French nation.

This broad overview of the main topics of Le Pen's Twitter communication during the campaign shows the centrality of ethnic messaging, but it does not tell us a great deal about the *content* of the messaging or *why* Le Pen's campaign reverberated with a large swath of the population. Stepping back, and applying our framework and an ethno-symbolic lens, we can see that Le Pen's entire campaign was structured by a process of building an image of a virtuous in-group through a series of ethnic myths and symbols, contrasted with a villainous out-group.

"Us"

Le Pen's Twitter communication sought to build a base of support—an image of the true France that she was seeking to lead—through a series of related ideas that clearly drew from the foundational set of ethnic myths and symbols we outlined earlier in this chapter. When she used these myths, she tended to paint the in-group in highly positive terms. While some of her messaging did express negative sentiment, this was generally to signal displeasure with the situation or threats facing the in-group. And so even these messages were about constructing a positive image of the in-group and reinforcing its validity and standing as a legitimate political entity.

By some measure, the primary means Le Pen used to define her in-group was to reinforce an ethnic conception of the French people. She constructed this group by centering "the French" (*les Français*) in her program—using the image of a homogeneous nation that owned the country (April 4, 2017, 10:36 p.m.). At the same time, she alluded to a core ethnic, white majority by using the phrasing of "the silent France" (*la France silencieuse*) and "the silent majority" (April 13, 2017, 5:24 p.m.; April 4, 2017, 6:16 a.m.). She traced the lineage of this majority back to the Gauls and the Romans (April 13, 2017, 5, 27 p.m.). She emphasized the perceived grievances and threats to this ethnic majority's identity—how it was being dispossessed of its culture, lifestyle, and identity (April 25, 2017, 7:18 p.m., 7:19 p.m.; April 19, 2017, 6:50 a.m.). Often Le Pen would argue that the ethnic white majority was tired of immigration and that migrants were the cause of their perceived decline (February 26, 2017, 248 p.m.; April 17, 2017, 7:38 p.m). And so she presented herself as the leader of this white majority, resisting these changes and seeking to recapture France for the French, to give them the keys back to their own house—to make France French, again (April 20, 2017, 6:40 p.m.; April 19, 2017, 7:25 p.m., 6:52 a.m.; April 17, 2017, 8:06 p.m).

Le Pen layered on top of this image of the people two other long-standing ideas that reinforce an ethnic basis for French identity. First was the ethnic limit of French citizenship. She linked true citizenship to ancestry (*jus sanguinis*), as something that is inherited or earned through sacrifice (April 20, 2017, 6:51 p.m.; January 3, 2017, 8:15 a.m.). She regularly criticized birth on soil as creating citizens in name only and as favoring those who do not want to assimilate (April 19, 2017, 6:41 a.m.; November 29, 2016, 251 p.m.). In a similar maneuver, Le Pen reinforced the difference between the *Pieds-Noir* and migrants from North Africa: she depicted the *Pieds-Noir* as true French citizens and compatriots, while implying that migrants from North Africa could not be true citizens (April 19, 2017, 7:14 a.m.; March 19, 2017, 7:52 a.m.).

Second, Le Pen aggrandized the French as a hard-working people. Part of her focus on the middle and working class was clearly an attempt to inject some economic populism into the National Front campaign, but her discussion of the economy often sought to reinforce an ethnic notion of the French people set against Others. She would regularly highlight how migrants, the EU, and globalization were threatening the jobs and fortunes of French workers (April 25, 2017, 7:11 p.m.; March 15, 2017 6:37 p.m., 6:51 p.m.). In this respect she associated workers with the French people. Here, she highlighted farmers and workers in the agricultural sector as archetypes of how global and foreign forces were destroying the true France and the livelihood of French people (March 30, 2017, 10:13 a.m.; March 2, 2017, 7:55 a.m.; February 17, 2017, 5:49 p.m.).

Le Pen's focus on the middle and working class, along with farmers and agriculture, also drew from a set of myths and symbols about the French homeland. She invoked the idea that farming was a core component of the French way of life—that farmers were protectors of France's cultural heritage (March 30, 2017, 10:13 a.m., 10:33 a.m., 6:43 p.m.). She rooted these traditions and way of life in particular regions (*appellations*) and the unique attributes of French soil—arguing they were under threat from global forces and the EU (April 8, 2017, 2:20 p.m.; April 2, 2107, 1:53 p.m.). These ideas were part of a larger strategy of playing into the long-standing myth that the true France is found in the rural countryside, in *la France profonde*. Le Pen regularly evoked the imagery that the real French can be found in the villages and countryside (April 19, 2017, 8:05 p.m.; April 4, 2017, 6:16 a.m.; April 3, 2017, 5:05 p.m.). She also lamented its decline and said she would lead the resistance to revitalize these parts of France (April 13, 2017, 5:08 p.m.; March 12, 2017, 11:47 a.m.; March 4, 2017, 3:50 p.m.). At the same time, Le Pen did play into the myth that the entire French territory was the home of all French. She drew from the idea that the homeland (*patrie*) and that the defense and love for the homeland (*patriotisme*) were core elements of being French (February 24, 2017, 6:35 p.m.; November 20, 2016, 11:12 a.m.)—and she drove home the difference between the French rooted in their place in the world and globalists who were threatening their way of life (May 7, 2017, 6:14 p.m.; April 24, 2017, 6:33 p.m.). These themes were further reinforced by a consistent focus on the need to thicken and defend the borders of France against incursions from migrants and exploitive global capitalists (May 1, 2017, 6:26 a.m.; April 25, 2017, 7:11 p.m.).

Le Pen also used two core myths about the religious foundations of French identity to reinforce her in-group. She used Catholicism and Christianity as key boundary markers—repeatedly asserting that the cultural and historical roots of France were Christian (April 13, 2017, 5:27 p.m.; February 9, 2017, 9:04 p.m.). She actively sought to protect and promote this Christian heritage, even in the public space (March 18, 2017, 3:02 p.m.). But Le Pen also recognized—and tied together—her views on the Christian foundations of French identity with its long-running tradition of secularism. As she herself stated, "Our country obviously has a Christian heritage, secularized by the Enlightenment, which shapes our worldview" (April 10, 2017, 10:08 a.m.). This support for secularism (or more precisely, the separation of non-Christian religions from public space) was the other key myth Le Pen used to build an image of the French in-group. As we will discuss shortly, the vast majority of instances where Le Pen invoked the notion of secularism (*laïcité*) sought to frame Muslims as outsiders, who are incompatible with French values. However, she also sought to build boundaries for the in-group by praising secularism as a core *French* value and setting herself

Figure 6.1 Examples of Marine Le Pen's Tweets constructing an ethnic in-group

up as the candidate who would fiercely defend and apply this most French ideal (April 18, 2017, 6:38 p.m.; March 12, 2017, 11:51 a.m.).

Le Pen would often combine religious myths and symbols with ethnic notions of the French ethos to build her in-group. She explicitly linked the principle of *laïcité* to French republicanism—identifying both as key pillars of French identity (April 21, 2017, 8:23 a.m.). She signaled her support for republicanism, claiming that she would be its defender, and thus the defender of French values (April 25, 2017, 8:48 p.m.). In doing so, though, she situated republicanism as an invention and virtue of the French people, for example associating traditional republican slogans (*Vive la République*) alongside more populist ideas (*Vive le Peuple*) (April 27, 2017, 8:06 p.m.; March 26, 2017, 2:19 p.m.).

The most common way Le Pen sought to frame the French ethos, though, was by promoting French exceptionalism. She regularly pointed to the past glory and the innate greatness and superiority of the French people (February 26, 2017, 3:11 p.m.; February 27, 2017, 10:05 a.m.; March 27, 2017, 4:51 p.m.). She said she would lead the country back to this greatness (April 19, 2017, 8:05 p.m.; February 17, 2017, 6:17 p.m.). In essence, her vision—her summation of the French ethos—was that her leadership would allow the French to return as one of the great and "rightful actors of history" (April 27, 2017, 7:36 p.m.). This line of thought manifested itself as a consistent argument that the nation ought to be prioritized in international and domestic policy (April 25, 2017, 7:35 p.m.; March 20, 2017, 10:12 p.m.; March 5, 2017, 11:53 a.m.). She argued that she would always put France, and its people, "first" (April 20, 2017, 6:54 p.m.; April 6, 2017, 5:44 p.m.; January 16, 2017, 6:46 a.m.). Another way this manifested was Le Pen's promotion of the superiority of French culture. She praised the nation's cultural identity as an important heritage that is passed down from generation to generation (May 1, 2017, 11:09 a.m.; Mach 11, 2017, 3:07 p.m.). But she also argued it was in decline and that the people feel their identity has been disposed of, and so only her steadfast leadership would protect French culture (April 25, 2017, 7:19 p.m.; April 4, 2017, 9:24 p.m.; February 17, 2017, 6:10 p.m.). This focus on culture included consistent messaging that France was a great civilization (April 25, 2017, 8:48 p.m.; April 8, 2017, 1:57 p.m.). A common refrain here was that France has long been a civilized nation—a world-leading example—but again that this status was in jeopardy from outside forces (May 1, 2017, 11:14 a.m.; April 19, 2017, 19:23 p.m.). And so, she set up the election as a choice about the very future of civilization itself (January 20, 2017, 7:56 a.m.).

This same theme—past greatness, present decline, and possible future greatness under her leadership—was also the most common way Le Pen tapped into the repository of historical myths and symbols to construct an in-group. She regularly painted an image of past French glory. She envisioned a nation with a long past, where the French once ruled their own country, suffered to achieve its status, had a rich culture, and were the epitome of civilization (April 27, 2017, 7:36 p.m.; April 17, 2017, 7:15 p.m.; November 8, 2016, 4:22 p.m.). But, as we will discuss shortly, the campaign argued this greatness has been muted and is constantly under threat. It is only through her leadership of a new resistance that the French could turn the tide and return to greatness once again (April 30, 2017, 6:22 p.m.; April 19, 2017, 8:05 p.m.). And so she urged the French to just "keep courage: in the end the eternal France always wins" (March 27, 2017, 4:56 p.m.). In short, Le Pen presented herself as the modern-day Joan of Arc leading the French resistance back to glory—although she did not directly employ the symbolism of Joan of Arc (perhaps because of the association with her father).

"Them"

While Le Pen spent a good deal of her energy on Twitter trying to construct a positive image of her in-group, the majority of her tweets using ethnic motifs were about identifying and vilifying outsiders. These tweets were largely negative, framing members of the out-group as dangerous, as heretics who were threatening the French way of life from afar and at home.

Le Pen primarily targeted migrants as a group that simply could not become French. Her rhetoric sought to dehumanize them, othering migrants as savages living in "jungles" and taking over whole neighborhoods, making them foreign (April 19, 2017, 7:23 p.m.; January 24, 2017, 3:32 p.m.). This othering linked migration to the decay of French society and social values—presenting it as a detrimental force of "globalization from below" that was forever changing the French way of life (February 5, 2017, 2:18 p.m.). To justify her focus on migration, Le Pen regularly argued France was taking in too many people and that even greater numbers were looming (May 4, 2017, 6:39 a.m., 7:22; May 1, 2017, 11:04 a.m.; April 19, 2017, 5:51 a.m.; April 18, 2017, 6:25 p.m.). At times she made the racial undertones of these threats more explicit; for example, she raised the potential of a growing number of people from the "third world" using a "highway" of migration from Algeria to France (May 3, 2017, 9:31 p.m.; April 19, 2017, 7:22 p.m.; April 10, 2017, 10:20 a.m.).

Le Pen's strategy when discussing migrants was to argue they threatened the French majority in three related ways. First, she said migrants were threatening the safety and security of the French—that migrants were putting France in "great danger" (April 9, 2017, 11:08 a.m.), associating foreigners with criminals (April 10, 2017, 10:12 a.m.; February 14, 2017, 6:52 a.m.), and arguing that uncontrolled migration was leading to chaos, violence, and insecurity (April 11,

2017, 6:12 a.m.; March 28, 2017, 6:26 p.m.; November 27, 2016, 3:18 p.m.). As we discuss in a moment, she linked migration and terrorism by saying that dangerous Islamic fundamentalists and jihadists were slipping into the country through illegal flows and as asylum seekers (April 18, 2017, 6:22 p.m.; March 20, 2017, 8:58 p.m.). Second, Le Pen consistently linked increased migration with the economic hardships of French people (February 9, 2017; 8:20 p.m.; November 29, 2016, 2:40 p.m.). She argued that migrants were suppressing wages and displacing the French from their rightful jobs (February 7, 2017, 7:45 a.m.), and so she proposed a policy that would prioritize hiring French people over migrants (April 19, 2017, 7:44 p.m.; April 4, 2017, 7:16 p.m.). Third, she promoted "welfare chauvinism." She said that migrants were taking social housing spots from French people (March 5, 2017, 3:30 p.m.) and straining social services like welfare (April 13, 2017, 5:15 p.m.) and healthcare (March 23, 2017, 8:14 a.m.). She argued for a prioritization of French people in receiving social services (February 17, 2017, 6:03 p.m.), often in conjunction with calls for the same type of priority in economic matters (February 5, 2017, 2:36 p.m.). Together, these three prongs of Le Pen's attack on migrants explicitly and implicitly drove home the message that migrants are not really French—that the good, productive and deserving French people do not come from migrant stock.

Le Pen's othering of migrants was closely related to how she used religion to build an out-group that threatened the French majority. Along with migrants, Muslims and Islam were among her favored targets on Twitter. Indeed, she would often imply that Muslims were by nature foreigners and migrants (that true French were not Muslims). Her tweets on Islam were universally negative. By far and away her most common refrain here was to link Islam with terrorism (April 21, 2017, 5:52 a.m.; 10:10 p.m.; April 14, 2017, 6:37 a.m.; February 5, 2017, 2:53 p.m.). When raising Islam, she would invariably use the phrasing of fundamentalism (linking the two concepts over forty times), explicitly and implicitly arguing that Muslims inside France were terrorists or terrorist sympathizers. One of the main ways she built an image of an Islamic threat to the majority group was through her discussion of "file S" (*fiché S*). "File S" refers to individuals designated as a potential threat to national security, and are thus under investigation by the state. Le Pen claimed that there were more than 10,000 people associated with Islam who carried this designation (April 20, 2017, 6:19 a.m.; April 14, 2017, 6:40 a.m.). She used "file S" as a totem for the Islamic terrorist threat inside the French borders. And so she repeatedly said that Muslims with a "file S" designation were dangerous and needed to be arrested, stripped of their nationality, and deported (May 3, 2017, 7:58 p.m.; February 26, 2017, 3:09 p.m.). It bares noting that a "file S" designation means an individual is under investigation, but it does not mean they have a warrant for their arrest. In a similar and related line of argument, she often targeted mosques and imams as symbols of the Islamic enemy within—calling for their closure and removal from France (May 3, 2017, 8:00 p.m.; April 21, 2017, 8:23 a.m.). In short, she made a concerted case that Muslims were not French and did not deserve their citizenship, a view often pushed in calls to strip citizenship from Islamic fundamentalists and deport them (March 21, 2017, 9:19 a.m.). Of course, this implies that they have a "real" home to go back to and that France is not their country.

In addition to this link between Islam and terrorism, Le Pen promoted a vision that Islam was incompatible with the values of the French people and held that Muslims are not able to truly integrate into French society. She tapped into this myth through three related types of tweets. Le Pen consistently noted that Islam was not compatible with French values—that there was a civilizational struggle going on and that the ideology of Islam posed an existential threat to the French people (May 1, 2017, 11:14 a.m.; February 26, 2017, 2:36 p.m.). She said, "Islamism is a monstrous, hegemonic ideology that has declared war on our nation, on reason, on civilization" (April 21, 2017, 8:17 a.m.). She gave tangible form to this line of argument by talking about how Islam threatens women's equality and rights in France. She regularly argued that Islam is a repressive ideology (December 7, 2016, 7:20 p.m.), fiercely criticized the practice of wearing a veil (March 20, 2017, 9:18 p.m.), and said that doing so was not French (April 17, 2017, 7:11 p.m.). In a similar vein, she would often link these critiques to a perceived crisis for secularism—that the Islamic presence in France was endangering the principle and practice of *laïcité*. She gave form to this idea by railing against "burkinis" (April 8, 2017, 2:47 p.m.), decrying the growth of religious symbols in the public sphere (April 2, 2017, 2:35 p.m.; November 29, 2016, 2:54 p.m.), and vowing to defend secularism against the Islamic threat (April 18, 2017, 6:38 p.m.).

Here, we can also see how Le Pen sought to weave together the myths and symbols of religion with the French ethos. She would often combine these two categories to reinforce a boundary between her idea of the French in-group and outsiders. She consistently lamented public expressions of Islamic faith as perceived attacks on French identity and the foundations of French republicanism (April 21, 2017, 8:23 a.m.; April 17, 2017, 7:11 p.m.; February 5, 2017, 2:19 p.m.). She targeted Muslim's praying in the street—holding them up as the symbol of anti-French behavior and a dangerous shift in French society (April 7, 2017, 6:14 p.m.; March 27, 2017, 6:27 a.m.). She worried about the creep of Islamic practices into the sacred sphere of republican schooling (March 20, 2017, 8:26 p.m., 8:41 p.m.). Le Pen would link these themes together through her anger at a perceived, wider turn away from republicanism toward multiculturalism and "communitarianism" (*communautarisme*) (March 20, 2017, 9:03 p.m.; November 20, 2017, 2:54 p.m.). She asked, "[W]ill France remain the France that the French love, or will it be subjected to communitarianism?"

(April 30, 2017, 6:34 p.m.). She attributed the growth of a dangerous communitarianism to migration (April 19, 2017, 5:51 a.m.). And she pointed toward Islam as the true culprit in spreading this anti-French worldview (February 17, 2017, 6:12 p.m.), saying that the growing acceptance of communitarianism is why France has suffered so much from terrorism (March 27, 2017, 4:26 p.m.; November 15, 2017, 5:09 p.m.).

After setting up this existential threat of a growing communitarianism and Islam, Le Pen then embraced the idea that she was leading France on a new civilizing mission. She presented herself and her party as the bulwark against this growing dangerous tide, saying "I will be the President of secularism" (April 27, 2017, 7:14 p.m.). She said she would lead the fight against Islam as the savior of the true French nation (April 27, 2017, 7:09 p.m.; April 3, 2017, 5:34 p.m.). She planned to double down on secularism as the guiding principle of French society—extending the ban on religious symbols instituted in French schools to the entire public sphere (April 2, 2017, 2:35 p.m.; March 26, 2017, 1:18 p.m.). In short, Le Pen promoted a fierce nationalized republicanism—along with the idea that only this pathway would make France French again by ridding the nation of the foreigners who were jeopardizing these values and the French way of life.

A central plank of her argument here was that foreigners were already inside the proverbial gate and had invaded and taken over parts of the homeland. In contrast with her framing of the rural countryside as the real, peaceful, and productive France, she painted a much more negative picture of the urban suburbs (*banlieues*). She played off the common image of the suburbs as overrun by migrants, as places where French feel like "strangers in their own country" (April 19, 2017, 7:23 p.m.; April 17, 2017, 7:40 p.m.). She depicted them as dangerous, "lawless" zones—as homes of rioters and thugs (February, 2017, 6:06 p.m.; February 12, 2017, 9:13 a.m.). She claimed they were havens for jihadists and the incubators of Islamic terrorism inside France (April 19, 2017, 7:51 p.m.; November 15, 2016, 5:14 p.m.). And she argued that these pockets of France were more than a local issue—they represent a threat to the very civilization values of the French republic and its people (April 19, 2017, 7:23 p.m.; December 11, 2016, 12:25 p.m.).

In making these points, Le Pen often argued that the French people have a long history of resisting these dangers and threats. In this respect, when building the out-group, she consistently tapped the historical mythology of French resistance to foreign invaders and threats to its civilization. To do this, she adopted the terminology of warfare—saying the nation was at war with terrorists, but also with a vague collection of other threats (April 21, 2017, 8:17 a.m., 1:18 a.m., 8:25 a.m.). Predictably, her main targets were migrants and Islam and terrorism (April 19, 2017, 6:46 a.m.; April 8, 2017, 8:14 a.m.; April 21, 2017, 8:17

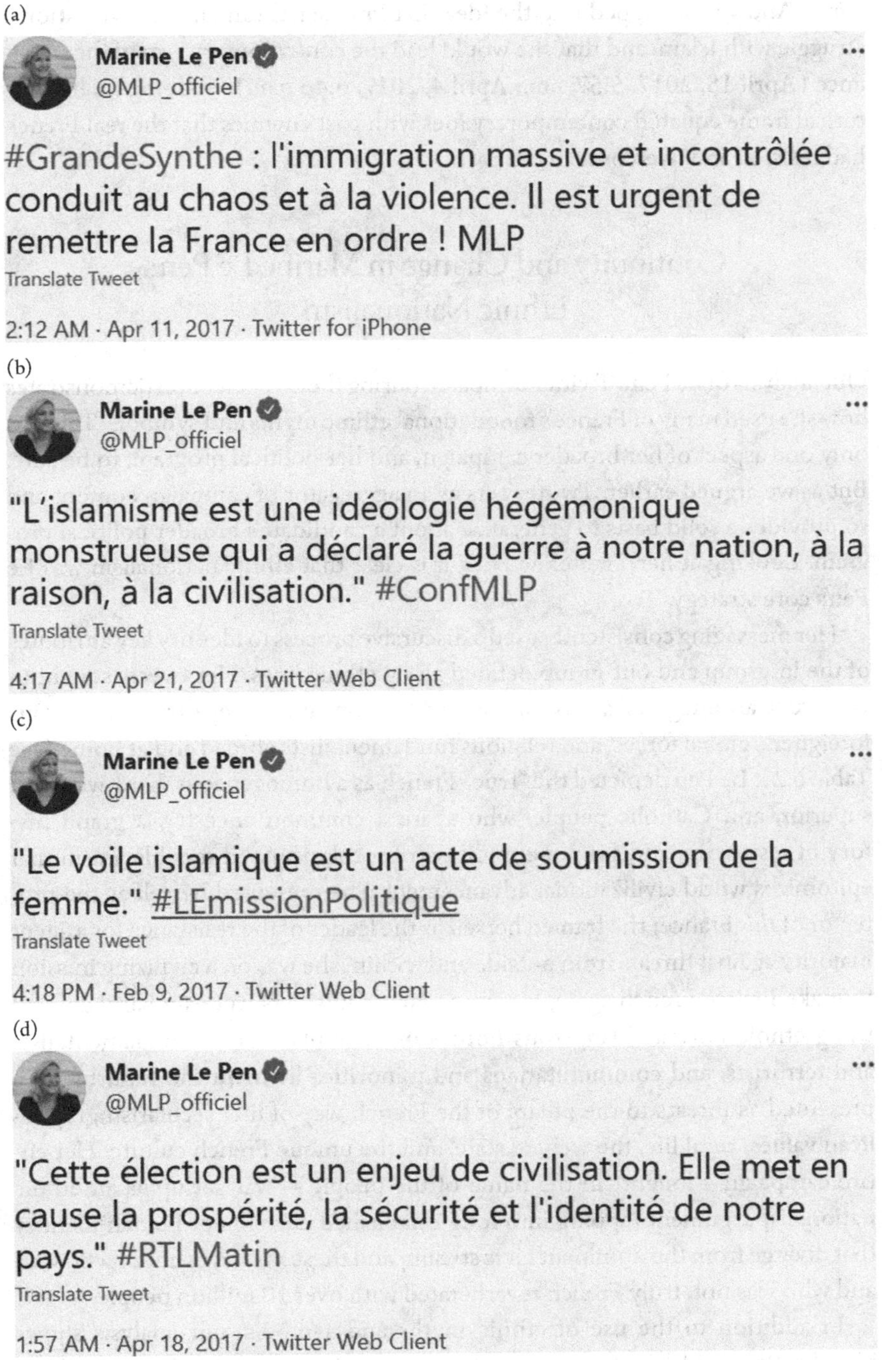
(a)
Marine Le Pen
@MLP_officiel
#GrandeSynthe : l'immigration massive et incontrôlée conduit au chaos et à la violence. Il est urgent de remettre la France en ordre ! MLP
Translate Tweet
2:12 AM · Apr 11, 2017 · Twitter for iPhone
(b)
Marine Le Pen
@MLP_officiel
"L'islamisme est une idéologie hégémonique monstrueuse qui a déclaré la guerre à notre nation, à la raison, à la civilisation." #ConfMLP
Translate Tweet
4:17 AM · Apr 21, 2017 · Twitter Web Client
(c)
Marine Le Pen
@MLP_officiel
"Le voile islamique est un acte de soumission de la femme." #LEmissionPolitique
Translate Tweet
4:18 PM · Feb 9, 2017 · Twitter Web Client
(d)
Marine Le Pen
@MLP_officiel
"Cette élection est un enjeu de civilisation. Elle met en cause la prospérité, la sécurité et l'identité de notre pays." #RTLMatin
Translate Tweet
1:57 AM · Apr 18, 2017 · Twitter Web Client

Figure 6.2 Examples of Marine Le Pen's Tweets constructing an ethnic out-group

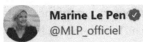

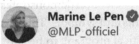

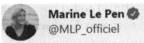

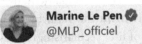

a.m.). And so she tapped into the idea that France has long had a civilizational struggle with Islam, and that she would lead the contemporary arm of the resistance (April 18, 2017, 5:57 a.m.; April 4, 2017, 6:46 p.m.). In doing so, her historical frame equated contemporary foes with past enemies that the real French had resisted and overcome in the past.

Continuity and Change in Marine Le Pen's Ethnic Nationalism

Our analysis of Le Pen's Twitter campaign during the 2017 election demonstrates how she used many of France's foundational ethnic myths and symbols. This was only one aspect of her broader campaign, and her political program, to be sure. But as we argued earlier, Twitter acts as an aggregator of campaign content and so provides a solid basis to generalize about a candidate's broader political program. Looking at her Twitter activity, it is clear that ethnic nationalism was Le Pen's core strategy.

Her messaging consistently used a discursive process to identify key attributes of the in-group and out-group defined along ethnic lines. Her tweets sought to construct an image of a virtuous French nation under siege from dangerous foreigners, global forces, and religious fundamentalists abroad and at home (see Table 6.2). Le Pen depicted the "true" French as a homogeneous, hard-working, superior, and Catholic people, who share a common ancestry, a grand history of resistance, and a unique tradition of secularism and republicanism that epitomizes world civilizational advancement. She presented herself as the protector of *this* France; she framed herself as the leader of the resistance for a silent majority against threats from outside and within; she was on a civilizing mission to make France French again, for the French. Outsiders were similarly defined using ethnic criteria. Dangerous hordes of migrants, Islamic fundamentalists and terrorists, and communitarians and minorities living in the suburbs were presented as threats to the pillars of the French way of life: secularism, republican values, rural life, the welfare state, and the unique French culture. Her entire campaign—fought "in the name of the people"—was set up as an ethnic nationalist argument tapping into long-established currents of French identity that diverge from the dominant civic stream; and these messages about who was, and who was not, truly French reverberated with over 10 million people.

In addition to the use of ethnic myths and symbols, our analysis shows how Le Pen used largely positive and sympathetic language when discussing the in-group, and more negative and aggressive language when discussing the out-group. For example, in messages that evoked the republican ethos, Le Pen

Table 6.2 **Key Distinctions in Marine Le Pen's Ethnic Conception of the In- and Out-Group in Her Twitter Communication in the 2017 Presidential Election**

"Virtuous" In-Group	"Villainous" Out-Group
Silent majority/Silent France	Migrants
Middle and working class	Job stealers and welfare recipients
Rural	Suburban
Christian	Muslim
Secular	Fundamentalists
Republican	Communitarian

tended to be more positive (nearly 70% of the time). Of course, because she was often lamenting the situation of the in-group, even her more positive in-group messages at times expressed negative language and tones. For example, about one-third of her tweets about rural France had negative associations, while about two-thirds were positive. The use of negative framing here was indicative of the overall trend in Le Pen's Twitter campaign—her tweets tended to be more negative than positive and tended to focus more on vilifying the out-group. This was evident in how she framed Islam and Muslims: over 95 percent of her tweets about Islam were highly negative. Similarly, when discussing migration, she was overwhelmingly negative (almost 70% of the time she used highly negative messaging).

This strategy—creating an in-group and an out-group through positive and negative messaging—is standard fare in contemporary politics and campaigns. What our analysis here shows, though, is the centrality of ethnic myths and symbols as the *content* that gives substantive meaning to this process. By historically situating these myths and symbols, we have also shown the rather remarkable historical continuity in Le Pen's ethnic nationalism. Many of her key campaign messages echoed long-standing ethnic ideas rooted deep in French political culture. France's foundational ethnic myths were core to her campaign: the ethnic origins of the French people; the importance of blood in citizenship; the historical struggle and resistance against foreign invaders; the superiority of French *terroir*, and that *la France profonde* is the real France; the French as both deeply Christian and secular; France's civilizing mission to battle Islam and spread the virtues of its republican values. As we noted, many of these themes were also present in her father's campaigns. In this respect, the purported departure from overt ethnic nationalism when Marine took over the party from Jean-Marie may be overstated (see Hutchins and Halikiopoulou 2018; Stockemer

2017). As we show here, there is clear continuity in both how Marine Le Pen used long-standing ethnic myths and symbols of French political culture, and in how she retained core aspects of the traditional National Front program.

As the same time, there are changes in Marine Le Pen's ethnic nationalism. She has deviated from her father's more overtly racist and anti-Semitic positions. One example of this is her positive messaging in support of Jews during the 2017 campaign: she denounced the Vichy regime (April 10, 2017, 10:04 a.m.), at times included Jews alongside Christians as members of the in-group (April 15, 2017, 1:32 p.m.), and would often argue that Jews were being persecuted and threatened by Islamic fundamentalists (May 3, 2017, 8:01 p.m.; April 17, 2017, 7:48 p.m.). These are clear breaks from the approach of the National Front under Jean-Marie Le Pen. In a related, but more profound shift, Marine Le Pen changed her party's position on republicanism. As shown earlier, she embraced language and ideas that foreground the defense of republican ideals and more civic conceptions of French identity. This development is in keeping with a broader shift of far-right parties in western Europe to embrace the language of civic nationalism (Halikiopoulou, Mock, and Vasilopoulou 2013). But what is also clear is that Le Pen has promoted a particularistic "national republicanism." It is a political program that includes opposition to (Muslim) immigration, national preference for social services (welfare chauvinism), restrictive citizenship policies (rejecting birth on soil), and the promotion of ideals like *laïcité* as the hallmarks of a civilized society, and views these as innately French ideas that need to be protected from dangerous outside forces (e.g., globalization, the EU, and Islamic fundamentalism). In this respect she has embraced a form of illiberal liberalism (Triadafilopoulos 2011)—one that has been shaped by cultural and ethnic foundations of French identity rooted deep in the nation's past. Thus, even in this change we can see continuity with the past in how Le Pen presented her vision of national republicanism. She used the wellspring of ethnic myths and symbols to powerfully bridge the classical divide between ethnic and civic forms of identity in France. Le Pen did eschew, in some instances, more overtly racist language, opting for a more political and cultural set of frames on a number of topics (Hutchins and Halikiopoulou 2018). But, as we show here, these cultural and political frames are also deeply ethnic in their historical roots—they draw from long-established ethnic myths and symbols about the French nation. And, these myths and symbols provided Le Pen with a measure of authenticity and legitimacy among members of the majority group, which clearly helped her to secure the highest-ever level of support for a National Front candidate in 2017.

7

English Nationalism and the Campaign for Brexit

In this chapter, we discuss the role of English nationalism in the campaign for Brexit during the 2016 referendum on leaving the EU. To do so, we focus on the Twitter communication of the two most prominent Leave campaigns: Vote Leave and Leave.EU. Although the referendum led to a different type of campaign than the American and French presidential elections, it provides an excellent opportunity—perhaps more so than the other cases—for examining nationalism. This is because the very *raison d'être* of the referendum was to decide upon the future of the United Kingdom, which inevitably brought nationalist ideas about "who we are" to the forefront of debates. Most significant here was the way in which these debates aligned with an ethnic nationalist vision of England. The particularities of the UK also make it an interesting case for exploring our approach. Unlike the US or France, the UK is a multinational state (comprising England, Wales, Scotland, and Northern Ireland). Furthermore, until recently, the most powerful constituent nation—England—was long noted for its apparent lack of nationalism. Brexit therefore offers a unique window into the dynamics of the new nationalism.

Our argument is that the Leave campaign's success among white English voters was partly the result of the way in which their messaging tapped into long-standing ethnic myths and symbols of English identity. Of course, these campaigns also addressed other social and economic policy issues. However, even these issues tended to be presented through a framework of ethnic English nationalism. In making this argument, we join several others who argue that "Brexit was made in England," or, more precisely, that English nationalism was the key driver of support for Brexit (Henderson et al. 2017; Henderson and Wyn Jones 2021; Sobolewska and Ford 2020; Calhoun 2017). Most people who make this argument rely on public opinion and survey data to show how English identity played a role in Brexit. Our analysis brings a longer historical dimension into the discussion. By showing where the content of English nationalism comes from, we hope to explain why it resonated in the Brexit referendum. To make this case, we show how the two main Leave campaigns (Vote Leave and Leave.EU) were structured around a message that the English had to "take back control" of their sovereignty from the EU in order to protect their nation from invading migrants, dangerous Muslims, and the impacts of unfettered globalization, and thereby restore their lost glory as a great nation.

This chapter is divided into two parts. The first part describes the foundational myths and symbols of English ethnic nationalism. The second part analyzes how Vote Leave and Leave.EU employed this myth-symbol complex through a comprehensive analysis of their Twitter communication.

The Ethnic Foundations of English Nationalism

English nationalism has long been notoriously difficult to parse.[1] This is because it has tended to be intertwined with British nationalism. Much like the ethnic majorities in the US and France that we discussed in the previous chapters, English people have historically tended not to distinguish between their particular national identity and that of the state as a whole. From their perspective, English and British were, and often still are, largely synonymous (Kumar 2003, 1–3; Henderson and Wyn Jones 2021). This tendency is amplified by the fact that England is a dominant nation within a multinational state. Generally, dominant nations are distinguished by a propensity to favor ideologies that promote pan-state unity, such as civic nationalism. As such, they tend to disavow an ethnic identity for their group, instead associating ethnicity with minority nations and seeing it as a dangerous and centrifugal force (Kaufmann 2004a; Kaufmann and Haklai 2008; Lecours and Nootens 2009; Schertzer and Woods 2011). To complicate this situation further, by the nineteenth century, England was not just the center of a multinational state, it was also the seat of the most powerful empire in the world. In this context, English elites perceived themselves to be in the business of building worlds, not just their own community (Kumar 2003, 178–79).

However, against this long historical tendency, recent decades have witnessed the surfacing of a distinct, self-conscious English nationalism. As one report put it, the "dog has finally barked" (Wyn Jones et al. 2012). The turn toward Englishness is partly a response to the dissolution of the British Empire and the attendant loss of prestige associated with Britishness (Gilroy 2005), and partly to mass immigration from the former colonies and the European Union (Kenny 2016). For many English people, these social changes have triggered a disorienting "ontological uncertainty" (Skey 2010) and a heightened perception that their collective identity is under threat (Aughey 2010). Immigrants have borne the brunt of this perception. In the press and among political elites, migrants have increasingly loomed large as threatening Others (McLaren and Johnson 2004; McLaren, Boomgaarden, and Vliegenthart 2018). Relatedly, the European Union (prior to Brexit) also featured prominently as a threatening Other, which was depicted not only as enabling the free flow of European migrants into the UK, but also as impinging upon the nation's autonomy (Wellings 2010).

Although a distinctively *English* ethnic nationalism is a relatively new development, the complex of myths and symbols upon which it is based is not. In the following sections, we use our schema of ethnic identity to map out the core features of this historically constituted myth-symbol complex. In doing so, we should make clear that our aim is to identify the core ethno-cultural components of English identity, not to intervene in debates over its origins (see Breuilly 2005; Hastings 1997; Greenfeld 1992; Kumar 2003; Reynolds 1997; Smith 2006). In this undertaking, we are particularly indebted to the work of Krishan Kumar (2003, 2015). However, there is one important area where we part ways from Kumar. Kumar generally does not elaborate on the role of whiteness in the making of English identity. Nevertheless, it is clear that the idea that English people are "white" was already in circulation at the end of the nineteenth century—as exemplified most famously in Rudyard Kipling's poem *The White Man's Burden* (1899). As such, we also examine the significance of whiteness to the ethnic conception of English identity.

People

The central myth of English peoplehood is that their ancestors were Anglo-Saxon. This idea is at the center of a dense web of linked mytho-symbolic content depicting the origins, boundaries, and character of the English people. More recently, the idea that the English are white has also come to provide a core myth of English peoplehood. These myths of peoplehood arose through interactions with several sets of significant Others, including non-Anglo British communities of Britain and Ireland, continental Europeans (principally French people), and colonized people of color. In addition to Anglo-Saxonness and whiteness, the idea that the English are a Protestant people has long been central to their identity. However, as with the cases of ethnic nationalism in the US and France, the religious element of English identity is so important that we discuss it in a separate subsection.

The myth that the English are Anglo-Saxon arose primarily through conflictual relations with the British communities that were already residing in the

"British Isles" at the time of the migration of Germanic tribes from northern Europe in the fifth century. Conflictual relations with these perceived outgroups prompted the formation of an in-group among the newcomers, who by the time of Bede's *Ecclesiastical History of the English People* in 731 had developed several shared ethno-cultural features, including a common language (Hastings 1997; Smith 2006, 441–42; Davies 1998, 199–200). They were further unified by "Alfred the Great" during his rule at end of the ninth century. Alfred proved to be an auspicious myth-maker. He translated Bede's work into English and used it to reinforce his legitimacy by depicting his kingship as the culmination of the development of the Anglo-Saxons (Hastings 1997, 39; Kumar 2003, 42). This myth of origins proved to be remarkably resilient. The symbolic boundaries between the Anglo-Saxons and the other British communities also endured: even today, they broadly serve to define the UK's internal national boundaries. Many persistent myths of the English "character" also arose through the relations among these ethnic communities. Generally, these myths centered on the perceived superiority of the English vis-à-vis the inferior "Celtic fringe." Thus, the English were "rational and restrained," "open and generous," as well as "plain-speaking and direct," as opposed to the "wild and lawless" Irish, the "canny and tight-fisted" Scots, and the "cunning and calculating" Welsh (Kumar 2003, 62).

The myth of Anglo-Saxon ancestry took on renewed importance after the Norman Conquest of 1066. There is much debate about whether the Anglo-Saxons and Normans remained distinct communities following the Conquest (see, Hastings 1997, 43; Breuilly 2005, 23), but what is undoubtedly true is that it provided the Anglo-Saxon myth with an enduring source of cultural content. The Conquest provided the foundations for the idea that Anglo-Saxons (*qua* English) were imbued with an innate love of liberty and democracy, which they needed to protect against tyrannical outsiders, particularly from mainland Europe. This idea came to the fore during the Glorious Revolution of 1688, when the proponents of parliamentary democracy represented it as the return of ancient Anglo-Saxon rights that had long been stymied by the "Norman yoke" (Hill 1997). The Whig historians of the nineteenth century also made this idea central to their accounts of English history, focusing upon the enduring Anglo-Saxon values of liberty and freedom in the face of malevolent outsiders (Kumar 2015, 81, 208–9, 225). More recently, this idea resurfaced to great effect in the twentieth century during the First and Second World Wars, such as when Winston Churchill urged his follow Britons to defend the world's freedom and "wage war against a monstrous tyranny" in his famous "Blood, Toil, Tears and Sweat" speech in May 1940. The idea was even used to justify imperial expansion. In this regard, the British Empire was not subjugating non-English people; it was uplifting them by endowing them with the unique English capacity for civilization, liberty, and democracy (Kumar 2003, 191). As we discuss further in the subsection on "ethos," what is notable about this addition to the Anglo-Saxon myth is that, much like the cases of the Anglo-Americans and the French, it imbued seeming political principles with ethnic characteristics. Liberty and democracy were depicted as innately Anglo-Saxon/English traits.

The idea of the "Norman yoke" points to the importance of conflictual relations with Europeans from the mainland, particularly the French, for English identity. The very real threat from France came into sharp relief with the Hundred Years' War of the fourteenth and fifteenth centuries. The war marked a milestone in the development of an English identity that was increasingly based upon its opposition to France (Hutchinson 2017, 24–26, 58, 80; Hastings 1997, 48; Kumar 2003, 53–54). The symbolic significance of France as an outgroup was subsequently reinforced in the seventeenth and eighteenth centuries during the long imperial rivalry over possession of North America (Kumar 2015, 50–51; Greenfeld 1992). In the twentieth century, persistent conflict and competition with Germany—notably through the world wars—reinforced the English perception that the European continent represented a threat. As with their relations with the British outgroups, English intellectuals and politicians drew upon their relations with the "Continent" to mythologize their superiority. Thus, the English were "manly" vis-à-vis the "effeminate" French (Breuilly 2005, 27; Kumar 2015, 48), they were "prudent" vis-à-vis the Italians, and they were peaceable vis-à-vis the militaristic Germans (Kumar 2003, 62).

The imperial competition with France draws our attention to the role of the British Empire in defining the English as an ethnic group. A view of the empire as a benevolent mechanism for imparting to the world the fruits of "civilization" are key elements of an ethnic English *ethos*. But the overseas empire also reinforced an ethnic understanding of the English *people*. Empire had a multifaceted effect on English identity. From one angle, it triggered the development of an expansive conception of Englishness, in which English people would, by settling ever larger swaths of the world, create a "Greater Britain" (Kumar 2003, 189). However, while empire provoked a more expansive view of Englishness, it also hardened their cultural boundaries, particularly vis-à-vis colonized peoples of color. In these interactions, whiteness increasingly joined Anglo-Saxonness as key symbolic criterion of English identity.

Racism did not initially characterize English relations with the peoples they encountered in their exploits. For example, as we detailed in our history of Anglo-American identity in chapter 4, Indigenous Americans were not initially seen to be racially different from the English (in the sense of being immutably and biologically distinct). Rather, their differences were thought to be due to environmental factors. As such, it was widely believed that Indigenous Americans could become English if they were properly inculcated into the beliefs and practices of English "civilization." However, the rise of scientific racism in the nineteenth century marked a definitive and lasting shift toward biological understandings of race. In sum, "race" was perceived to be fixed at birth—no matter how much someone from one race learned the cultural trappings of another race, they could never truly escape their biological destiny. This conception of race was also inflected by social Darwinism, which interpreted the success of white people relative to other races to be a result of their innate racial superiority. English intellectuals contributed to, and were influenced by, this new racism (Bonnett 2003). As a result, empire was reconceived along racial lines, with many English writers now perceiving their role at its helm to be a "natural" outcome of their inherent racial superiority. By contrast, the perceived racial inferiority of nonwhite people made their capacity for "responsible government" unlikely. This understanding underpinned the view that the "white dominions" should have a degree of self-rule, whereas the colonial "dependencies" should not (see Haseler 1996, 17–49).

As whiteness took on increasing significance for English intellectuals, it generally became intertwined with, rather than replacing, existing ethnic myths and symbols of peoplehood. In this regard, Englishness came to be seen as a variant of whiteness. Moreover, whiteness reinforced the English myth of superiority: the "English race" was generally depicted to be the very apex of the racial hierarchy, superior even to other white races (Bonnett 2003, 323; 1998, 320). What is more, existing cultural boundaries with long maligned out-groups, particularly Irish Catholics—who were phenotypically indistinct from English people, and therefore might have been accepted as white—were instead infused with the new racism, such that they were redefined as nonwhite people (Hickman 1995; Laughlin 1999). Among English people, the new myths of whiteness also did not initially overturn internal cultural boundaries, particularly with regard to social class. Thus, there was initially much discussion over the extent to which working-class English people should be considered white. For many intellectuals, they were not fully white—rather, they were a kind of degenerated form of "sub-man" (Bonnett 2003, 328). It was not until the twentieth century that working-class people were fully accepted into the white English in-group, a process that was greatly bolstered by the postwar migration of nonwhite British subjects to the UK from the former colonies.

The myth of whiteness did not just increasingly characterize English perceptions of the external empire, it also became hugely significant for cultural politics within the UK. While postwar migrants from the former colonies had initially been encouraged to come to the UK, upon arrival they were perceived by many English and British people as a "threat," resulting in episodic racist violence, the formation of new racist political movements (e.g., the British National Party), and, ultimately, the creation of a British citizenship regime, beginning with the Immigration Act of 1971, which sought to deny automatic citizenship to British subjects from the former colonies (Solomos 1993). The new outgroups were largely perceived through a racial lens. What made them threatening to many English and British people was that they were not *white* (Gilroy 2005; Brah 2005). Recent research suggests that the importance of whiteness as a signifier of English identity within the UK has endured into the twenty-first century (Leddy-Owen 2013, 2014; Valluvan 2021).

Homeland

There are many persistent myths and symbols about how the English territory shapes English identity. We highlight here two of the most recurrent themes: that it is an island nation, and that it is rural nation.

The myth of England as an island, onto itself, which is protected by the sea from threatening Others, is among the most enduring ideas used to define Englishness (Abell, Condor, and Stevenson 2006). Of course, this idea flies in the face of the fact that England shares the island of Britain with several other national communities. However, the tendency for the English to elide those other national communities is associated with their status as the dominant nation within Britain. Anthony Smith has traced the origins and dimensions of the island mythology, finding evidence as far back as the writings of Gildas in the sixth century, who wrote that the island lay "at the end of the world . . . fortified on all sides by a vast and more or less uncrossable ring of sea, apart from the straits on the south" (cited in Smith 2006, 438). This vision of England as a solitary island protected from a threatening outside world was subsequently immortalized by Shakespeare in the late sixteenth century:

> This royal throne of kings, this scepter'd isle, This earth of majesty, this seat of Mars, This other Eden, demi-paradise, This fortress built by Nature for herself Against infection and the hand of war, This happy breed of men, this little world, This precious stone set in the silver sea, Which serves it in the office of a wall, Or as a moat defensive to a house, Against the envy of less happier lands, This blessed plot, this earth, this realm, this England . . .
> —*Richard II*, Act II, Scene I

Although there is considerable debate over whether Shakespeare wrote from a nationalist perspective, there is no doubt that his works have provided ample fodder for subsequent generations of English nationalists (Kumar 2003, 117–20). The passage cited here has provided a long-standing source of content for the representation of English identity—in many ways, it might even be described as the urtext of Englishness. It encapsulates how the mythology and symbolism of England as an "island" reinforces a closed, ethnic conception of English identity. It depicts England's homeland as a "fortress," as their "little world" set in the "silver sea," which serves as a "wall" and defensive "moat" against the "infection" and invasion of foreigners from "less happier lands." As Smith (2006, 438–39) shows, this has been a recurrent set of ideas about the island as a natural boundary—a physical border—between the home of the English and malevolent outsiders, particularly from the continent. Other themes have been layered onto the myth of England as an island nation, notably its historic concern with being a foremost naval power (Smith 2006, 440), the building of an "overseas empire" (reinforcing cultural boundaries between "us" at home and "them" out there), and eventually the decline of empire and naval supremacy precipitating a turn inward to our "little world" (Kumar 2003, 198). The world wars and myths associated with Dunkirk and the Blitz only added to the symbolism of England as an island—framing the nation as closely linked with, but also apart from, the continent separated from it by the channel (Kumar 2003, 233).

The second core myth of England's homeland is that it is a rural nation characterized by a bucolic countryside—that it is a "green and pleasant land," as the poet William Blake famously put it in 1804. This idealized depiction of the English countryside has long provided a source of content for English identity, but it really took hold in the nineteenth century amid Romantic intellectuals and artists who, like Blake, were nostalgically reacting to the perceived deleterious impact of industrialization and urbanization (Wiener 2004; Lucas 1990). This counter-current against the idea of England as the leader of the Industrial Revolution has remained a powerful theme into the twentieth century, returning to the fore particularly during the world wars—when soldiers were exhorted to remember what it was "they were fighting for" (Berberich 2006, 208; Kumar 2015, 125–26; Kenny 2014, 10–13). The cultural works of the nineteenth century established the symbolism of pastures, cottages, small towns, abbeys, and rolling hills of England as the essence of Englishness. Frank Newbould's painting *South Downs* encapsulates this imagery and has become one of the most reproduced images of England (Kumar 2003, 209–10). This idea of England *as* the countryside—not the red, white, and blue of Great Britain, but the green of England (Paxman 1999, 265)—reinforces the linkage between the English of today and their Anglo-Saxons ancestors who lived in the countryside (Kumar 2015, 213).

The myth of England as a rural nation is bound up with the cultural politics of modern England, particularly in the way that it serves to reinforce conceptions about who is authentically English. Most significantly, the symbolic elevation of rural life against city life implies that it is in the former where "true" English people live. As Kumar (2015, 226–28) has shown, this is among the central themes of the influential work of artists and authors like William Morris. In this respect, the myth of the countryside perpetuates the view that the regions outside the cities (especially London), represent the true England (Kumar 2015, 145). The message here is that the metropole is global, but the rural is national. In the twentieth century, this message has become intertwined with the ethnonationalist reaction to postcolonial migrants, many of whom settled in large city centers, especially London.

Religion

Religion, specifically Protestantism, has been a central part of an ethnic English nationalism. Henry the Eighth's break with the Roman Catholic Church played a foundational role in shaping English national consciousness (Greenfeld 1992, 51). Establishing the Church of England with the monarch at its head also ensured that the nation was aligned with, rather than opposed to, the sacred (Smith 2006, 436). Beyond Henry the Eighth, the symbolism and mythology of Queen Elizabeth the First—the Protestant Queen, the Virgin Queen, the first monarch to have an age of their own—reinforced the bind between nation and sacred (Kumar 2003, 93). More generally, the translation of the Bible into English as part of the Protestant Reformation similarly grounded religion in the nation: Tyndale's Bible tied Protestantism to the English language and identity (Greenfeld 1992, 52–53). In short, in England, Protestantism and nationalism were mutually reinforcing ideologies.

The upshot of English identity becoming intertwined with Protestantism was that it was infused with a religious sense of destiny in the world. English people were, from this perspective, a "chosen people." The myth of chosenness is a recurring theme in ethnic nationalism, which draws upon the biblical story of Jewish people's covenant with God (Smith 2003). We have already discussed how this myth was also foundational to Anglo-American identity (which was largely derived from English identity). The myth of chosenness has a long history in England, showing up in the Old English poem *Exodus* to describe the migration of the Saxons to Britain, which "depicted a latter-day chosen people who, like the ancient Israelites at the Red Sea, crossed the waters in their ships to a promised land" (Smith 2006, 439, 442–43; Colley 1992, 29–30). But this idea really gained traction through conflict with Catholic Europe. In this regard, the English increasingly depicted themselves as an "elect nation," who had a special mission from God to resist Roman Catholicism and the tyranny of the pope.

The perceived threat of Roman Catholicism has long shaped English cultural boundaries, within Britain and further afield. Within Britain, it helped unite various factions of Protestants, which ultimately provided the basis for the rise of an overarching British identity (Colley 1992). However, it also led to the long-term persecution and exclusion of British and Irish Catholics (Colley 1992, 19–25). In short, they were redefined as a foreign Other, who did not represent an authentic Englishness/Britishness. This was partly fueled by a fear that they wanted to re-establish Roman Catholic supremacy in Britain—a fear that was ritually enacted each fifth of November through the burning of effigies of Guy Fawkes, a Catholic who was convicted of treason following the failed "Gunpowder Plot" of 1605. Outside of Britain, antipathy toward Roman Catholicism principally took shape through the long-standing conflict with France, which subsequently, through imperial competition, was translated into a global struggle for the defense of the "true" religion against "papist tyranny."

Roman Catholics endured as a significant out-group long into the twentieth century. This was partly the result of ongoing violent conflict in Northern Ireland, which would frequently spill over into Britain and enflame tensions with Catholics (Ghaill 2000; Hickman et al. 2005). However, the attenuation of violence following the 1998 Good Friday Agreement, alongside a steep decline in religiosity in the UK, softened perceived boundaries with Catholics. Also, as we discuss shortly, the rise of Islam as a perceived threat to English identity created a new significant Other, which has drawn British Catholics closer to the in-group.

Ethos

There are a number of overlapping themes that together form an ethos of English identity. We focus upon two particularly recurrent and linked ideas: the myth of English exceptionalism and the myth that the English have a special destiny to defend liberal democracy and the rule of law in the world. Unsurprisingly, this ethos shares much with American and French ethnic nationalism. We have seen how both of those cases emphasize their unique role in bringing about, and defending, key aspects of modernity, particularly liberal democracy. Both cases also have a strong tendency toward "ethnicizing" this myth, in the sense that the nation's greatness is the result of their innate, and inherently superior, ethno-cultural characteristics. In these respects, English ethnic nationalism is broadly similar.

The roots of English exceptionalism lie in some of the dynamics we have already highlighted. Most important here is the myth that England is an island, unto itself, which acts as a bulwark against (European) tyranny. The Protestant Reformation and establishment of the Church of England reinforced this myth by adding a sacred element (Smith 2006, 445). These ideas of English exceptionalism were also combined with a myth that the English were superior to all nations in the world—they were the "top nation," as the popular 1930 satire *1066 and All That* put it. This latter idea initially came to the fore as a result of England's dominance over its British neighbors (Kumar 2003, chap. 4). When England/Britain became a leading economic power through the Industrial Revolution, and then subsequently became *the* global imperial power in the nineteenth century, descriptions of its unique superiority swelled. England was now represented as a special instrument of world historical change. Thomas Carlyle encapsulated this idea in 1840, when he loftily declared:

> The stream of World-History has altered its complexion; Romans are dead out, English are come in.... To this English People in World-History, there have been ... two grand tasks assigned: the grand Industrial task of conquering some half or more of this Terraqueous Plant for the use of man; then secondly, the grand Constitutional task of sharing, in some pacific endurable manner, the fruit of said conquest, and showing all people how it might be done. (cited in Kumar 2003, 175)

As Carlyle and many of his contemporaries saw it, England's special destiny was to uplift the world—it was England's version of France's *mission civilisatrice*. And while it is true that in the high point of empire, references to England were largely replaced by references to Britain, this did not mean that the English stopped emphasizing their central role in the empire—quite the opposite. Depictions of the English in relation to the empire in the mid- to late nineteenth century tended to place them at its center, as its forebearers (Kumar 2003, 191–92). These descriptions often combined with ideas about England's special ingenuity and creativity—symbolized by reference to literary giants like Shakespeare, Tennyson, and Chaucer (117–19, 220–21).

Myths of English exceptionalism are also closely related to the idea that they have a special role to defend liberal democracy and the rule of law. As with the Anglo-Americans, this seemingly civic idea became "ethnicized" through its imagined link to Anglo-Saxonness. Recall our discussion in chapter 4 about how the Anglo-Saxon myth partly came to England via the writings of Tacitus, who described the ancient Saxons as an innately freedom-loving and democratic people. In the nineteenth century, Whig historians drew upon these ideas to portray the English as having a unique predisposition to liberty and democracy. Indeed, for these historians, liberalism was so closely linked to Englishness that they became synonymous concepts (Kumar 2003, 214). From the Whig perspective, the development of parliamentary democracy and the rule of law in England was not simply the result of contingent processes—it could *only* have happened in England because of English people's special affinity for these institutions.

For our purposes, one major consequence of linking liberalism to Englishness is that it raises the possibility that non-English groups could be represented as having an innate antipathy to liberal ideas. In turn, this creates a logic that these groups need to be vanquished in order for liberalism to triumph. As we have seen, this was a common way of depicting England's perceived enemies, particularly Catholics. In the present day, it is Muslims who risk being portrayed in this way, as we shall demonstrate in our analysis of the Brexit campaigns.

History

Of course, English identity has also been crafted through historical narrative. At its core, the historical image of the English is that the nation has ancient roots, that the ancestors of the English were Anglo-Saxon. The Whig historiography of the nineteenth century picked up on this idea of a long lineage of the English moving through time, imbuing this narrative with a sense of progress. English history, in this regard, was depicted as a story of *becoming* (Kumar 2003). This idea was further combined with the ethos of English exceptionalism and, especially, the myth that they had a special role to defend liberty and democracy. Historical progress, in this sense, was not simply a story about the English accumulating power, status, and resources. More importantly, it was also a story about the triumph of liberty. From this perspective, throwing off the "Norman yoke" in 1066 was but a stage in the progress of liberty, which would eventually culminate, through the British Empire, in its worldwide triumph. However, although this was a narrative of progress, it also contained a certain circularity. This was because, as we have seen, the ancient Anglo-Saxons were mythologized as having once embraced the values of liberty and democracy. The triumph of these values therefore represented a return to England's ancient roots—to its "authentic" self.

Whig historiography was remarkably influential in shaping how English history was understood in the public sphere until the unraveling of the empire in the twentieth century. Previous research has demonstrated how the catastrophic loss of status associated with this development has triggered a widespread sense of anxiety among the English "about losing ground, both economically and culturally vis-à-vis other groups" (Garner 2012; Skey 2011; Kenny 2014). Paul Gilroy (2005) has even posited that the loss of empire engendered a kind of collective trauma—a "postcolonial melancholia." Furthermore, these developments have fed a nostalgic myth of the "golden age," that the best days of England are in the past (Black 2019; Byrne 2007; Wellings 2010). The Whig myth of English progress has been, in this sense, challenged by a myth of decline. In our view, this idea is central to understanding the resurgence of English nationalism and, as we shall discuss in the next section of this chapter, on the vote for Brexit.

To conclude this discussion of the core myths and symbol of English ethnic identity, we have provided a summary of the myths in the table (Table 7.1), followed by a list of symbols.

Table 7.1 **Foundational Ethnic Myths of English Identity**

People	Religion	Homeland	History	Ethos
The Anglo-Saxons are the ancestors of the English, who bequeathed to the English an enduring affinity for liberty and democracy	The English are a Protestant people whose successes and failures are guided by God	England is an island, unto itself, which is protected by the sea from a threatening outside world	The English have a long history that reaches back to the ancient Saxons	The English are an exceptional people—the "top nation"—who are inherently superior to all other nations
The English are an inherently superior people, with a special capacity for civilization, reason, creativity, and restraint	The English have been chosen by God to defend the "true" religion in the world In so doing, the English resist the heathens, especially Roman Catholicism	The "true" English homeland is rural, which is defined by a bucolic countryside and agricultural work	The English have a glorious past with many victories over their foes, foreign and domestic English history is characterized by the progressive movement toward the fulfillment of liberty, democracy, and rule of law	The English have bequeathed liberty, democracy, and the rule of law to the world, and they therefore have a special role to play in spreading them
The English are defined by their whiteness—a biological category that unites them by blood and proves their inherent superiority			While once a great economic and imperial power, Britain's place in the world has declined	The British Empire was a vehicle for spreading these values to lesser developed regions

These myths are linked to numerous symbols. Of course, the meaning of many of these symbols are multivocal and contested (see Kenny 2014). However, there are a few symbols of Englishness whose meanings have been particularly stable. Some of the most prevalent include:

- Anglo-Saxons—as the ancestors of the English
- King Alfred the Great—as the first ruler of a unified England
- Henry the Eighth—as the leader who broke with Rome
- The monarchy—as the representative of the people, and as link between sacred and secular
- The island, the cliffs of Dover, and the channel—symbols of England's place in the world as a fortress set apart from the continent and foreigners
- Green, bucolic countryside—as the true place of the English
- St George's Cross—as a political symbol of the English
- The Church of England—the institution and its churches across the country as a symbol of the sacredness of the English
- Shakespeare—the nation's poet, a symbol of an English special capacity for creativity and beauty
- Empire—a symbol of England's exceptionalism and role in creating the modern world
- Magna Carta—an attenuation of absolute power that reflects an English enduring affinity for liberalism and rule of law
- Parliament and Palace of Westminster—as symbols of English exceptionalism and its historical role in creating democracy

The foregoing discussion outlined several historically constituted, ethnocultural elements of English identity. As several observers have noted, these elements of English identity have rarely coalesced into a self-conscious, ethnic nationalist movement. Instead, they have provided a largely unconscious worldview, or diffuse set of sentiments (Aughey 2010; Kenny 2014). But the absence of a history of nationalist politics does not necessarily imply that the myths and symbols of English identity do not have the affective power to move English people. As we will now discuss, recent events suggest otherwise.

Brexit and English Nationalism

Brexit occurred at a particularly fraught time for the EU. It is true that, in some respects, the EU is in a semi-permanent state of crisis (Habermas 2012). However, the years preceding Brexit were especially tumultuous. The Great Recession of 2007–2008 and the ensuing Sovereign Debt Crisis accentuated economic inequality across the EU, and triggered a steep rise in anti-EU sentiment (Gomez 2015). At the same time, many Europeans felt that they faced a migration crisis, particularly following the rapid increase of asylum seekers after the outbreak of civil war in Syria in 2011. In the view of a growing number of Europeans, their respective national states were better placed to manage migration than the EU (Baubock 2018; Guild et al. 2015).

In the run-up to the 2016 referendum over the UK's membership in the EU, the context of these perceived crises largely structured debates, with the two camps—"Remain" and "Leave"—clashing over how to respond. Underpinning the policy debates was a deeper divide over the identity of the UK. In stable times, national identity is largely unconscious, routinized, and apolitical—it is, as we discussed in chapter 2, reproduced via "banal nationalism" (Billig 1995). Amid the growing sense of crisis, and in light of the question posed by the referendum, Brexit triggered a break from banal nationalism. Nationalist questions about "who we are" became a framework for navigating the debate over whether the UK should remain in, or leave, Europe. It is in this respect that a sense of English identity was especially pertinent.

The results of the referendum were very close: the Leave side won with 51.9 percent of the vote, against 48.1 percent in favor of Remain. However, when we drill down into the data and look at how each constitutive nation voted, the results appear much less close. The Leave side lost by large margins in both Northern Ireland (44.2% to 55.8%) and Scotland (38% to 62%), but it won comfortably in Wales (52.5% to 47.5%) and England (53.4 to 46.6). Given that the population of England (approximately 67.6 million) far outweighs that of Wales (approximately 3.2 million), it is clear that England was the driver of Brexit (Henderson et al. 2017; Henderson and Wyn Jones 2021). Furthermore, if we drill down even further into the data, and look at how the various regions of England voted, we can see that is the rural regions and smaller cities that really broke for Leave: the West Midlands voted 59.3 percent in favor of leave, followed closely by the East Midlands (58%), the North East (58%), and East England (56.5%) (Goodwin and Heath 2016, 324).

The common factor across the English regions that voted for Leave was a high proportion of voters who identified with English identity. Among those who declared an intention to vote Leave, English national identity was among the clearest variables that indicated their likelihood to support Brexit: a YouGov survey conducted immediately prior to the vote found that a staggering 73 percent of people who prioritized their English identity intended to vote Leave, while only 35 percent of those who prioritized British identity intended to vote Leave (Henderson et al. 2017, 639–40). Other leading polls following the referendum reinforced the idea that Leave supporters were motivated by long-standing pillars of English national identity: the two top reasons given for voting leave were to regain parliamentary sovereignty and to regain control over immigration (Lord Ashcroft poll, cited in Hearn 2017, 20).

There were, of course, other factors influencing voting patterns. Economic forces, including unemployment and income inequality, were also important drivers of support for Brexit (Becker, Fetzer, and Novy 2017; Colantone and Stanig 2018). There is strong evidence that non-nationalist cultural factors, particularly authoritarian and populist values, motivated Leave voters (Norris and Inglehart 2019, chap. 11). Demographic factors, especially age, were also key variables: overwhelmingly it was the older generations that voted to leave (Henderson et al. 2017, 641; Norris and Inglehart 2019, 385). As Craig Calhoun put it, Brexit was a vote for the past not the future (Calhoun 2017, 60). The significance of the ethnic and racial backgrounds of voters has also been explored, and while it is not clear that identification as white *alone* predicts support for Brexit (Norris and Inglehart 2019, 387), we do know that black, Asian, and Muslim voters were much more likely to vote Remain (Hearn 2017, 20). There are also findings that the "othering" of racialized groups was central to the Leave campaigns (Virdee and McGeever 2018, 1803). While each of these explanations for why Leave won provides important insights, on their own they can contradict one another or lack a compelling, comprehensive account that explains why support for Brexit was so high among certain English populations—this is particularly apparent in the tension between economic and cultural explanations (Carreras, Carreras, and Bowler 2019, 1397).

In our view, focusing on national identity, particularly English identity, can help tie these threads of analysis together. Viewing Brexit as a moment when a hotter nationalism arose as a structuring force over politics—and using a lens sensitive to how ethnicity, culture, and history shape politics—can help us to see how the Leave campaigns capitalized on economic and cultural grievances in the population. We can better account for how the Leave campaigns used these grievances to mobilize voters against the EU—particularly English voters outside London—if we pay attention to how they used ethnic nationalist messaging. In short, we know quite a bit now about *who* voted for Brexit, but there is still a need to explore *why* it was that specifically *English* voters were mobilized. We think that by exploring how the Leave campaigns used ethnic myths and symbols of English nationalism we can better understand why their messages reverberated.

The English Nationalism of the Leave Campaigns on Twitter

For the remainder of this chapter, we unpack how the Leave campaigns used the core mytho-symbolic elements of English identity in their social media strategy. To do so, we analyze all the tweets sent directly from the two main Leave accounts (Vote Leave and Leave.EU) for the six months prior to the referendum vote on June 23, 2016.[2] Vote Leave (VL) was officially recognized by the Electoral Commission. It was a cross-partisan group including leading Conservatives and Labour members. Leave.EU (LEU) did not have an official designation, but its funding and backing by UKIP (the UK Independence Party) meant that it also provided a powerful voice for Leave. Both campaigns had highly visible social media campaigns. Together, they tweeted over 7,000 times in the six months prior to the vote: Vote Leave tweeted 2,957 times and Leave.EU tweeted 4,416 times.[3] There were differences, which we will discuss, in how Vote Leave and Leave.EU used these myths and symbols in their overall communication strategies; however, we analyze them together as the leading representatives of the Leave campaign.

Although both campaigns generally referred to the "British" people (for reasons that we have already discussed), our analysis demonstrates that myths and symbols of English identity were central to the campaigns of both Vote Leave and Leave.EU. Combined, the two camps invoked ethnic myths and symbols in almost 2,150 tweets (approximately 30% of the time). Among these 2,150 tweets, the campaigns drew from different myths and symbols of English identity almost 2,800 times. Of the two campaigns, Vote Leave turned to an ethnic nationalist message more often, drawing on these ideas over a third of the time. Leave.EU relied upon them in about a quarter of their tweets.

Both campaigns used English myths and symbols—primarily ones that relate to *people* and *ethos*—to create a dividing line between "us" and "them." The campaigns regularly defined the British people through an English ethnic lens (in almost 15% of all tweets). They largely did this by juxtaposing British people against foreigners and immigrants, who were represented as threats to economic and physical security. This strategy was closely followed by tweets that argued that leaving the EU was the only way to protect and recapture the nation's *ethos* (in almost 11% of tweets); central to this message was a focus on "taking back control" of "our" destiny by regaining parliamentary sovereignty. In addition to these two lines of argument, the Leave campaigns also tapped into ethnic mythologies about the nation's *history*, highlighting that Britain could recapture its lost imperial glory as a world leader (in almost 4% of tweets); the *religion* of "us" and "them," focusing on the threat of Turkey and its neighbors with large Muslim populations joining the EU (in almost 4% of tweets); and the importance of protecting the *homeland* and its borders to keep out dangerous foreigners (in over 3% of tweets).

Of course, substantive public policy issues were also important themes (featuring in almost 37% of tweets). The policy topic that both campaigns discussed most, by some measure, was the economic threat of staying in the EU.

A related theme was the advantages for trade that would be incurred by leaving the EU (roughly 22% of tweets). As we discuss later, migration was also central to the campaigns (about 12% of tweets). After these clear foci, the campaigns discussed a diverse set of other policy areas: they argued that staying in the EU jeopardized the healthcare system (almost 11% of Vote Leave tweets), that the EU threatened democratic governance (3.4% of all tweets), and that leaving would improve law and order (2.6% of all tweets). Other topics included foreign policy (about 2% of tweets), the courts (approximately 1.5% of tweets), and terrorism (just over 1% of tweets). Unsurprisingly, these more specific policy discussions were also paired with direct attacks on the EU as an institution. For example, the campaigns argued the EU was anti-democratic and created unfair rules and regulations (themes that appeared in over 11% of all tweets). Attacks on political opponents—whether from the Remain camp or those associated with the EU—were also common (about 15% of all tweets). Populist themes, including attacking elites and criticizing globalization, were also present in the campaigns; about 4 percent of tweets had *overt* populist messages, and about 3 percent were anti-globalist. Of course, as we discuss later, the focus on the economy and migration, as well as the general narrative of "taking back control," also has strong populist and anti-globalist connotations.

While these substantive policy discussions were significant aspects of the Leave message, they were often embedded within an ethnic nationalist logic: approximately one-third of all public policy tweets were underpinned by ethnic myths and symbols. Both campaigns argued that "uncontrolled" migration was threatening the safety and welfare of the British people—that the current approach to migration was not in the national interest (@LeaveEUOfficial, April 19, 2016, 11:04 a.m.; @vote_leave, May 29, 2016, 7:34 p.m.).[4] These arguments were extended to many aspects of public policy: both campaigns argued that staying in the EU meant foreigners were migrating to the UK at unsustainable levels and jeopardizing the wages, jobs, housing, schooling, and healthcare of British people (VL, June 21, 2016, 7:20 p.m.; April 28, 2016, 11:32 a.m.; LEU, April 29, 2016, 9:47 a.m.; May 8, 2016, 9:15 p.m.). A similar "us" versus "them" logic underpinned the criticism of the EU as an institution: the EU was cast as an imperial, anti-democratic body controlled by foreigners, which blocked the inherent sovereignty of the British people, and their ability to control their destiny through their model of parliamentary democracy (VL, June 22, 2016, 8:55 p.m.; LEU, May 12, 2016, 835 p.m.).

The campaigns similarly rooted their political attacks and populist messages in ethnic nationalist themes. For example, Vote Leave questioned whether the people could trust David Cameron on immigration and Turkish membership in the EU—arguing he wanted to "pave the road from Ankara" (VL, June 15, 2016, 6:17 p.m.). A similar anti-elite populism was used to pit the British people against the politicians and EU bureaucrats (LEU, April 29, 2016, 8:29 a.m.), a sentiment that was often underpinned with an element of ethnic nationalism that emphasized that the EU elites were foreigners working against the interests of the British people (VL, June 12, 2016, 7:27 p.m.). Indeed, the Vote Leave slogan of "take back control" epitomized how the campaigns used ethnic nationalism to frame other topics. The Leave side was arguing that "we" (the British) needed to take back control from "them" (the EU and the foreigners who controlled the institution, working for the interests of other nations). The idea of "taking back control" was often directly paired with arguments that it was the only way to protect "our" jobs, health, and physical safety from the invading threat of dangerous migrants.

This overview of the main themes of the Leave side's social media campaign shows the centrality of ethnic nationalism—and how it anchored the framing of many topics. However, this high-level description does not tell us specifically how the campaigns used ethnic myths and symbolism in their messaging. To better understand the content of the Leave campaign—to unpack how they tapped into well-established ethnic ideas of English identity—we need to look deeper into the process by which they constructed a sense of "us" and "them" using ethnic nationalism.

"Us"

The Leave campaigns often relied upon negative messaging when using ethnic myths and symbols. They tended to depict groups as a perceived threat to the British people, rather than putting forward a positive national self-image. Indeed, the primary message of the Leave campaigns—that "we" must take back control—was constructed to communicate that the nation was under threat. In other words, the central idea was that British people must "take back control" in order to protect "our" physical safety, economic well-being, and way of life. Nevertheless, both campaigns did still construct an image of "us" through ethnic myths and symbols.

The ways in which the Leave campaigns used ethnic ideas of Englishness to construct an image of "us" were often subtle. Racist language was avoided—the campaigns did not *explicitly* point to whiteness or common ancestry as defining features of the in-group. They did, however, craft an image of the British people as being largely homogeneous—not as a collection of diversities, but rather as a nation defined by its commonalities (LEU, June 2, 2016, 10:24 a.m.). Messages focused on the idea that this largely homogeneous nation was losing its sense of commonality because of the EU. Leaving the EU would therefore give the *English* a voice (LEU, June 20, 2017, 7:43 p.m.) and help them to regain their identity and power (VL, June 19, 2016, 10:50 a.m.). The symbolism of the English lion as the fighting spirit of a fierce nation was evoked (LEU, June 6, 2016, 5:00 p.m.). Similarly, the idea that the nation had been forged through a history of successful wars was also often employed (LEU, June 4, 2016, 1:41 p.m.). The campaigns also emphasized historical continuity with their ancestors through the idea that "we're a proud nation, with a proud history, let's not give it away" (LEU, February 19, 2016, 7:51 p.m.). From this perspective, the EU was just the most recent foe in a long history of existential threats that had come from the European continent (LEU, May 9, 2016, 10:28 a.m.). Here a key part of building a sense of "us" was to stress that British people are not European (LEU, June 9, 2016, 10:21 p.m.). Leaving was an opportunity for the British people to reassert their cultural boundaries with Europe, and thereby be reborn (LEU, April 8, 2016, 8:28 a.m.; VL, June 4, 2016, 6:44 a.m.).

Underpinning this messaging was the notion that the Leave campaign was spearheaded by "true" British people. For example, Leave.EU argued that it was giving a voice to a "grassroots movement" (LEU, March 1, 2016, 11:09 a.m.). The visuals promoted through their account often included a claim that they were the "fastest growing grassroots movement" in the nation (LEU, May 3, 2016, 11:00 a.m.). Both campaigns built on this idea by playing up that "real" people support leaving (LEU, February 19, 2016, 7:39 p.m., 8:01 p.m.). They argued that staying in the EU imperiled the lives of "normal working people" (VL, June 8, 2016, 12:04 a.m.). The campaigns also regularly tapped into myths that these "normal" British people were "hard working." Threats to their livelihoods were therefore not a result of a lack of effort, but rather because of the EU and its open border policies (VL, June 16, 2016, 12:39 p.m.; LEU, April 19, 2016, 10:09 a.m.). Together, the two campaigns invoked the idea of the everyday, working person as the definitive, "true" British person over 100 times.

The Leave campaigns also emphasized the "threat" of migration to build an in-group. Both campaigns argued that leaving the EU was necessary to reform the UK's immigration system—to establish a controlled, economic migration system based on the human capital model (e.g., a "skills" or "points" based system) (VL, May 31, 2016, 9:12 p.m.; LEU January 14, 2016, 7:00 a.m.). They claimed they were not anti-immigrant; they simply wanted to control immigration through a fair system (VL, April 16, 2016, 5:03 p.m.; LEU, June 21, 2016, 7:46 p.m.). As part of this message, the campaigns often pointed to other liberal democracies that use a points-based approach to control immigration (VL, June 21, 2016, 7:45 p.m.). Australia was singled out as the model to emulate (VL, June 21, 2016, 7:44 a.m.; LEU, January 26, 2016, 12:05 p.m.). While subtle, coded in this message was the idea that white-majority countries like Australia ought to control their migration—to do otherwise and allow uncontrolled migration is not only illogical, but also threatens the host nation's sense of community over time (LEU, June 20, 2016, 9:38 p.m.; 201; January 23, 2016, 3:23 p.m.). Other aspects of the narrative on controlling immigration reinforced this messaging. Central to the Leave campaigns' discussion of migration was the idea that if nothing was done, large swaths of the country—and particularly regional centers in England—would be overrun by migrants from southern and eastern Europe and Turkey, "chang[ing] the face of England forever" (LEU, June 9, 2016, 9:58 p.m.; May 25, 9:12 p.m.; VL, June 8, 2016, 6:54 p.m.; March 21, 2016, 9:14 p.m.). The message here was that the "real" British people were at risk of being displaced if they did not take back control of immigration.

The slogan "take back control" was central to the campaigns' messaging. Both campaigns embraced the slogan: the phrasing and formulation appeared in almost 500 tweets (over 380 Vote Leave and over 100 Leave.EU tweets). It was Vote Leave's most common message. Ostensibly, this slogan was about regaining political power from the EU. But it was also about the survival of the nation. Early on, the campaigns argued that taking back control was the "safer" option for Brits by pointing to various national security and economic threats from outsiders (VL, April 6, 2016, 6:42 a.m.; LEU, May 17, 2016, 3:09 p.m.). Vote Leave built on these ideas to claim that "taking back control" of immigration, healthcare, and economic and national security would protect British people from foreign outsiders (VL, June 4, 5:00 p.m.). The ethnic nationalist elements here were clearest in tweets about immigration, where taking back control was consistently presented as the means by which "we" would control who, and how many of "them," entered the country (LEU, April 19, 2016, 6:00 a.m.; VL, March 24, 2016, 8:08 a.m.). Ethnic undertones were also present in tweets about the National Healthcare Service (NHS), a revered symbol of national solidarity. The Leave campaigns both argued that the NHS was being overrun by migration (VL, March 27, 2016, 3:47 p.m.; LEU, June 14, 2016, 7:00 p.m.). From this position, both campaigns argued that "taking back control" was the only way to save the NHS and protect "our" health. In short, a central theme of both campaigns was that "we" needed to protect "ourselves" from "them" by taking back "our" rightful place as the true holders of power in the UK.

Closely linked to this message was the notion that the sovereignty of parliament—Westminster—needed to be reasserted. The Leave side regularly tapped into the mythology of parliamentary sovereignty as a unique and ingenious English idea (LEU, June 19, 2016, 8:51 a.m.; February 19, 2016, 9:09 p.m.; VL, June 19, 2016, 8:59 a.m.). Both accounts centered parliamentary sovereignty in their campaigns (LEU, June 13, 2016, 11:06 a.m.; VL, June 21, 2016, 8:35 p.m.). They made an instrumental case for regaining sovereignty as a way of achieving goals in "our" national interest (LEU, May 13, 2016, 11:22 a.m.), as well as emphasizing that British sovereignty was an end unto itself (LEU, June 22, 2016, 10:02 a.m.). In this respect, they argued that regaining full sovereignty was the only way to protect and actualize English national identity (LEU, May 24, 2016, 1:27 p.m.; VL, June 13, 20167, 9:18 p.m.). Here parliamentary sovereignty was presented as a core reflection of the nation's spirit—and so to attenuate its power through the EU put the nation itself at risk (LEU, May 12, 2016, 8:35 p.m.; VL, June 13, 2016, 2:49 p.m.; June 19, 2016, 10:50 a.m.).

In making their case for taking back control and the importance of parliamentary sovereignty, both campaigns also tapped into elements of English exceptionalism. Here they drew upon myths of Great Britain as an exceptional, leading nation in the world (LEU, June 16, 2016, 12:16 p.m.; February 5, 2016, 9:10 p.m.). They repeatedly pointed to its status as the fifth largest economy—as an economic and political force (LEU, June 20, 2016, 7:14 p.m.; VL, April 16, 2016, 3:58 p.m.). They made the case that Leave supporters were the only ones who believed in this greatness (LEU, June 20, 2016, 6:56 p.m.; VL, June 19, 2016, 11:19 a.m.). In these tweets the EU was cast as a barrier, which was blocking the UK from achieving its destined greatness (LEU, June 22, 2016, 8:30 p.m.; VL, April 16, 2016, 3:58 p.m.). In this respect, Brexit was presented as the necessary step for the nation to regain its rightful place in the world as "top nation."

The campaigns also drew from these themes when employing historical myths about the nation and its future. In this respect, both campaigns used nostalgic messaging that emphasized that Brexit would enable it to recover its lost glory, when it was a great imperial power. Leave.EU referred to the Commonwealth—the international association of former colonial holdings—as a symbol of this past (LEU, April 25, 2016, 4:30 p.m.; February 5, 2016, 9:12 p.m.). It argued that the UK should resume its rightful place, leading the Commonwealth to regain its prominence on the world stage (LEU, March 14, 2016, 11:01 a.m.). Often this kind of messaging was linked to a second, related, idea that the UK could return to greatness on the world stage once it left the EU. Elements of imperialism underpinned these arguments, with tweets emphasizing that the "world can be our oyster" again, and that there are "opportunities there for the taking," with references to former colonies in Africa and India (LEU, June 22, 2016, 6:37 a.m.; June 18, 2016, 12:00 p.m.; May 12, 2016, 8:06 a.m.; May 7, 2016, 1:00 p.m.). More generally, though, the campaigns spoke about how the UK—as one of the largest economies of the world—would prosper after leaving (VL, June 21, 2016, 7:37 p.m.). They argued that Brexit would enable the UK to regain its influence in many of the world's important institutions, rather than being subsumed within the EU (VL, June 9, 2016, 8:28 p.m.; LEU, April 12, 2016, 7:56 a.m.). Once again, the UK could be a global leader (VL, June 22, 2016, 8:54 p.m.; LEU, June 22, 2016, 8:30 p.m.). In short, the campaigns argued the referendum was a once in a lifetime opportunity for voters to change the course of the nation (VL, June 19, 2016, 5:35 p.m.)—the "time has come for our nation to make its greatest decision for a generation . . . for our nation to take control of its destiny" (LEU, February 19, 2016, 9:07 p.m.). Boris Johnson summed up the general historical position of the campaigns on the eve of the election: the success of the nation after it left the EU would be vindicated in time (VL, June 23, 2016, 11:59 a.m.).

"Them"

In contrast to the sometimes subtle building of an in-group, the Leave campaigns were more explicit in identifying out-groups. Together, the campaigns framed migrants—and particularly people from Turkey and neighboring Muslim-majority countries of Iraq and Syria—as invaders who were endangering the physical and economic security of the nation. One of the central planks of the campaigns was that British people could only properly protect themselves from this threat by leaving the EU.

Both campaigns regularly used coded ethnic myths and symbols when discussing migration. Together, they tweeted about immigration well over 800 times—it was among the most common topics. They overwhelmingly used negative language that reinforced migrants were a threat to the British people. Approximately 71 percent of tweets on migration were explicitly negative (72% for Vote Leave and 70% for Leave.EU). The campaigns consistently linked membership in the EU with unsustainable levels of migration (VL, June 20, 2016, 1:21 p.m.; LEU, May 11, 2016, 6:00 p.m.). Central to this messaging was the idea that the EU had enabled a chaotic and uncontrolled system of immigration (VL, June 3, 2016, 6:56 p.m.; January 14, 2016, 7:00 p.m.). Tweets often focused on the number of migrants entering the UK. A key argument here was that current levels of migration were changing the face of the nation—that whole "cities" of migrants were entering the country each year (VL, March 24, 2016, 10:39 a.m.; LEU, May 26, 2016, 10:23 a.m.). Speculation about massive population movements—often focusing on what would happen when Turkey joined the EU—was also common. At various points, the campaigns cited figures like "5.23 million" migrants would enter by 2030 (VL, May 26, 2016, 4:25 p.m.), that "76 million" people would be able to access UK benefits when Turkey joined the EU (VL, June 2, 2016, 7:31 p.m.), and that staying in the EU could mean "100 million people in this country" (LEU, May 30, 8:17 p.m.). Leaving was also depicted as the only way that Britain could insulate itself from the refugee "crisis" that was ostensibly engulfing the EU (LEU, March 6, 2016, 10:45 a.m.; VL, June 7, 2016, 10:19 p.m.). Leave.EU further linked refugees to Islamic terrorism by arguing there was a " 'staggering number' of EU-born Islamists posing as refugees [and that the] migrant crisis [was] now a security crisis" (LEU, April 5, 2016, 8:27 p.m.).

This last tweet by Leave.EU is also indicative of how the campaign tended to blur the boundaries between different types of migration. The campaign would periodically refer to refugees and asylum seekers in their social media communication. Predictably, these messages were aimed at stoking fear over the scale and impact of refugees coming to the UK (LEU, March 21, 2016, 11:00 a.m.; January 28, 2016, 1:00 p.m.). However, even when using the imagery and idea of crisis, Leave.EU used the broader term "migrant" much more often (LEU, May 11, 2016, 6:00 p.m.; March 26, 2016, 11:00 a.m., 12:16 p.m.). Indeed, even when talking directly about the "crisis," they would use "migrant" or "illegal immigrant" in place of "refugee" to describe the people (LEU, May 2, 2016, 1:30 p.m.; April 6, 2016, 2:00 p.m.). In this respect, the campaign sought to lump together population movements associated with membership in the EU and broader movements associated with asylum seekers. They capitalized on the sometimes opaque and complicated immigration system to paint a picture that *all types* of migration were out of control, and that migrants from undesirable locations were entering through the EU to threaten the nation.

The campaigns built upon this general position to target migrants as a threatening Other. They scapegoated migrants through a politics of blame, attributing many of the nation's perceived ills to them. They argued that these dangerous migrants needed to be expunged through deportation or kept out by reducing immigration levels in order to protect the nation (VL, June 21, 2016, 7:49 p.m.; June 15, 2016, 6:20 p.m.; LEU, May 26, 2016, 4:12 p.m.). This politics of blame manifested itself through three related messages about migrants.

First, migrants were repeatedly blamed for economic hardships faced by the British people. Both campaigns argued that migration was suppressing the wages of British workers (VL, June 21, 2016, 7:20 p.m.; LEU, June 21, 2016, 11:00 a.m.). This was linked to the idea that migration was generally a problem for working people—that migrants were making income inequality worse and keeping the poor poor (VL, June 22, 2016, 2:45 p.m.; LEU, May 29, 2016, 8:00 a.m.). More generally, the campaigns claimed that migration was bad for the economy—that it cost the UK millions of pounds per day (LEU, June 20, 2016, 12:25 p.m.; May 29, 2016, 9:45 a.m.; May 17, 2016, 11:39 a.m.).

Second, the campaigns linked these economic arguments to a form of "welfare chauvinism." Both campaigns claimed migrants were endangering the social services of the country, saturating the education system, and contributing to housing shortages (VL, June 21, 2016, 7:47 p.m.; May 8, 2016, 7:47 a.m.; May 26, 2016, 9:53 p.m.; April 29, 2016, 9:48 a.m.). But the overwhelming focus here was on how migration was perceived to threaten the NHS. Vote Leave tweeted about healthcare over 300 times, and in many of these tweets it claimed uncontrolled migration was putting the NHS in crisis (VL, June 14, 2016, 8:14 p.m.; May 10, 5:39 p.m.). These messages used inflammatory language and images to claim that the NHS would not be able to cope once countries like Albania, Macedonia, Montenegro, Serbia, and Turkey joined the EU (VL, June 15, 2016, 6:57 p.m.; May 1, 2016, 9:18 p.m.).

Third, the campaigns blamed the EU for blocking the UK's ability to deport dangerous migrant criminals (VL, June 21, 2016, 7:49 p.m., 8:31 p.m.). Leave.EU claimed that dangerous foreigners had infiltrated the rest of Europe, and so were going to make their way to the UK (LEU, May 24, 2016, 1:34 p.m.; May 20, 2016, 9:03 a.m.). Both campaigns raised the specter of terrorists moving freely throughout the EU with impunity and making their way to the UK (LEU, June 13, 2016, 4:30 p.m.; VL, June 21, 2016, 8:29 p.m.). These lines of argument were brought together with the refrain that it would be "safer to take back control" (VL, April 6, 2016, 6:42 a.m.).

Tweets about migration were often paired with messages about the potential threat posed by Turkey joining the EU. Both campaigns made the case that Turkey's accession was an inevitability, and indeed that this was supported by the EU, Prime Minister David Cameron, and the Remain campaigners (VL, June 22, 10:27 p.m.; June 7, 2016, 10:57 p.m.; LEU, June 13, 2016, 9:33 a.m.). Implicit in these tweets about Turkey joining the EU was the idea that it would enable Muslims to freely migrate to the UK. In this respect, the campaigns used Turkey as a symbol to capitalize on fears of Islam. Both campaigns used imagery and language that implied that Turkish people were dangerous Muslims. For example, Leave.EU tweeted images that portrayed Turkish people as hooded, sword-wielding criminals and terrorists (LEU, May 17, 2016, 3:09 p.m.). Other tweets portrayed them as undemocratic extremists, who mobilized in the streets and acted violently in their own parliament (LEU, March 11, 2016, 1:21 p.m.; May 3, 2016, 12:51 p.m.). More directly, Leave.EU argued that once Turkey acceded, Europe would literally burn (LEU, May 17, 2016, 6:45 p.m.). Both campaigns also emphasized that Turkey would be a gateway for Islamic extremists and terrorists from the Middle East to enter the EU and, following that, the UK (VL, June 2, 2016, 7:35 p.m.; April 23, 2016, 6:12 a.m.; LEU, March 22, 2016, 5:30 p.m.). Both campaigns tweeted maps highlighting the fact that Turkey borders Syria and Iraq (VL, May 4, 2016, 2:16 p.m.). These maps had prominent red arrows showing how people from these countries would pour into the UK (VL, May 7, 2016, 9:09 a.m.; LEU, May 3, 2016, 11:00 a.m.). The message was clear: once Turkey joined the EU, there would be an open door for terrorists to enter the UK.

At the same time, the Leave campaigns' depiction of Turkey was about more than raising the threat of Islamic terrorism (see Figure 7.1). The rhetoric about Turkey also stoked fear that the white, Christian majority in the UK was being replaced by Muslim migrants. Here, long-standing religious myths about the nation's role as God's "chosen" defender of the true faith against dangerous

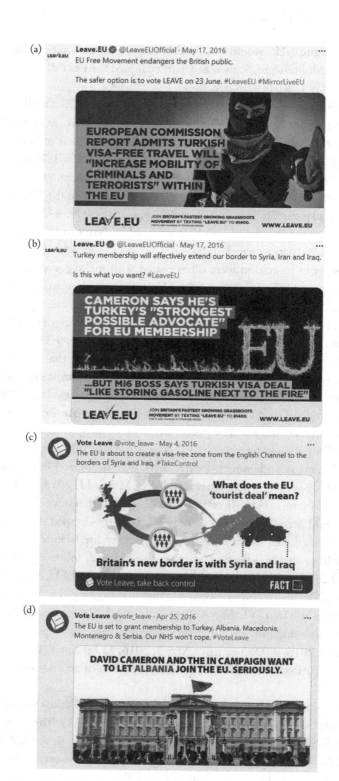

Figure 7.1 Tweets depicting Turkey and Muslims as Threats

heathens provided a framework for depicting Muslims. Both campaigns raised the specter of massive flows of Turkish people invading the UK. They tweeted pictures of long lines of migrants in caravans (LEU, March 9, 2016, 7:01 a.m.) and standing for visa applications (LEU, May 4, 2016, 4:13 p.m.). They implied that once Turkey joined the EU, its entire population—all 76 million people—would walk through an open door to enter the UK (VL, May 23, 2016, 8:37 a.m.). In addition to Turkey, both campaigns often raised fears that Albania—a Muslim-majority country, was also likely to join the EU (VL, April 27, 2016, 2:16 p.m.). Both campaigns referred to Muslim migration to the UK to argue that key elements of British identity were in jeopardy (LEU, March 8, 2016, 10:55 p.m.). For example, Vote Leave used imagery showing how these migrations would change the face of the nation—publishing a picture of Buckingham Palace flying the Albanian flag (VL, April 25, 2016, 2:23 p.m.). Leave.EU argued that if nothing were done, Christmas messages would soon have Arabic subtitles (LEU, December 25, 2015, 6:58 a.m.).

The campaigns also drew upon myths and symbols of the peaceful "island nation" to oppose the "threat" of Muslim migration. Here, the symbolism that the borders of the nation were under siege by migrant invaders was a common theme, particularly for Leave.EU. They tweeted imagery of raucous crowds of people appearing to storm border gates (LEU, December 28, 2015, 7:01 a.m.). Alongside an image of crowds of excited men at a fence, they claimed that a "staggering number" of refugees were from the terrorist group ISIS (LEU, April 6, 2016, 2:00 p.m.). They also promoted UKIP's infamous "Breaking Point" billboard that depicted a line of asylum seekers and included text about how the UK had to take back control of its borders (LEU, June 16, 2016, 10:35 a.m.). Both campaigns built on this idea to argue that the UK needed to leave the EU to take back control of its border and thereby take back "our" country—with the veiled message here being that "our country" does not include Muslims (VL, June 23, 2016, 1:58 p.m.; LEU, May 24, 2016, 1:32 p.m.). In this respect, the symbolism of the border played a central role in Leave's argument—that a strong border (our island fortress) is what protects "us" from "them."

The Leave campaigns also often combined ethnic nationalist themes with a populist framework. EU officials were consistently portrayed as anti-democratic, unelected foreigners, who had no connection to the UK (VL, May 6, 2016, 10:12 p.m.; LEU, June 3, 2016, 7:40 p.m.). In short, they depicted the EU as a set of elites—a modern-day Norman yoke—who threatened the interest of "real" British people (VL, June 21, 2016, 8:19 p.m.; June 12, 2016, 7:27 p.m.; LEU, June 22, 2016, 5:46 p.m.; June 14, 2016, 9:31 a.m.). Attacks on the EU took on a particularly strident tone when it was identified as an imperialist institution. Here the long-standing myths of the "island nation" standing as a liberal bulwark against the aggression of tyrannical (French) outsiders were invoked.

For example, Leave.EU recalled the symbolism of Napoleon to emphasize that the EU was a modern-day empire (LEU, May 14, 2016, 4:24 p.m.). Additional tweets likened the "chaos" of the EU to the "death throes" of a "racist, imperialist" order (LEU, June 19, 2016, 8:11 a.m.; June 16, 2016, 8:57 a.m.). Against this purported new European imperialism, Leave.EU drew upon the words of Shakespeare to declare that "England never did, nor never shall, lie at the proud foot of a conqueror" (LEU, April 26, 2016, 8:50 a.m.). Playing on these same themes, both campaigns emphasized the idea that the EU was in reality controlled by France and Germany, the UK's traditional adversaries (VL, March 10, 2016, 8:21 p.m.; June 11, 2016, 9:23 a.m.). They further implied that the EU was a cover for recurring German aggression, by asking rhetorically "who had won the Second World War?" (LEU, May 10, 2016, 11:36 a.m.). These positions accentuate how many of the populist claims about the EU's threats to the British people drew their content from the myths and symbols of English identity. Thus, the anti-migrant, anti-Muslim and pro–strong border messaging was paired with a populist message that blamed a foreign institution, controlled by foreigners working for their own interests, for the ills of the nation. In other words, the threat was not only dangerous migrants and Muslims, but also their elite allies in Brussels.

Continuity and Change in the Leave Campaigns' Ethnic Nationalism

This overview of the two Leave campaigns' tweets shows how they relied on an ethnic English nationalism to make a case for Brexit. They both drew from a wellspring of ethnic myths and symbols of English identity to build a sense of the in-group that they were seeking to protect by leaving the EU, while also constructing the out-group that was threatening the nation if it stayed in the union (see Table 7.2). The campaigns promoted the idea that working people in the rural regions of the country were the true heart of the nation, and that Britain had a proud history leading the world as a powerful empire. They argued that the only way to regain this prominent position as "top nation"—and to protect the prosperity and way of life for ordinary Britons—was to reassert their long-standing tradition of parliamentary sovereignty. Here is where "taking back control" from the EU played such a central role in the Leave campaigns: it was a pivot between the identification of "us" and what "we" needed to do to protect "ourselves" from "them."

The campaigns also depicted this "Other" by drawing on long-standing myths and symbols of historic threats to the English nation. The continent and

Table 7.2 **Key Distinctions in the Leave Campaigns' Conception of the In- and Out-Group in Their Twitter Communication in the 2016 Brexit Referendum Campaign**

"Virtuous" In-Group	"Villainous" Out-Group
British people (as a movement)	Migrants and Refugees
Working people	Healthcare and social service free riders
A glorious imperial past/a great nation/leader in the West	Muslims and terrorists (from Turkey and its Middle Eastern neighbors)
Inventors of liberal democracy and parliamentary sovereignty	EU elites and bureaucrats as foreign enemies of the nation

the imperial yoke remained common themes, but the Normans, the French, and the papacy of old were replaced by the European Union of today. And the ethnic Others here also shifted, with migrants becoming the most prominent target. The Leave campaigns framed migration as an existential danger for the people of Britain—arguing that migrants were causing the ills for working people, that they were eroding the welfare state, and that they were dangerous. The campaigns often paired these negative arguments with an implicit point that when Turkey and other Muslim-majority countries inevitably joined the EU, the situation would only get worse, particularly the threat of Islamic fundamentalist terrorism. Here, clearly, the history of religious strife between Protestants and Catholics, and the idea of the English as a "chosen" people, was adapted to portray Islam as the religious Other of the English. This scapegoating of migrants through ethnic nationalist themes was a key—if not *the* key—theme of the Leave campaigns. "Taking back control" was therefore not only about sovereignty, or about controlling economic decisions, but also about stopping migration and enforcing a strong border between "us" and "them."

Despite this dichotomy, Leave's case for who they were seeking to represent and protect—the in-group—was at times ambiguous. Their language reflected the sometimes obscure relationship between Englishness and Britishness that we discussed earlier in the chapter, with the demonyms "English" people and "British" people often used synonymously. Generally, however, they favored "Brits," British people, and Britain more often than the English and England. However, as our analysis shows, despite this tendency to favor Britain, the core myth-symbols that they relied upon were English. In this respect, the Leave campaigns implicitly adopted a position that British identity should reflect English identity. One of the telling points here is that *direct* appeals to other nations within the UK were very circumspect. Only about 60 tweets between both campaigns mentioned how Brexit was supported by, or would impact, the minority nations of Scotland, Wales, or Northern Ireland. In short, while the campaigns adopted language that spoke about the British people and Britain, their target constituency and the national identity that structured their communication most forcefully was the English. Nevertheless, our analysis also shows that the primary focus of the campaigns was on building a sense of a threatening Other—that leaving the EU was required to protect the nation from dangerous migrants, Muslims, and their elite allies in the EU.

This dichotomy between a virtuous "us" and a villainous "them" was particularly evident in how the campaigns used negative and positive language to reinforce the boundary between the two groups. Overall, the two campaigns were quite negative. Over half of their tweets used overtly negative language and ideas, whereas only about a third were clearly positive.[5] These patterns largely held when the campaigns used ethnic myths and symbols in their tweets, as about 45 percent were negative and about 32 percent were positive. Negative framing was most obvious in how the campaigns targeted migrants and Muslims as outsiders: over 70 percent of tweets about migrants were clearly negative, and over 75 percent of tweets about Turkey and Muslims were negative. Perhaps even more telling, only about 5 percent of tweets that mentioned Turkey or Islam were clearly positive. This overwhelmingly negative depiction of migrants and Muslims contrasts with how the campaigns depicted English and British identity. Over 90 percent of tweets about recapturing Britain's place in the world—evoking ideas about returning to its past imperial stature—were positive. Similarly, nearly 80 percent of tweets about the Commonwealth were positive. In other areas, the campaigns were more balanced. For example, when the campaigns invoked myths and symbols of parliamentary sovereignty, they tended to balance negative messages with positive ones (roughly half of these tweets were positive and half were negative). In short, the campaigns' discourse reinforced their oppositional strategy, targeting migrants and Muslims as threats to the nation.

We analyzed the two Leave campaigns together. Approaching both campaigns as representative of the "Leave" campaign does obscure some of the differences in their rhetoric and strategy. For example, Vote Leave focused more often on immigration than Leave.EU: 16 percent of Vote Leave tweets referenced migration, compared to about 9 percent of Leave.EU tweets. At the same time, some of Leave.EU's messages on migrants were highly visible—and as the above examples show, at times they could be more inflammatory in their messages about the threat posed by migrants. Similarly, Vote Leave was more focused on Turkey joining the EU—about 5 percent of their tweets were about Turkey, while about 2 percent of Leave.EU's touched on the topic. Vote Leave was also more focused on the EU, while Leave.EU focused more broadly on globalization. Leave.EU also tweeted more often about the border (they tweeted about the "homeland" almost twice as many times as Vote Leave). Leave.EU was also more focused on Britain's historical standing, particularly drawing from myths of its imperial past and its potential return to greatness (they referenced these ideas in about 4.5% of their tweets, whereas Vote Leave touched upon similar ideas about 3% of the time). All told, Vote Leave was more likely to rely on ethnic ideas in their messaging: over a third of Vote Leave tweets employed ethnic myth-symbols compared to about a quarter of Leave.EU tweets. Vote Leave was also more likely to focus on public policy issues: about 41 percent of their tweets engaged with a substantive public policy issue, whereas roughly 34 percent of Leave.EU tweets touched on public policy. In terms of actual issues, though, there was not much difference between the focus of the two campaigns, other than Vote Leave's tendency to focus more on healthcare (almost 11% of their tweets referenced healthcare or the NHS, compared to just 2% of Leave.EU's).

On most other fronts, the two campaigns were relatively aligned in their focus on Twitter. Their general patterns, tactics, and topics were quite similar. Both similarly used negative messaging (both campaigns did so in about 52% of their tweets). However, Leave.EU was much less positive (only about 29% of their messages were clearly positive, compared to about 42% of Vote Leave's tweets). Perhaps most important, though is that both campaigns played a prominent role in representing the Leave side in the referendum. For example, as others have noted, together Vote Leave and Leave.EU at the time of the vote had more than three times the number of Twitter followers than Remain (Usherwood and Wright 2017, 377). They also tweeted roughly two times more than Remain. Of course, as we discussed in chapter 3, followers and tweet volumes are not necessarily a good measure of impact. However, the relative prominence of the two Leave campaigns enabled them to play central roles in setting and communicating the Brexit agenda through similar, if sometimes subtly different, campaigns. All this being said, the main takeaway from their social media messaging is that both Leave campaigns centered ethnic nationalism in their political communication. This messaging clearly reverberated with, and mobilized, the white, English majority to vote to leave the EU.

Conclusion

The Deep Roots of the New Nationalism

The case we have made in this book is that the "new nationalism" that has recently swept through the West is, in fact, not so new. In America, there has long been a tradition of ethnic nationalism—from its founding right through to today. Donald Trump capitalized on, and reinvigorated, this element of American political culture. His political messaging was anchored by an ethnic conception of the American people that pitted the white majority against various purportedly threatening Others. His strategy was remarkably successful: white Americans were central to his victory in 2016, and made up the majority of his over 74 million voters in 2020. Similarly, while France is generally understood as a civic nation *par excellence*, there is also a long-standing and powerful conception of the French people as an ethnic group. Marine Le Pen tapped into this stream of identity, garnering remarkable results in her 2017 presidential bid. And while a self-conscious English ethnic nationalism is relatively new—having long been subsumed within an overarching British nationalism—the identity upon which it is based is not. The Leave campaigners embraced this identity to bring together enough English voters to win the Brexit referendum.

The takeaway from our exploration of the US, UK, and France is that ethnic nationalism in these cases has deep historical roots. These roots lie in the cultures of the white majorities. Today's ethnic nationalists have recognized this, and are cultivating support from these groups by drawing from long-standing myths and symbols to construct an image of the nation as an ethnic community. Our analysis of Donald Trump, Marine Le Pen, and the Leave campaigns show us how leaders today are speaking to the white majorities in their own codes using digital media, and drawing from a wellspring of long-established ideas about their membership, aspirations, fears, histories, and futures. It is this connection to the past that gives today's ethnic nationalism perceived legitimacy as an authentic reflection of the nation's character. In this way, the historical foundations of ethnic identity have been carried through time and are influencing contemporary politics.

Recognizing these deep roots helps to demystify the resurgence of the new nationalism. The seeming inexorable rise of ethnic nationalists and populists across the globe since 2016 has taken many people aback. The shock has been most acute in the bastions of liberal democracy and pluralism. For many liberal observers, Trump's win, Le Pen's showing in 2017, and the vote for Brexit were jarring. But we have tried to show here that these are only puzzling events if we forget our history. Ethnic nationalism has been a recurring part of politics in some of the most liberal, pluralist countries in the world. Its particulars have changed in sometimes subtle ways over time, but its foundations have endured. It is a core part of politics in the West, emerging at times of perceived crisis time and time again. In short, the new nationalism is not new, nor is it exceptional.

Acknowledging that ethnic nationalism is an endemic feature of politics in the West helps us to better understand the phenomenon. It can correct the tendency to over-attribute the rise and success of ethnic nationalists and populists to structural changes in social, economic, and technological conditions. Of course, we agree that the growth of economic inequality and a corresponding backlash to liberalization and immigration have shaped contemporary politics. Attention to these factors is particularly helpful in showing us why support for ethnic nationalism and populism has grown at this point in time. The advent of social media has also enabled ethnic nationalist leaders and movements to reach their supporters in greater numbers. But if we focus upon these structural factors too much, ethnic nationalism begins to appear as an aberration—as a "one-off" event that occurs in exceptional circumstances, rather than as a core aspect of political culture. Highlighting the deep roots of ethnic nationalism—showing how ethnic identity solidified and developed over *la longue durée*, and how political leaders today tap into these cultural foundations—augments our understanding of the new nationalism. Furthermore, if we overemphasize structural factors, we can lose sight of the *ideas* that the new nationalism seeks to convey. Clearly these ideas matter; for example, it is notable that rising socioeconomic inequality has not triggered a renewed embrace of socialist internationalism on nearly the same scale that nationalism has been embraced. Thus, by focusing squarely on the ideational content of the new nationalism, we can shed new light on why it reverberates with its target populations.

Taking this longer view of the new nationalism's ethno-cultural content showcases the potential of our theoretical approach. By foregrounding the cultural foundations of nationalism—adopting an ethno-symbolic approach—we have tried to draw attention back to the power of these identities to shape politics. As such, this book has sought to highlight the role of ethnicity, culture, and history in today's politics. The new nationalists may rely heavily on digital mediums, but we can only understand the content of their messaging, and its symbolic power, by paying attention to its links to history. This has been one of our primary aims: to demonstrate the analytical potential of ethno-symbolism.

In making our case about the deep cultural roots of the new nationalism, we hope we have shed some light on the two questions we posed at the outset of the book: (1) Why is ethnic nationalism gaining currency across the West, particularly among the white majorities, and (2) how and why do these movements differ across countries? We want to close by reflecting on these questions more directly, drawing from our analysis. We will start with a discussion of the dynamics of persistence and change in the ethnic nationalism of the US, UK, and France. We will then comment on the similarities and differences across the three cases.

The Persistence and Adaptability of Ethnic Nationalism in the West

Our analysis of the US, UK, and France highlighted that in each country there is a foundational set of myths and symbols that defines the dominant majority in ethnic terms. This ethnic "myth-symbol complex" ties together cultural content that gives these communities a sense of meaning. In other words, these myths and symbols reflect a set of beliefs that these communities hold about themselves (Schöpflin 1997). While not necessarily based on historical truths (Kumar 2015, 199–200), these myth-symbol complexes have played an important legitimating function by providing a long-standing set of stories about how and why the community exists. At times of crisis, we have seen how they have even provided these communities with a perceived legitimacy to protect their way of life by excluding, vilifying, and attacking people who are defined as outsiders. In this respect, the foundational set of myths and symbols we traced in each case have played a critical role in constructing a sense of the nation that is rooted in a strong ethnic core—even if this more ascriptive ethnicity has at times receded into the background, or has been hidden from view through a veil of purported civic ideals.

In all three cases, the nation's ethnic identity is centered on the white majority. These white majorities are key players in the rise of the new nationalism. Their support has propelled nationalist leaders to new heights. It is their myths and symbols that leaders draw from to cultivate this support. This is most apparent in America, where "race" is an especially powerful symbol of identity. But we have shown here that ethnic nationalism in the West is about more than just racism. To be sure, whiteness is a central identity marker for the majority group in all three of our case studies: it helps shape who is perceived to belong to the in-group and who does not. But we have also shown how a related complex of identity markers combine to create a deeper sense of "us" and "them." These markers go beyond just race to include other ascriptive criteria for defining the people, their homeland, their religion, their history, and their ethos. In our view, focusing on how leaders tap into this wellspring of identity helps us understand why their ethnic nationalist messaging is resonating with their target communities. Of course, not all members of the white majorities in the US, UK, and France identify with this ethnic nationalism. National and ethnic groups are inherently heterogeneous, with many competing sets of ideas on their nature (Schertzer and Woods 2011; Hutchinson 2005). Significant numbers of white voters in all three countries embrace civic ideals. Similarly, members of the purported out-groups can and do support new nationalists. A fair number of Hispanic and black voters sided with Trump in 2020. But this heterogeneity does not diminish our main point that the dominant, white majority in each of our cases has a decidedly ethnic core. And the roots of today's ethnic nationalism are deeply embedded in the culture of these white majorities.

The specific ways in which leaders are using these identities demonstrates just how remarkably persistent their core myths and symbols have been through time. All three of our case studies reinforce the argument that core cultural elements of ethnic identity can be remarkably durable once they have taken shape. Once these identities were ingrained in a set of "institutional carriers" (Hutchinson 2005), they endured for centuries. Additionally, our analyses underscored the long-standing power that these identities have to mobilize people, even after lengthy periods of seeming dormancy. Time and again, when faced with some perceived threat, these identities have suddenly been rushed to the forefront of politics in the form of a virulent ethnic nationalism—before receding again after the threat perception has abated. In our view, the diminution of ethnic nationalism in the second half of the twentieth century should be read in this light. It did not signal that it had reached its historical endpoint. Rather, it had simply entered a period of abatement. Furthermore, the sudden return of ethnic nationalism in the 2010s should not be seen as a "new" development—it reflects a recurring historical pattern.

At the same time, the durability of the identities that we analyzed is partly due to their adaptability. While firmly rooted in a foundational, core set of ethnic myths and symbols, in each case we saw how the precise content of this myth-symbol complex adapted over time in sometimes subtle, and sometimes less subtle, ways. These adaptations were most often provoked by relatively rapid changes in who, or what, was perceived as a threat to the majority group. Here, we saw how different identity markers became salient depending on the relational context. This process, over time, also fed longer-term adaptations to the structure of the myth-symbol complex. These two types of adaptation can be illustrated through Clifford Geertz's (1973) concept of cultural "depth"; adaptations in the *salience* of different myths and symbols occurred at the "surface" level of political culture, whereas adaptations in the myth-symbol complex represented changes to the "deep" content of political culture.

In our view, this dual process of adaptation is key to understanding the enduring symbolic power of ethnic nationalism in the West. In our analyses, the content of ethnic nationalism was never simply "invented" *tout court*—it was always built upon preexisting ideas that defined who "we" are, and why "they" do not belong. And this is what links the deep roots of ethnic nationalism to the politics of today: the new nationalists we examined in this book successfully tapped into a wellspring of ethnic myths and symbols, and adapted them for the digital age and in response to new sets of perceived threats.

As we showed in chapter 4, these dynamics have been hallmarks of American ethnic nationalism. In the eighteenth and early nineteenth centuries, a decidedly ethnic understanding of the American nation crystallized, centering around Anglo-Saxon heritage and a related sense of superiority, combined with Protestantism and a perceived covenant with God. This conception of the in-group was constructed in relation to different sets of threatening Others, namely metropolitan English, black people, Indigenous communities, Catholics, Jews, and various other European migrants. The foundational set of myths and symbols associated with this identity were mobilized at moments of perceived crisis in the ensuing nineteenth and twentieth centuries, notably during the increase in immigration from southern and eastern Europe, Asia, Latin America, and other countries; during the Mexican-American War and the Civil War; and in the wake of the civil rights movement. During these events, different myths and symbols became salient, depending on who, or what, was perceived as a threat. Alongside this process, a longer-term adaptation of dominant group identity also occurred, from being based on "Anglo-American" myths and symbols to being grounded in a broader, but equally powerful, "white American" identity.

As we argued in chapter 5, Donald Trump is the most recent iteration in a long line of ethnic nationalists who have tapped into this stream of American political culture. His political program epitomized the dynamics of persistence, but also adaptation. He drew from well-trodden myths and symbols to construct an in-group and an out-group. Trump courted the white majority—his "silent majority" and "movement"—identifying them as the "real" Americans because they lived in the rural heartland and were good Christians and Jews. He built on the trends of the late twentieth and early twenty-first centuries to identify a set of outsiders—dangerous Hispanic migrants, Islamic terrorists, and global elites—who were depicted as threats to the white majority's way of life. The core of his political messaging throughout his first presidential campaign and time in government was an argument that he alone could protect the white majority from these threats and, in doing so, "make America great again" (at least for white Americans). We think it is the deep roots of Trump's ethnic nationalism, adapted to the current context, that helped him cultivate support from a majority of white Americans.

In chapters 6 and 7 we showed a similar pattern of persistence and change in the ethnic nationalism of France and the UK. We traced the well-established, if sometimes quiescent, stream of ethnic identity that traces French ancestry to the Gauls, who are a people who live in *la France profonde*, and who have a long history of defeat and resistance to foreign invaders. In this ethnic understanding of the French, they are seen as both fiercely Catholic and as defenders of a unique French ethos of secularism in the public sphere, while also being champions of liberty through a *mission civilisatrice*. Marine Le Pen tapped into these ideas by building upon, but also adapting, these foundational ideas and her father's overt ethnic nationalism. As we showed, Le Pen constructed a sense of the in-group as a homogeneous, hard-working, Catholic people, who share a common ancestry and a grand history of resistance, cultural superiority, and a unique tradition of secularism and republicanism that epitomizes civilizational advancement. She presented herself as protecting this group—working "in the name of the people"—against dangerous hordes of migrants, Islamic fundamentalists and terrorists, communitarians, and minorities living in the suburbs that she said were trying to tear down the pillars of the French way of life: secularism, republican values, rural life, the welfare state, and the unique French culture.

In our case study of the UK, we showed there is a deep-seated sense of English people as an ethnic group. This ethnic understanding of the English emerged through often conflicted relations with the other ethnic groups of the British Isles, through conflict with continental Europe (especially France), and through the colonization of peoples abroad in the building of empire. Through these relations, a complex of ethnic myths and symbols coalesced that depicted the English in-group as the descendants of the Anglo-Saxons, and as a free and superior people, whose innate genius and greatness thrust them forward as world leaders and as a "civilizing" force through their empire, and as people chosen by God to defend the "true" religion. This myth-symbol complex also evoked strong boundaries, which presented the island as a fortress (imagined to be inhabited solely by Protestant English), which protected them from a dangerous world of tyranny and heathenism. The Brexit campaigners built on these foundational elements of English nationalism and adapted them in relation to the growing stream of Euroskepticism and anti-immigrant ideas in the twentieth century. We showed how the Leave campaigns depicted the English as a hard-working people, fighting to take back control of their sovereignty, so they could once again return to glory at home and abroad. The campaigns further argued that leaving the EU was necessary to protect the English from dangerous migrants and Muslims, whose free entry into the UK was backed by corrupt and anti-democratic powers on the continent.

In his pathbreaking work on "invented traditions," Eric Hobsbawm conceded that nationalist messaging must hit the right "wavelength" in order to be able to mobilize people (Hobsbawm and Ranger 1983). But this raises a question: What enables a message to hit the right wavelength? In this book, we have drawn from the ethno-symbolist approach of Smith and Hutchinson (Smith 2009; Hutchinson 2005) to argue that ethnic nationalist messaging must be grounded in the historically established myth-symbol complex of the target population if it is to be seen by that population as legitimate and authentic. But this leads to a second question: How can historic ideas reverberate with people *today*? We have tried to show that these ideas have been remarkably consistent in their foundational elements: that the main parameters of the ethnic myth-symbol complex for our three cases endured over large swaths of time. But we have also tried to show that they have adapted to new circumstances and contexts. Indeed, our research design for this book was in part motivated to respond to this question of whether historic myths and symbols still matter today. This is partly why we chose to focus on Twitter: we wanted to see whether historically rooted ideas about the nation were manifesting themselves in the most modern of mediums. And we found them. Even on a digital, micro-blogging platform, foundational ethnic myths and symbols were a central—indeed, *the central*—theme of political communication for all three of our case studies. This leads us to the second theme we want to highlight: that it is not just the medium that matters, but also the message.

The Form and Content of the New Nationalism in the West

Much has been made of how the new nationalists of our era seemed to suddenly arrive on the political scene in quick succession. The cover of the *Economist* in November 2016 pictured a new band of leaders marching together—led by Trump, along with contemporaries Nigel Farage, Marine Le Pen, and Vladimir Putin—beating the drum of a dangerous new nationalism. Academics opined on the seeming global-level nationalist resurgence (Bieber 2018; Halikiopoulou and Vlandas 2019; Brubaker 2017). Generally, the view in this literature is that the new nationalism is a global movement—that we are in a moment where ethnic nationalists and populists have emerged together, borrowing strategies and ideas to capture a zeitgeist sweeping across the West and beyond.

There is, of course, truth behind this view. The Brexit vote, Donald Trump's victory, and Marine Le Pen's strong showing all happened within a short eighteen-month span. As we have shown, their campaigns all focused on ethnic nationalism. But beyond the clear similarities in the general form of their political communication, the actual content of their messaging varied in important, if sometimes subtle, ways. We think both aspects—their common discursive form and their context-dependent content—help explain the resurgence and success of the new nationalism.

As our empirical analysis of Donald Trump, Marine Le Pen, and the Leave campaigns shows, all three were informed by the *logical structure* of ethnic nationalism. Each campaign was built upon the creation of an in-group set against an out-group. These groups were invariably defined through ethnic identity markers drawn from the dominant majority group's myths and symbols. The common theme in each case was that "we" (the white majority) were under threat from "them" (religious and ethnic minorities, and their purported elite allies). And each campaign was largely an argument about how only a nationalist leader could protect the white majority against the threat from the out-groups. In this respect, our analysis adds to the argument that discourse is critical to the success of ethnic nationalists and populists (Wodak 2015). Similarly, our analysis of Twitter aligns with previous work showing the centrality of this medium for contemporary politics, particularly for ethnic nationalists and populists (Gerbaudo 2018). Social media was a foundational pillar of each campaign in our case studies: it was a cornerstone of their political strategy, and it was used in similar ways. Of course, this is true of virtually all successful political campaigns today, which is one of the reasons we are skeptical of claims that social media is the primary driver of the new nationalism.

We expected to see these kinds of commonalities for the US, France, and UK. These are, after all, broadly similar cases, which share a long and intertwined history with one another. And, as we have said throughout, all three cases are also all widely seen as the forerunners of liberal democracy and as archetypes of civic nationalism. Indeed, on this score, we found remarkable congruence in the way that liberal democratic ideas were incorporated into a decidedly *ethnic* sense of identity. In each of the three cases, liberalism had a long history of being depicted not only as universal political principles, but also as a unique characteristic of their ethnic identities. From this perspective, the development of liberalism and democracy in the US, France, and England was mythologized to have occurred because of their innate, ethnic affinity for these ideas. It was, in this sense, a "natural" development.

The "ethnicization" of liberalism in the US, France, and England had two significant consequences for ethnic nationalism in these places. First, it added fuel to existing religious beliefs that they had a special mission from God to defend and promulgate the "true" religion. To this religious mission was added a secular belief (or "ethos," as we defined it in this book), that they had a mission to defend and promulgate liberalism and democracy in the world. This "civilizing mission" was seen to be specifically entrusted to them because liberalism itself was a unique characteristic of their ethnic identities—it was their gift to share with the world. Second, while the ethnicization of liberalism enabled a more expansive ethnic nationalism to develop in each of the three cases, it also provided new resources for constructing a more restrictive ethnic nationalism. Because their communities were perceived to have an innate affinity for liberalism and democracy, it raised the possibility that outsiders could be depicted as having an innate antipathy to these ideas. This created a logic that these outsiders needed to be excluded or vanquished for liberalism and democracy to triumph. As we have seen, this was a common way of depicting perceived Others in the US, France, and England.

Attention to the way in which liberalism has long been mythologized as an ethnic characteristic in each of the three cases helps to explain the rise of "illiberalism liberalism" across the West, which has become an important boundary mechanism for excluding migrants and Muslims (see Triadafilopoulos 2011). Here, as we also saw in our analysis of the three cases, Muslims are depicted as innately opposed to liberalism and democracy, as a threat to "our" communities and even Western civilization. While this kind of discourse has been characterized as a relatively new development in far-right and ethnic nationalist politics (Halikiopoulou, Mock, and Vasilopoulou 2013), our book demonstrates that it actually has a long and recurrent history. For example, we discussed how in the US and England this was how Roman Catholics were historically depicted, and it was how Protestants were historically depicted in France. The relational context of the present day may have changed, but the underlying ethnic myths and symbols remain largely the same.

Alongside these similarities in the three cases, we also found several important differences. These differences were most evident in how the in-group was constructed. Each campaign drew from particular myths and symbols of their nation's dominant ethnic group. As a result, how they depicted the core attributes of the nation's identity were highly context-dependent. For example, in each case the "real" members of the nation were largely seen through the prism of whiteness, but the substantive attributes of this symbol were presented slightly differently. Trump used long-standing Anglo-American myths about the group's inherent greatness, while also focusing on how the white majority has recently been silenced and forgotten. Le Pen picked up on some of these themes about a silenced majority, but she tended to depict the majority as a homogeneous, united, and hard-working group of people being thwarted by malign foreign forces. The Leave campaigners tapped into some similar ideas about how the majority is threatened by foreign elites, but they also used myths about the innate genius of the English as the inventors of parliamentary sovereignty and as world leaders. This was wrapped within a historical idea that this greatness had lately declined, but could be recaptured upon leaving the EU. In France, Le Pen relied upon a much different historical narrative of defeat, paired with myths of historic episodes of resistance in the face of threats to the nation. One of Trump's central messages merged these two themes: arguing that America had once been great but had now declined, and that the white majority needed to take back power to return to greatness. Similar variation is evident in how the campaigns referred to their homeland. Le Pen relied heavily on the notion that the "real" French are in the rural countryside, whereas the Leave campaigns were more focused on presenting Britain as an island fortress. Across the three cases, the unique ethos of the ethnic groups was also rooted in different cultural content. Le Pen reinforced the idea that the French had a great civilizing mission, and that the pillars of republicanism—liberty, equality, and fraternity, along with a strong secularism—were innate French values and principles. The Leave campaigners played up the idea that parliamentary democracy and sovereignty are core to the English spirit. Trump was focused more on how the majority had to, once again, put "America first" to become great again.

These different ways of constructing the in-group were paired with variations on who were depicted as threatening Others. Trump, for instance, repeatedly claimed Mexican migrants were dangerous criminals—drug dealers and rapists—threatening the white majority. For Le Pen, the threatening Others were Muslims, largely from North Africa. For the Leave Campaigners, the term "migrant" was often used to describe hordes of people coming from far-off lands, namely refugees from Syria, Muslims from Turkey, and laborers from southern and eastern Europe. In each case, migrants were seen as a threat in different ways. In the US, migrants were equated with dangerous criminals and terrorists; in France, migration was depicted an existential threat that challenged the homogeneity and secularism of the nation; in the UK, migration—particularly from Turkey—was seen as an unsustainable invasion that would overrun the English and erode their way of life. Of course, the common theme is that migrants were presented as a major cause of each nation's woes. But there is still variation here, as there was in other areas when constructing the out-group. Predictably, race was a more overt boundary mechanism in the US: Trump tweeted about how America's inner cities with high African American populations were rat-infested centers of crime. Le Pen, meanwhile, depicted the suburbs of Paris as lawless zones overrun with terrorists. Whereas in the UK, race was not explicitly linked by the Leave campaigns to perceived ghettoization and crime.

At the same time, Muslims were a commonly perceived foe. They were the clear out-group for each campaign. As we have discussed, the previous antagonism within Christianity and between Christians and Jews is giving way to Muslims as the religious Other. But, even here, context mattered in how the campaigns presented Islam and Muslims. In the US, Trump portrayed Muslims as terrorists—nearly every time he spoke about Islam or Muslims he evoked the threat of terrorism, jihad, or radicalism. Le Pen tapped into the threat of terrorism, but she also relied heavily on the idea that Islam itself was an existential threat to French values. In the UK, the Leave campaigners also stoked fears about how a Muslim invasion would threaten the English way of life, but they were more focused on the sheer size of the Muslim population in places like Turkey, which they said needed to be kept out of the country to protect the health and prosperity of the British people. In short, as with other out-groups, the specific content of the messages varied to fit the context.

In our view, this variation is part of why so many members of the white majorities are responding affirmatively to the new nationalists. We are often quick to identify political messaging that evokes ethnic nationalist ideas, puzzling at how these "dog-whistle," "race-baiting," or "culture war" tactics attract so many people. As others have shown, their discursive form—particularly the use of an "us" versus "them" structure—go some way to helping us understand the success. But we also think that the specific cultural content matters a great deal. It is the context-specific content that enables the messaging to hit the "right wavelength."

This Is Not the End

Many liberals have expressed hope that the years 2016–2021 were an aberration. Nowhere is this view more apparent than in the United States. The 2020 presidential election was billed as the chance to right the wrongs of Donald Trump. In Joe Biden's own words, the election was a battle for the "soul of the nation." For many observers, Biden's victory signaled that the forces of liberalism, democracy, and progressive ideas won in the end. But we have to remember that Trump also promoted the election as a battle for the soul of America (Dias 2020). The 74 million people that voted for Trump show us this battle is far from over. These people voted knowing virtually everything there is to know about the man and his politics. His ethnic nationalism, racism, misogyny, and anti-democratic views were documented, daily, through his tweets and the media coverage those tweets instigated. Our takeaway from the 2020 election is not that it was a capstone on an exceptional period; rather, it showed the continued strength and resonance of the new nationalism in America. The events on January 6, 2021, reinforced this: the Capitol siege was not the dying breath of the ethnic nationalist movement in the US, but rather another example of how much these ideas continue to resonate. If 2020 was a battle for the soul of the nation, it is not clear who won.

The upshot of seeing ethnic nationalism as an endemic feature of politics in the US, and in other nations across the West, is that we cannot just will it into oblivion. It is not going anywhere, at least anytime soon. Ethnic nationalism is recurrent. It is not always the primary mover of politics. Over long periods of time, it can recede into the background. But even when it is far from sight, its ideas remain embedded in our institutions, available for "rediscovery" by enterprising political actors. We have seen how crises can play a powerful role in providing political opportunities for activating these ideas. The heightened uncertainty and the disruption that comes with a crisis can shift the context within which politics occurs, creating conditions that allow new political leaders and movements to gain traction (Brecher 2019; Falleti and Lynch 2009).

The years 2020 and 2021 were defined by crisis. The COVID-19 pandemic is a paradigm-shifting, global public health catastrophe. The sheer scale of the health crisis is, in turn, leading to a cascade of related economic, social, and political crises throughout the world. In short, the COVID-19 pandemic has the potential to upend politics. On this front, we need to remember that COVID-19 emerged into a world where the new nationalism had already taken hold. Whether the pandemic will further deepen, or weaken, nationalism's hold on world politics is still unclear (Woods et al. 2020). That being said, some trends have started to emerge. On one hand, the pandemic has stimulated international collaboration and reinforced the value of liberal international institutions. It has also shone a light on the value of good, stable governance. On the other hand, for many states, COVID-19 has triggered a turn inward. The pandemic has emboldened nation-states: they have strengthened and closed borders, curtailed migration, increased public spending, and enhanced social control over their citizens. Racism and xenophobia—particularly directed at Asians—have risen across the West.

We will not know for some time whether COVID-19 will ultimately amplify existing liberal norms or ethnic nationalism. But we do know that COVID-19 has shown us how quickly things can change in the face of a crisis. Just as ethnic nationalism is endemic to politics in the West, crisis is endemic to politics in general. In our view, these two forces are mutually constitutive and reinforcing. Even if ethnic nationalism is on the wane now, new crises can quickly arise and reinvigorate its appeal.

This being said, we are not convinced that the West has left the current nationalist moment. Just looking across our three cases, there are signals that the new nationalism is still a strong force. In the UK, Brexit has come to pass. British politics now takes place in this new, nationalized context. And within this context, it appears that English nationalism is a strong and growing force. For example, in local elections in 2021, English Leave supporters flocked to the Conservatives, turning away from Labour and reversing previously powerful class divides in order to back the party that delivered Brexit (Ford 2021). In the US, Trump's departure from the White House and social media may be a short-lived reprieve. Trump's influence over the Republican Party in the short term was evident with the ouster of Representative Liz Cheney from the party's leadership following her criticism of Trump's contestation of the 2020 election results (Rogers 2021). While Trump's future electoral fortunes are opaque, deeper fault lines remain. These are most evident in the "culture wars" and debates about "cancel culture" that are hotter than ever in the US. In France, Marine Le Pen is set to run for president again in 2022. One year out from voting, polling shows she could defeat current president Emmanuel Macron in the first round—a historic level of support for the leader and her party (Benoit 2021). But even beyond Le Pen's support, shifts in the political discourse indicate how the new nationalism is shaping French politics. Macron has even adopted a hardline stance defending *laïcité*, positioning himself as a protector of this most French set of values in an attempt to attract Le Pen's supporters (Onishi and Meheut 2021). And even if we are wrong here and ethnic nationalism is receding across the West, this does not mean it will necessarily disappear. It has receded before, many times, only to emerge again.

So, what is to be done? Well, one of the ways to approach this question is to look at what *can* be done.

For those who see economic inequality, political alienation, and anxiety over immigration as the drivers of the new nationalism, a set of clear-headed policy interventions that can weaken the appeal of ethnic nationalism and populism makes sense. Focusing on addressing things that create grievances among ethnic majority groups is certainly a good starting point. Policies that bolster the social safety net and ease the transition into the information-based labor market can reduce inequality. Pilot studies testing the effects of a universal basic income that protects workers from large-scale labor market transitions could help to show these benefits. The massive interventions of governments to support out-of-work people during COVID-19 could open space for these types of programs. A redoubling of efforts to promote transparency and accountability in government institutions could help re-establish connections between the public and their representatives. Brexit, on its face, was largely motivated by the view that Brussels did not represent the interests of British citizens in decision-making. A focus on how immigration can benefit both migrants and the host society through logical, managed, and well-resourced selection and settlement policies can alleviate anxiety about its impact. But these kinds of policies take time to implement, and it is unclear if politicians and parties will be able to generate consensus around their value.

Similarly, those who see the rise of social media as the force driving the new nationalism are pushing for strong regulations. But, as we have tried to show here, simply calling for social media to either banish or control ethnic nationalism and the far right will not solve the problem. Trump's ban from social media does seem to have reduced his exposure in the short term. But it remains to be seen how this will impact his fortunes over the longer term, and there are real democratic concerns with private technology firms having the power to limit public debate. More to the point, technology is not deterministic: it is a tool that humans use toward some other end. While people are (rightly) taking a hard look at the role of Twitter and Facebook as threats to liberal democracy, we should also remember their potential for increasing engagement. Their power to mobilize people can be used for both progressive and regressive purposes. Of course, we could and should regulate platforms to be more responsible for both the data of their users and their content, as we do with more mainstream publishers of information.

This leaves us in a rather bleak place. Large-scale changes like addressing inequality through redistribution take time and can be controversial. Small-scale changes like regulating social media may help, but are not necessarily the answer. But, perhaps even more critically, these kinds of proposals are largely focused on the proximate drivers of the new nationalism. In our view, the path forward for the liberal democracies of the West starts by properly diagnosing the causes and consequences of the new nationalism. While specific policy prescriptions are beyond the scope of our study here, we do think that our analysis sheds some light on the emerging debates about how to respond to the new nationalism and perhaps opens a few new avenues. In short, we hope that our analysis can help us better understand—and thus respond to—ethnic nationalism in the West.

There is an emerging debate about how liberal democracies should respond to the stream of ethnic nationalism we have identified. The first perspective is to combat nationalism by redoubling our commitment to liberal values and a civic identity. Francis Fukuyama's (2018) recent work exemplifies this line of argument. In essence, the approach here is to embrace a patriotism rooted in the institutions, values, and practices of democratic citizenship. The second perspective is to embrace nationalism and take on board the concerns and anxieties of ethnic majority groups. Eric Kaufmann's (2018) defense of white identity exemplifies this position. The approach here calls for controls on immigration, protections for majority group identities, and protectionist economic policies.

In our view, the prudent course of action probably lies somewhere between these arguments. What is likely needed is a politics that acknowledges the deep divides in our political cultures. Simply calling for people to not be nationalists is not going to work. History has shown us its resiliency. At the same time, giving in to the darker, exclusionary tendencies of the ideology can lead to barriers and violence against perceived Others. Progress on human rights and pluralism cannot be washed away in the name of placating an anxious majority.

Regardless of what path we take and what happens next, one of the takeaways from our analysis of the new nationalism is that it is unlikely to fade away entirely. Its myths and symbols have proven to be remarkably resilient. Donald Trump, Marine Le Pen, and the Leave campaigns did not succeed in spite of their use of these ideas; they succeeded in part because they tapped into their power to mobilize the white majorities of the West. As we have shown, this is just the most recent iteration in a long line of recurring upsurges of ethnic nationalism. The new nationalism is not new. It is not going away. This is not the end.

NOTES

Chapter 3

1. The Trump Twitter Archive is available at www.trumptwitterarchive.com; it has been used and cited by numerous popular presses.
2. The tweets were collected using the Rtweet package, with the script written by Alexandre Fortier-Chouniard and Catherine Ouellet from the University of Toronto.
3. These coding frameworks for the US, France, and UK are explained further in the subsequent chapters, with details for each available online through the Harvard Dataverse site at https://dataverse.harvard.edu/dataverse/newnationalism. .
4. The members of our research team who assisted with constructing the frameworks and coding tweets include: Javier Carbonell Castañer, Alexandre Fortier-Chouniard, Fasial Kamal, Catherine Ouellet, and Amedeo Varriale.

Chapter 4

1. These ideas were also combined with a Protestant myth that Anglo-Americans were a "chosen" people, but we will return to this in our discussion of religion.
2. We discuss this mythology in greater detail in chapter 7.
3. However, in the ensuing presidential election, Bush himself also played on white identity by leaning into fears over the "threat" of black criminality in the infamous Willie Horton commercials.

Chapter 5

1. All tweets cited in this chapter are from @realDonaldTrump, using dates and time to indicate when they were sent, as appropriate. The text and supplementary material for all cited and coded tweets in this chapter are available through the supplementary material provided online through the Harvard Dataverse site at https://dataverse.harvard.edu/dataverse/newnationalism. Alternatively, the tweets can be found at www.thetrumparchive.com, following Donald Trump's ban from the platform.
2. As discussed in chapter 3, this number excludes retweets. Each tweet was coded and reviewed by the two authors.
3. The difference between the number of tweets and the number of topics (e.g., an ethnic myth or symbol) reflects Trump's tendency to incorporate numerous themes and topics in a single tweet.
4. Asian Americans make up approximately 6 percent of the US population, but Trump largely ignored them. He only mentioned Asian Americans in two tweets that we can find during the 2016 election (which were about criticizing Jeb Bush).

Chapter 6

1. We are grateful to Javier Carbonell Castañer for his research support and assistance with this section.
2. We use the term "Frenchmen" purposefully. The relationship between French identity and the homeland often reflects a gendered vision of the nation. The territory is referred to as the "fatherland" more often than the "motherland" and the progeny of the land are often seen as Frenchmen.
3. Members from our research team, along with ourselves, coded the tweets using NVivo. We are grateful to Alex Fortier-Chouinard and Catherine Ouellet for their research support and assistance with this work. All coded tweets were reviewed by at least three individuals, always including one of the authors, to increase inter-coder reliability. Supporting material can be found at online through the Harvard Dataverse site at https://dataverse.harvard.edu/dataverse/new nationalism.
4. This excludes retweets. They were captured using an application to access the Twitter API designed by Alex Fortier-Chouinard and Catherine Ouellet, members of our research team from the University of Toronto. All tweets are in French; translations appearing here are the authors'.
5. All tweets cited in this chapter are from @MLP_officiel.

Chapter 7

1. We are grateful to Amedeo Varriale for his research support and assistance with this section.
2. Members from our research team, along with ourselves, coded the tweets using NVivo. We are grateful to Alex Fortier-Chouinard and Catherine Ouellet for their research support and assistance with this work. All coded tweets were reviewed by at least three individuals, always including one of the authors, to increase inter-coder reliability. Supporting material can be found online through the Harvard Dataverse site at https://dataverse.harvard.edu/dataverse/new nationalism.
3. These figures exclude retweets. The totals when including retweets is 5,919 from Vote Leave and 6,772 from Leave.EU. The tweets were captured using an application to access the Twitter API designed by Alex Fortier-Chouinard and Catherine Ouellet, members of our research team from the University of Toronto.
4. Tweets cited in this chapter are from @vote_leave and @LeaveEUOfficial, using the date and time, where applicable. All @vote_leave tweets will be signified by VL, and @LeaveEUOfficial tweets by LEU.
5. The totals do not add up to 100 percent, because some tweets were neutral.

REFERENCES

Aalberg, Toril, Frank Esser, Carsten Reinemann, Jesper Strömbäck, and Claes de Vreese. 2016. *Populist Political Communication in Europe.* New York: Routledge.

Abell, Jackie, Susan Condor, and Clifford Stevenson. 2006. "'We Are an Island:' Geographical Imagery in Accounts of Citizensship, Civil Society, and National Identity in Scotland and England." *Political Psychology* 27 (2): 207–26.

Abizadeh, Arash. 2005. "Was Fichte an Ethnic Nationalist? On Cultural Nationalism and Its Double." *History of Political Thought* 26 (2): 334–59.

Abramitzky, Ran, Leah Boustan, and Katherine Eriksson. 2020. "Do Immigrants Assimilate More Slowly Today Than in the Past?" *American Economic Review: Insights* 2 (1): 125–41. https://doi.org/10.1257/aeri.20190079.

Abramowitz, Alan. 2011. "Partisan Polarization and the Rise of the Tea Party Movement." In *Annual Meeting of the American Political Science Association*, edited by Frances Hagopian and Bonnie Honig. Washington, DC: American Political Science Association.

Abramowitz, Alan. 2018. *The Great Alignment: Race, Party Transformation, and the Rise of Donald Trump.* New Haven, CT: Yale University Press.

Abromeit, John. 2017. "A Critical Review of Recent Literature on Populism." *Politics and Governance* 5 (4): 177–86.

Abts, Koen, and Stefan Rummens. 2007. "Populism versus Democracy." *Political Studies* 55 (2): 405–24.

Ahmadian, Sara, Sara Azarshahi, and Delroy L. Paulhus. 2017. "Explaining Donald Trump via Communication Style: Grandiosity, Informality, and Dynamism." *Personality and Individual Differences* 107 (March): 49–53.

Aisch, Gregor, Matthew Bloch, K. K. Lai, and Benoit Morenne. 2017. "How France Voted." *New York Times*, May 7, 2017.

Alexander, Jeffery. 2002. "On the Social Construction of Moral Universals: The 'Holocaust' from War Crime to Trauma Drama." *European Journal of Social Theory* 5 (1): 5–85. https://doi.org/10.1177/1368431002005001001.

Alexander, Jeffery. 2003. *The Meanings of Social Life: A Cultural Sociology.* Oxford: Oxford University Press.

Allen, Theodore. 1994. *The Invention of the White Race.* London: Verso.

Almeida, Dimitri. 2014. "Decadence and Indifferentiation in the Ideology of the Front National." *French Cultural Studies* 25 (2): 221–32.

Almeida, Dimitri. 2017. "Exclusionary Secularism: The Front National and the Reinvention of Laicite." *Modern and Contemporary France* 25 (3): 249–63.

Alvarez, R. Michael, and Tara L. Butterfield. 2000. "The Resurgence of Nativism in California? The Case of Proposition 187 and Illegal Immigration." *Social Science Quarterly* 81 (1): 167–79.

Amengay, Abdelkarim, Anja Durovic, and Nonna Mayer. 2017. "L'impact Du Genre Sur Le Vote Marine Le Pen." *Revue Française de Science Politique* 67 (6): 1067–87.

Amnesty International. 2018. "Catastrophic Immigration Policies Resulted in More Family Separations than Previously Disclosed." London: Amnesty International, October 11, 2018.

Anderson, Benedict. 2006. *Imagined Communities: Reflections on the Origin and Spread of Nationalism*. 3rd ed. London: Verso Books.

Archard, David. 1995. "Myths, Lies and Historical Truth: A Defence of Nationalism." *Political Studies* 43: 472–81.

Arieli, Yehoshua. 1964. *Individualism and Nationalism in American Ideology*. Cambridge, MA: Harvard University Press.

Armstrong, John Alexander. 1982. *Nations before Nationalism*. Chapel Hill: University of North Carolina Press.

Aughey, Arthur. 2010. "Anxiety and Injustice: The Anatomy of Contemporary English Nationalism." *Nations and Nationalism* 16 (3): 506–24.

Babb, Valerie. 1998. *Whiteness Visible: The Meaning of Whiteness in American Literature*. New York: New York University Press.

Barth, Fredrik. 1969. *Ethnic Groups and Boundaries: The Social Organization of Culture Difference*. Long Grove, IL: Waveland Press.

Bastow, Steve. 2018. "The Front National under Marine Le Pen: A Mainstream Political Party?" *French Politics* 16 (1): 19–37.

Baubérot, Jean. 2004. *Laïcité 1905–2005, Entre Passion et Raison*. Paris: Seuil.

Baubock, Rainer. 2018. "Europe's Commitments and Failures in the Refugee Crisis." *European Political Science* 17 (1): 140–50.

BBC News. 2018. "Brad Parscale: Trump Names 2020 Election Campaign Chief." BBC News, February 27, 2018. https://www.bbc.com/news/world-us-canada-43214457.

Becker, Sascha, Thiemo Fetzer, and Dennis Novy. 2017. "Who Voted for Brexit? A Comprehensive District-Level Analysis." *Economic Policy* 32 (92): 601–50.

Beiner, Ronald. 2018. *Dangerous Minds: Nietzsche, Heidegger, and the Return of the Far Right*. Philadelphia: University of Pennsylvania Press.

Bell, David. 2001. *The Cult of the Nation in France: Inventing Nationalism, 1680–1800*. Cambridge, MA: Harvard University Press.

Benoit, Angeline. 2021. "France's Le Pen Gains Ground for 2022 Elections, Poll Shows." Bloomberg, April 11, 2021. https://www.bloomberg.com/news/articles/2021-04-11/france-s-le-pen-gains-ground-for-2022-elections-poll-shows.

Berberich, Christine. 2006. "This Green and Pleasant Land: Cultural Constructions of Englishness." In *Landscape and Englishness*, edited by Robert Burden and Stephan Kohl, 207–24. Amsterdam: Rodopi BV.

Bessi, Alessandro, and Emilio Ferrara. 2016. "Social Bots Distort the 2016 U.S. Presidential Election Online Discussion." *First Monday*, November 2016. https://doi.org/10.5210/fm.v21i11.7090.

Betz, Hans-Georg. 2018. "The New Front National: Still a Master Case?" In *Diversity and Contestation over Nationalism in Europe and Canada*, edited by John Fossum, Riva Kastoryano, and Birte Siim, 313–36. London: Palgrave Macmillan.

Bieber, Florian. 2018. "Is Nationalism on the Rise? Assessing Global Trends." *Ethnopolitics* 17 (5): 519–49.

Billig, Michael. 1995. *Banal Nationalism*. London: SAGE.

Black, Jack. 2019. "From Mood to Movement: English Nationalism, the European Union and Taking Back Control." *Innovation: The European Journal of Social Research* 32 (2): 191–210.

Blight, David. 2009. *Race and Reunion*. Cambridge, MA: Harvard University Press.

Blum, Edward. 2015. *Reforging the White Republic: Race, Religion, and American Nationalism*. Baton Rouge: LSU Press.

Blyer, David. 2020. "Trump Shocked the World with His Latino Support. Here's How It Happened." *Washington Post*, November 12, 2020.

REFERENCES

Bonacchi, Chiara, Mark Altaweel, and Marta Krzyzanska. 2018. "The Heritage of Brexit: Roles of the Past in the Construction of Political Identities through Social Media." *Journal of Social Archaeology* 18 (2): 174–92. https://doi.org/10.1177/1469605318759713.

Bonikowski, Bart. 2017. "Ethno-Nationalist Populism and the Mobilization of Collective Resentment." *British Journal of Sociology* 68 (S1): 181–213.

Bonikowski, Bart, and Paul DiMaggio. 2016. "Varieties of American Popular Nationalism." *American Sociological Review* 81 (5): 949–80.

Bonikowski, Bart, and Noam Gidron. 2016. "The Populist Style in American Politics: Presidential Campaign Discourse, 1952–1996." *Social Forces* 94 (4): 1593–621.

Bonnett, Alastair. 1998. "How the British Working Class Became White: The Symbolic (Re)Formation of Racialized Capitalism." *Journal of Historical Sociology* 11 (3): 316–40.

Bonnett, Alastair. 2003. "From White to Western: 'Racial Decline' and the Idea of the West in Britain, 1890–1930." *Journal of Historical Sociology* 16 (3): 320–48.

Bouchard, Gérard, ed. 2013. *National Myths: Constructed Pasts, Contested Presents*. London: Routledge.

Bouchard, Gérard. 2017. *Social Myths and Collective Imaginaries*. Toronto: University of Toronto Press.

Bouie, Jamelle. 2020. "The Myth of Trump's Political Genius, Exposed." *New York Times*, October 7, 2020.

Brah, Avtar. 2005. *Cartographies of Diaspora: Contesting Identities*. London: Routledge.

Brass, Paul. 1991. *Ethnicity and Nationalism: Theory and Comparison*. London: SAGE.

Brecher, Michael. 2019. *Crisis and Change in World Politics*. New York: Routledge.

Breen, T. H. 1997. "Ideology and Nationalism on the Eve of the American Revolution: Revisions Once More in Need of Revising." *Journal of American History* 84 (1): 13–39. https://doi.org/10.2307/2952733.

Breeze, Ruth. 2020. "Exploring Populist Styles of Political Discourse in Twitter." *World Englishes* 39 (4): 550–67. https://doi.org/10.1111/weng.12496.

Breuilly, John. 1993. *Nationalism and the State*. Manchester, UK: Manchester University Press.

Breuilly, John. 2005. "Dating the Nation: How Old Is an Old Nation?" In *When Is the Nation? Towards an Understanding of Theories of Nationalism*, edited by Atsuko Ichijo and Gordana Uzelac, 15–39. London: Routledge.

Brodkin, Karen. 1998. *How Jews Became White Folks and What That Says about Race in America*. New Brunswick, NJ: Rutgers University Press.

Brubaker, Rogers. 1992. *Citizenship and Nationhood in France and Germany*. Cambridge, MA: Harvard University Press.

Brubaker, Rogers. 1999. "The Manichean Myth: Rethinking the Distinction between 'Civic' and 'Ethnic' Nationalism." In *Nation and National Identity: The European Experience in Perspective*, edited by Hanspeter Kriesi, Klaus Armingeon, Hannes Slegrist, and Andreas Wimmer, 55–72. Zurich: Ruegger.

Brubaker, Rogers. 2004. *Ethnicity without Groups*. Cambridge, MA: Harvard University Press.

Brubaker, Rogers. 2017. "Between Nationalism and Civilizationalism: The European Populist Moment in Comparative Perspective." *Ethnic and Racial Studies* 40 (8): 1191–1226.

Brubaker, Rogers, Margit Feischmidt, Jon Fox, and Liana Grancea. 2006. *Nationalist Politics in and Everyday Ethnicity in a Transylvanian Town*. Princeton, NJ: Princeton University Press.

Bruns, Axel, Gunn Enli, Eli Skogerbø, Anders Olof Larsson, and Christian Christensen. 2015. *The Routledge Companion to Social Media and Politics*. New York: Routledge. https://doi.org/10.4324/9781315716299.

Buchanan, Patrick. 2011. *Suicide of a Superpower: Will America Survive to 2025?* New York: Thomas Dunne Books.

Bucy, Erik P., Jordan M. Foley, Josephine Lukito, Larissa Doroshenko, Dhavan V. Shah, Jon C.W. Pevehouse, and Chris Wells. 2020. "Performing Populism: Trump's Transgressive Debate Style and the Dynamics of Twitter Response." *New Media and Society* 22 (4): 634–58. https://doi.org/10.1177/1461444819893984.

Bump, Philip. 2020a. "Over and Over, Trump Has Focused on Black Lives Matter as a Target of Derision and Violence." *Washington Post*, September 1, 2020.

Bump, Philip. 2020b. "Donald Trump Doesn't Really Care about the White Supremacist Threat, and You're Not Going to Make Him." *Washington Post*, September 30, 2020.

Byrne, Bridget. 2007. "England—Whose England? Narratives of Nostalgia, Emptiness and Evasion in Imaginations of National Identity." *Sociological Review* 55 (3): 509–30.

Calhoun, Craig. 2017. "Populism, Nationalism and Brexit." In *Brexit: Sociological Responses*, edited by William Outhwaite, 57–76. London: Anthem Press.

Capoccia, Giovanni, and R. Daniel Kelemen. 2007. "The Study of Critical Junctures: Theory, Narrative, and Counterfactuals in Historical Institutionalism." *World Politics* 59 (3): 341–69.

Carreras, Miguel, Yasemin Irepoglu Carreras, and Shaun Bowler. 2019. "Long-Term Economic Distress, Cultural Backlash, and Support for Brexit." *Comparative Political Studies* 52 (9): 1396–1424.

Cave, Alfred. 2003. "Abuse of Power: Andrew Jackson and the Indian Removal Act of 1830." *The Historian* 65 (6): 1330–53. https://doi.org/10.1111/j.0018-2370.2003.00055.x.

Checkel, Jeffrey. 1998. "The Constructive Turn in International Theory." *World Politics* 50 (2): 324–48.

Choi, Matthew. 2020. "'She's Telling Us How to Run Our Country': Trump Again Goes after Ilhan Omar's Somali Roots." *Politico*, September 22, 2020. https://www.politico.com/news/2020/09/22/trump-attacks-ilhan-omar-420267.

Cineas, Fabiola, and Anna North. 2020. "We Need to Talk about the White People Who Voted for Donald Trump." *Vox*, November 7, 2020. https://www.vox.com/2020/11/7/21551364/white-trump-voters-2020.

Coaston, Jane. 2019. "Trump's New Defense of His Charlottesville Comments Is Incredibly False." *Vox*, April 26, 2019. https://www.vox.com/2019/4/26/18517980/trump-unite-the-right-racism-defense-charlottesville.

Cohen, Stanley. 1972. *Folk Devils and Moral Panics: The Creation of the Mods and Rockers*. London: Psychology Press.

Colantone, Italo, and Piero Stanig. 2018. "Global Competition and Brexit." *American Political Science Review* 112 (2): 201–18.

Colley, Linda. 1992. *Britons: Forging the Nation 1707–1837*. New Haven, CT: Yale University Press.

Conklin, Alice. 2005. *A Mission to Civilize: The Republican Idea of Empire in France and West Africa*. Stanford, CA: Stanford University Press.

Connor, Dylan Shane. 2019. "The Cream of the Crop? Geography, Networks, and Irish Migrant Selection in the Age of Mass Migration." *Journal of Economic History* 79 (1): 139–75.

Connor, Walker. 1994. *Ethnonationalism: The Quest for Understanding*. Princeton, NJ: Princeton University Press.

Crowder, Kyle, Matthew Hall, and Stewart E. Tolnay. 2011. "Neighborhood Immigration and Native Out-Migration." *American Sociological Review* 76 (1): 25–47.

Curiel, Concha Pérez. 2020. "Trend towards Extreme Right-Wing Populism on Twitter: An Analysis of the Influence on Leaders, Media and Users." *Communication and Society* 33 (2): 175–92. https://doi.org/10.15581/003.33.2.175-192.

Daily Kos. 2009. "Birther Americans Are Mostly Republican and Southern." *Daily Kos*, July 31, 2009. https://www.dailykos.com/stories/2009/7/31/760087/-.

Davies, Peter. 1999. *The National Front in France: Ideology, Discourse and Power*. New York: Routledge.

Davies, Peter. 2002. *The Extreme Right in France, 1789 to the Present: From de Maistre to Le Pen*. New York: Routledge.

Davies, Rees. 1998. *The First English Empire: Power and Identities in the British Isles, 1093–1343*. Oxford: Oxford University Press.

DeClair, Edward. 1999. *Politics on the Fringe: The People, Policies, and Organization of the French Front National*. Durham, NC: Duke University Press.

Della Posta, Daniel. 2013. "Immigration and the Front National: Competitive Threat, Intergroup Contact, or Both?" *Social Forces* 92 (1): 249–73.

REFERENCES

Deutsch, Karl. 1966. *Nationalism and Social Communication: An Inquiry into the Foundations of Nationality.* Cambridge, MA: MIT Press.

Dias, Elizabth. 2020. "Biden and Trump Say They're Fighting for America's 'Soul.' What Does That Mean?" *New York Times*, October 20, 2020.

Dietler, Michael. 1994. "'Our Ancestors the Gauls': Archaeology, Ethnic Nationalism, and the Manipulation of Celtic Identity in Modern Europe." *American Anthropologist* 96 (3): 584–605.

Doane, Ashley W. 1997. "Dominant Group Ethnic Identity in the United States: The Role of 'Hidden' Ethnicity in Intergroup Relations." *Sociological Quarterly* 38 (3): 375–97.

Doane, Ashley W. 2003. "Rethinking Whiteness Studies." In *White Out: The Continuing Significance of Racism*, edited by Ashley W. Doane and Eduardo Bonilla-Silva, 3–20. New York: Routledge.

Douglass, Frederick. 2000. *Frederick Douglass: Selected Speeches and Writings.* Edited by Philip Foner and Yuval Taylor. Chicago: Chicago Review Press.

Draper, Robert. 2018. "The Man behind the President's Tweets." *New York Times Magazine*, April 16, 2018. https://www.nytimes.com/2018/04/16/magazine/dan-scavino-the-secretary-of-offense.html.

Du Bois, W. E. B. 1935. *Reconstruct Democracy in America 1860–1880.* New York: Free Press.

Durkheim, Émile. 2001. *The Elementary Forms of Religious Life.* New York: The Free Press.

Eatwell, Roger, and Matthew Goodwin. 2018. *National Populism: The Revolt against Liberal Democracy.* London: Pelican.

The Economist. 2016. "Trump's World: The New Nationalism." *The Economist*, November 19, 2016. https://www.economist.com/leaders/2016/11/19/the-new-nationalism.

Edensor, Tim. 2002. *National Identity, Popular Culture and Everyday Life.* New York: Routledge.

Edison Research/CNN. 2016. "2016 Election Results: Exit Polls." CNN, 2016. http://www.cnn.com/election/2016/results/exit-polls.

Edison Research/CNN. 2020. "2020 Exit Polls." https://www.cnn.com/election/2020/exit-polls/president/national-results. CNN, 2020.

Engesser, Sven, Nicole Ernst, Frank Esser, and Florin Büchel. 2017. "Populism and Social Media: How Politicians Spread a Fragmented Ideology." *Information, Communication & Society* 20 (8): 1109–26.

Enli, Gunn. 2017. "Twitter as Arena for the Authentic Outsider: Exploring the Social Media Campaigns of Trump and Clinton in the 2016 US Presidential Election." *European Journal of Communication* 32 (1): 50–61.

Ernst, Nicole, Sven Engesser, Florin Büchel, Sina Blassnig, and Frank Esser. 2017. "Extreme Parties and Populism: An Analysis of Facebook and Twitter across Six Countries." *Information Communication and Society* 20 (9): 1347–64. https://doi.org/10.1080/1369118X.2017.1329333.

Falleti, Tulia, and Julia Lynch. 2009. "Context and Causal Mechanisms in Political Analysis." *Comparative Political Studies* 42 (9): 1143–66.

Farrell, Robert. 2019. "No Foreign Despots on Southern Soil: The Know-Nothing Party in Alabama, 1850–1857." *Alabama Review* 72 (2): 99–122. https://doi.org/10.1353/ala.2019.0001.

Farris, Sara. 2017. *In the Name of Women's Rights: The Rise of Femonationalism.* Durham, NC: Duke University Press.

FiveThirtyEight. 2021. "How (Un)Popular Is Donald Trump?" FiveThirtyEight, January 21, 2021. https://projects.fivethirtyeight.com/trump-approval-ratings/.

Foner, Eric. 1988. *Reconstruction: America's Unfinished Revolution, 1863–1877.* New York: Harper & Row.

Ford, Robert. 2021. "Labour Wants to Move on from Brexit, but English Voters Just Won't Let Them." *The Guardian*, May 9, 2021.

Fortin, Jacey. 2017. "The Statue at the Centre of Charlottesville's Storm." *New York Times*, August 13, 2017.

Fox, Jon. 2014. "National Holiday Commemorations: The View from Below." In *The Cultural Politics of Nationalism and Nation-Building: Ritual and Performance in the Forging of Nations*, edited by Rachel Tsang and Eric Taylor Woods, 38–54. London: Routledge.

Fox, Jon, and Cynthia Miller-Idriss. 2008. "Everyday Nationhood." *Ethnicities* 8 (4): 536–76.

Freeden, Michael. 1996. *Ideologies and Political Theory: A Conceptual Approach*. Oxford: Oxford University Press.

Freeden, Michael. 1998. "Is Nationalism a Distinct Ideology?" *Political Studies* 46 (4): 748–65.

Freeden, Michael. 2017. "After the Brexit Referendum: Revisiting Populism as an Ideology." *Journal of Political Ideologies* 22 (1): 1–11.

Fukuyama, Francis. 1992. *The End of History and the Last Man*. New York: Free Press.

Fukuyama, Francis. 2018. *Identity: The Demand for Dignity and the Politics of Resentment*. New York: Farrar, Straus and Giroux.

Gallup. n.d. "Presidential Approval Ratings—Donald Trump." https://news.gallup.com/poll/203198/presidential-approval-ratings-donald-trump.aspx.

Garner, Steve. 2012. "A Moral Economy of Whiteness: Behaviors, Belonging and Britishness." *Ethnicities* 12 (4): 445–64.

Gat, Azar. 2012. *Nations: The Long History and Deep Roots of Political Ethnicity and Nationalism*. Cambridge: Cambridge University Press.

Geertz, Clifford. 1973. *The Interpretation of Cultures: Selected Essays*. New York: Basic Books.

Gellner, Ernest. 1983. *Nations and Nationalism*. Oxford: Blackwell.

Gellner, Ernest. 1996. "Do Nations Have Navels?" *Nations and Nationalism* 2 (3): 366–70.

Gerbaudo, Paolo. 2012. *Tweets and the Streets: Social Media and Contemporary Activism*. London: Pluto Press.

Gerbaudo, Paolo. 2014. "Populism 2.0: Social Media Activism, the Generic Internet User and Interactive Direct Democracy." In *Social Media, Politics and the State*, edited by Daniel Trottier and Chrstian Fuchs, 67–87. New York: Routledge.

Gerbaudo, Paolo. 2018. "Social Media and Populism: An Elective Affinity?" *Media, Culture and Society* 40 (5): 745–53.

Gerstle, Gary. 1999. "Theodore Roosevelt and the Divided Character of American Nationalism." *Journal of American History* 86 (3): 1280–1307.

Gerstle, Gary. 2017. *American Crucible: Race and Nation in the Twentieth Century*. Princeton, NJ: Princeton University Press.

Geruso, Michael, Dean Spears, and Ishaana Talesara. 2019. "Inversions in US Presidential Elections: 1836–2016." Working Paper 26247. Cambridge, MA: National Bureau of Economic Research.

Geva, Dorit. 2020. "Daughter, Mother, Captain: Marine Le Pen, Gender, and Populism in the French National Front." *Social Politics: International Studies in Gender, State and Society* 27 (1): 1–26.

Ghaill, Mairtin. 2000. "The Irish in Britain: The Invisibility of Ethnicity and Anti-Irish Racism." *Journal of Ethnic and Migration Studies* 26 (1): 137–47.

Giddens, Anthony. 1986. *The Nation-State and Violence*. Berkeley: University of California Press.

Gilroy, Paul. 2005. *Postcolonial Melancholia*. New York: Columbia University Press.

Goldfarb, Zachary. 2006. "Va. Lawmaker's Remarks on Muslims Criticized." *Washington Post*, December 21, 2006.

Goldstein, Jared. 2018. "Unfit for the Constitution: Nativism and the Constitution, from the Founding Fathers to Donald Trump." *University of Pennsylvania Journal of Constitutional Law* 20 (3): 489–560.

Gómez, Laura. 2018. *Manifest Destinies: The Making of the Mexican American Race*. New York: New York University Press.

Gomez, Raul. 2015. "The Economy Strikes Back: Support for the EU during the Great Recession." *Journal of Common Market Studies* 53 (3): 577–92.

Gonawela, A'ndre, Joyojeet Pal, Udit Thawani, Elmer van der Vlugt, Wim Out, and Priyank Chandra. 2018. "Speaking Their Mind: Populist Style and Antagonistic Messaging in the

Tweets of Donald Trump, Narendra Modi, Nigel Farage, and Geert Wilders." *Computer Supported Cooperative Work: CSCW: An International Journal* 27 (3–6): 293–326. https://doi.org/10.1007/s10606-018-9316-2.

Goodwin, Matthew, and Oliver Heath. 2016. "The 2016 Referendum, Brexit and the Left Behind: An Aggregate-Level Analysis of the Result." *Political Quarterly* 87 (3): 323–32.

Goodwin, Matthew, and Caitlin Milazzo. 2017. "Taking Back Control? Investigating the Role of Immigration in the 2016 Vote for Brexit." *British Journal of Politics and International Relations* 19 (3): 450–64.

Gorski, Philip S. 2000. "The Mosaic Moment: An Early Modernist Critique of Modernist Theories of Nationalism." *American Journal of Sociology* 10 (5): 1428–68.

Gougou, Florent, and Simon Perisco. 2017. "A New Party System in the Making? The 2017 French Presidential Election." *French Politics* 15 (1): 303–21.

Grant, Susan Mary. 2012. *A Concise History of the United States of America*. Cambridge: Cambridge University Press.

Greenfeld, Liah. 1992. *Nationalism: Five Roads to Modernity*. Cambridge, MA: Harvard University Press.

Greenfeld, Liah. 2019. *Nationalism: A Short History*. Washington, DC: Brookings Institution Press.

Grosby, Steven. 2002. *Biblical Ideas of Nationality: Ancient and Modern*. Winona Lake, IN: Eisenbrauns.

Groshek, Jacob, and Karolina Koc-Michalska. 2017. "Helping Populism Win? Social Media Use, Filter Bubbles, and Support for Populist Presidential Candidates in the 2016 US Election Campaign." *Information Communication and Society* 20 (9): 1389–1407. https://doi.org/10.1080/1369118X.2017.1329334.

Guild, Elspeth, Cathryn Costello, Madeline Garlick, and Violeta Moreno-Lax. 2015. "The 2015 Refugee Crisis in the European Union." Policy Brief. Brussels: Centre for European Policy Studies.

Gunn, Jeremy. 2004. "Religious Freedom and *Laicite*: A Comparison of the United States and France." *Brigham Young University Law Review* 2: 419–506.

Gunn, Jeremy. 2005. "French Secularism at Utopia and Myth." *Houston Law Review* 42 (1): 81–102.

Haag, Matthew. 2019. "Thousands of Immigrant Children Said They Were Sexually Abused in U.S. Detention Centers, Report Says." *New York Times*, February 27, 2019. https://www.nytimes.com/2019/02/27/us/immigrant-children-sexual-abuse.html.

Habermas, Jurgen. 2012. "The Crisis of the European Union in the Light of a Constitutionalization of International Law." *European Journal of International Law* 23 (2): 335–48.

Hainsworth, Paul. 2008. *The Extreme Right in Western Europe*. New York: Routledge.

Halcoussis, Dennis, Anton Lowenberg, and Michael Phillips. 2019. "An Empirical Test of the Comey Effect on the 2016 Presidential Election." *Social Science Quarterly* 101 (1): 161–71.

Halikiopoulou, Daphne. 2018. "A Right-Wing Populist Moment? A Review of the 2017 Elections across Europe." *Journal of Common Market Studies* 56: 63–73.

Halikiopoulou, Daphne, Steven Mock, and Sofia Vasilopoulou. 2013. "The Civic Zeitgeist: Nationalism and Liberal Values in the European Radical Right." *Nations and Nationalism* 19 (1): 107–27.

Halikiopoulou, Daphne, and Tim Vlandas. 2019. "What Is New and What Is Nationalist about Europe's New Nationalism? Explaining the Rise of the Far Right in Europe." *Nations and Nationalism* 25 (2): 409–34.

Hall, Peter A., and Rosemary C. R. Taylor. 1996. "Political Science and the Three New Institutionalisms." *Political Studies* 44 (5): 936–57.

Hameleers, M. 2018. "A Typology of Populism: Toward a Revised Theoretical Framework on the Sender Side and Receiver Side of Communication." *International Journal of Communication* 12: 20.

Hancock, Ange-Marie. 2004. *The Politics of Disgust: The Public Identity of the Welfare Queen*. New York: New York University Press.

Hänska, Max, and Stefan Bauchowitz. 2017. "Tweeting Brexit: How Social Media Influenced the Referendum." In *Brexit, Trump and the Media*, edited by John Mair, Tor Clark, Neil Fowler, Raymond Snoddy, and Richard Tait, 31–35. Bury St. Edmunds, UK: Abramis Academic Publishing.

Hartz, Louis. 1955. *The Liberal Tradition in America: An Interpretation of American Political Thought since the Revolution*. Boston: Houghton Mifflin Harcourt.

Haseler, Stephen. 1996. *The English Tribe: Identity, Nation and Europe*. London: Macmillan.

Hastings, Adrian. 1997. *The Construction of Nationhood: Ethnicity, Religion and Nationalism*. Cambridge: Cambridge University Press.

Hawkins, Kirk, Ryan Carlin, Levente Littvay, and Cristóbal Rovira Kaltwasser. 2019. *The Ideational Approach to Populism: Concept, Theory and Analysis*. New York: Routledge.

Hawkins, Kirk, and Levente Littvay. 2019. *Contemporary US Populism in Comparative Perspective*. Cambridge: Cambridge University Press.

Hawkins, Kirk, and Cristóbal Rovira Kaltwasser. 2019. "Introduction: The Ideational Approach." In *The Ideational Approach to Populism*, edited by Kirk Hawkins, Ryan Carlin, Levente Littvay, and Cristóbal Rovira Kaltwasser, 1–25. New York: Routledge.

Hearn, Jonathan. 2017. "Vox Populi: Nationalism, Globalization and the Balance of Power in the Making of Brexit." In *Brexit: Sociological Responses*, edited by William Outhwaite, 19–30. Cambridge: Cambridge University Press.

Hechter, Michael. 1995. "Explaining Nationalist Violence." *Nations and Nationalism* 1 (1): 53–68.

Heimert, Alan. 1966. *Religion and the American Mind: From the Great Awakening to the Revolution*. Cambridge: Harvard University Press.

Hemmer, Nicole. 2016. *Messengers of the Right: Conservative Media and the Transformation of American Politics*. Philadelphia: University of Pennsylvania Press.

Henderson, Ailsa, Charlie Jeffery, Dan Wincott, and Richard Wyn Jones. 2017. "How Brexit Was Made in England." *British Journal of Politics and International Relations* 19 (4): 631–46.

Henderson, Ailsa, and Richard Wyn Jones. 2021. *Englishness: The Political Force Transforming Britain*. Oxford: Open University Press.

Hickman, Mary. 1995. "The Irish in Britain: Racism, Incorporation and Identity." *Irish Studies Review* 3 (10): 16–19.

Hickman, Mary, Sarah Morgan, Bronwyn Walter, and Joseph Bradley. 2005. "The Limitations of Whiteness and the Boundaries of Englishness: Second-Generation Irish Identifications and Positionings in Multiethnic Britain." *Ethnicities* 5 (2): 160–82.

Higham, John. 2002. *Strangers in the Land: Patterns of American Nativism, 1860–1925*. New Brunswick, NJ: Rutgers University Press.

Hill, Christopher. 1997. "The Norman Yoke." In *Puritanism and Revolution*, edited by Christopher Hill, 46–111. New York: Palgrave Macmillan.

Hill, James. 2019. "The War on Black Athletes." *The Atlantic*, January 13, 2019.

Hobsbawm, Eric. 1990. *Nations and Nationalism since 1780: Programme, Myth, Reality*. Cambridge: Cambridge University Press.

Hobsbawm, Eric, and Terence Ranger. 1983. *The Invention of Tradition*. Cambridge: Cambridge University Press.

Hochschild, Arlie. 2016. *Strangers in Their Own Land: Anger and Mourning on the American Right*. New York: The New Press.

Hofstadter, Richard. 1955. *The Age of Reform: From Bryan to F.D.R.* New York: Vintage Books.

Holan, Angie. 2019. "In Context: Donald Trump's 'Very Fine People on Both Sides' Remarks." *Politifact*, April 26, 2019. https://www.politifact.com/article/2019/apr/26/context-trumps-very-fine-people-both-sides-remarks/.

Horsman, Reginald. 1986. *Race and Manifest Destiny: The Origins of American Racial Anglo-Saxonism*. Cambridge, MA: Harvard University Press.

Hunt, Alfred. 2006. *Haiti's Influence on Antebellum America: Slumbering Volcano in the Caribbean*. Baton Rouge: LSU Press.

Hutchins, Rachel, and Daphne Halikiopoulou. 2018. "Enemies of Liberty? Nationalism, Immigration, and the Framing of Terrorism in the Agenda of the Front National." *Nations and Nationalism* 26 (1): 67–84.

Hutchinson, John. 1987. *Dynamics of Cultural Nationalism: The Gaelic Revival and the Creation of the Irish Nation State*. London: Routledge.

Hutchinson, John. 2005. *Nations as Zones of Conflict*. Thousand Oaks, CA: SAGE.

Hutchinson, John. 2017. *Nationalism and War*. Oxford: Oxford University Press.

Ignatiev, Noel. 1995. *How the Irish Became White*. Cambridge: Cambridge University Press.

Inglehart, Ronald, and Pippa Norris. 2016. "Trump, Brexit and the Rise of Populism: Economic Have-Nots and Cultural Backlash." HKS Working Paper RWP16-026. Cambridge, MA: Harvard Kennedy School.

Ivaldi, Gilles, and Maria Lanzone. 2016. "The French Front National: Organizational Change and Adaptation from Jean-Marie to Marine Le Pen." In *Understanding Populist Party Organization*, edited by Reinhard Heinisch and Oscar Mazzoleni, 131–58. London: Palgrave Macmillan.

Ivarsflaten, Elisabeth. 2008. "What Unites Right-Wing Populists in Western Europe?: Re-examining Grievance Mobilization Models in Seven Successful Cases." *Comparative Political Studies* 41 (1): 3–23.

Jacobson, Mattew Frye. 1999. *Whiteness of a Different Color: European Immigrants and the Alchemy of Race*. Cambridge, MA: Harvard University Press.

Jagers, Jan, and Stefaan Walgrave. 2007. "Populism as Political Communication Style: An Empirical Study of Political Parties' Discourse in Belgium." *European Journal of Political Research* 46 (3): 319–45.

Jamal, Amaney. 2008. *Civil Liberties and the Otherization of Arab and Muslim Americans*. Edited by Amaney Jamal and Nadine Naber. Syracuse, NY: Syracuse University Press.

Jamieson, Kathleen, and Joseph Cappella. 2008. *Echo Chamber: Rush Limbaugh and the Conservative Media Establishment*. Oxford: Oxford University Press.

Jardina, Ashley, and Michael Traugott. 2019. "The Genesis of the Birther Rumor: Partisanship, Racial Attitudes, and Political Knowledge." *Journal of Race, Ethnicity and Politics* 4 (1): 60–80. https://doi.org/10.1017/rep.2018.25.

Johnson, Jenna, and Abigail Hauslohner. 2017. "'I Think Islam Hates Us': A Timeline of Trump's Comments about Islam and Muslims." *Washington Post*, May 20, 2017.

Jones, Jeffrey. 2017. "Race, Education, Gender Key Factors in Trump Job Approval." Gallup, March 13, 2017.

Jones, Jeffrey. 2019a. "Non-College Whites Had Affinity for GOP before Trump." Gallup, April 12, 2019.

Jones, Jeffrey. 2019b. "Subgroup Differences in Trump Approval Mostly Party-Based." Gallup, March 29, 2019.

Jones, Rhys, and Peter Merriman. 2009. "Hot, Banal and Everyday Nationalism: Bilingual Road Signs in Wales." *Political Geography* 28 (3): 164–73.

Judis, John B. 2016. *The Populist Explosion: How the Great Recession Transformed American and European Politics*. New York: Columbia Global Reports.

Juge, Tony, and Michael Perez. 2006. "The Modern Colonial Politics of Citizenship and Whiteness in France." *Social Identities* 12 (2): 187–212.

Jusdanis, Gregory. 2001. *The Necessary Nation*. Princeton, NJ: Princeton University Press.

Kaldor, Mary. 2004. "Nationalism and Globalization." *Nations and Nationalism* 10 (1–2): 161–77.

Kandel, William. 2018. *The Trump Administration's 'Zero Tolerance' Immigration Enforcement Policy*. CRS Report R45266. Washington, DC: Congressional Research Service.

Kastor, Peter. 2008. *The Nation's Crucible: The Louisiana Purchase and the Creation of America*. New Haven, CT: Yale University Press.

Kaufmann, Eric. 1999. "American Exceptionalism Reconsidered: Anglo-Saxon Ethnogenesis in the 'Universal' Nation, 1776–1850." *Journal of American Studies* 33 (3): 437–57. https://doi.org/10.1017/S0021875899006180.

Kaufmann, Eric. 2004a. "Dominant Ethnicity: From Background to Foreground." In *Rethinking Ethnicity: Majority Groups and Dominant Minorities*, 1–12. London: Routledge.

Kaufmann, Eric. 2004b. *The Rise and Fall of Anglo-America*. Cambridge, MA: Harvard University Press.

Kaufmann, Eric. 2018. *Whiteshift: Populism, Immigration and the Future of White Majorities*. New York: Abrams.

Kaufmann, Eric, and Oded Haklai. 2008. "Dominant Ethnicity: From Minority to Majority." *Nations and Nationalism* 14 (4): 743–67.

Kendi, Ibram X. 2016. *Stamped from the Beginning: The Definitive History of Racist Ideas in America*. New York: Bold Type Books.

Kenny, Michael. 2014. *The Politics of English Nationhood*. Oxford: Oxford University Press.

Kenny, Michael. 2016. "The Genesis of English Nationalism." *Political Insight* 7 (2): 8–11.

Knott, Eleanor. 2015. "Everyday Nationalism: A Review of the Literature." *Studies on National Movements* 3.

Kohn, Hans. 1944. *The Idea of Nationalism: A Study of Its Origins and Background*. New York: Macmillan.

Kolchin, Peter. 2002. "Whiteness Studies: The New History of Race in America." *Journal of American History* 89 (1): 154–73.

Korteweg, Anna, and Gokce Yurdakul. 2014. *The Headscarf Debates: Conflicts of National Belonging*. Stanford, CA: Stanford University Press.

Krämer, Benjamin. 2017. "Populist Online Practices: The Function of the Internet in Right-Wing Populism." *Information Communication and Society* 20 (9): 1293–1309. https://doi.org/10.1080/1369118X.2017.1328520.

Kreis, Ramona. 2017. "The 'Tweet Politics' of President Trump." *Journal of Language and Politics* 16 (4): 607–18.

Krieg, Gregory. 2016. "It's Official: Clinton Swamps Trump in Popular Vote." CNN, December 22, 2016.

Kumar, Krishan. 2003. *The Making of English National Identity*. Cambridge: Cambridge University Press.

Kumar, Krishan. 2015. *The Idea of Englishness: English Culture, National Identity and Social Thought*. New York: Routledge.

Kuzio, Taras. 2002. "The Myth of the Civic State: A Critical Survey of Hans Kohn's Framework for Understanding Nationalism." *Ethnic and Racial Studies* 25 (1): 20–39.

Lacatus, Corina. 2019. "Populism and the 2016 American Election: Evidence from Official Press Releases and Twitter." *PS - Political Science and Politics* 52 (2): 223–28. https://doi.org/10.1017/S104909651800183X.

Lacatus, Corina. 2021. "Populism and President Trump's Approach to Foreign Policy: An Analysis of Tweets and Rally Speeches." *Politics* 41 (1): 31–47. https://doi.org/10.1177/0263395720935380.

Laforest, Guy, and Janique Dubois. 2017. "Justin Trudeau and Reconciliatory Federalism." *Policy Options*, June 19, 2017.

Lajevardi, Nazita, and Kassra Oskooii. 2018. "Old-Fashioned Racism, Contemporary Islamophobia, and the Isolation of Muslim Americans in the Age of Trump." *Journal of Race, Ethnicity and Politics* 3 (SP1): 112–52.

Laughlin, Jim Mac. 1999. "'Pestilence on Their Backs, Famine in Their Stomachs': The Racial Construction of Irishness and the Irish in Victorian Britain." In *Ireland and Cultural Theory*, edited by Colin Graham and Richard Kirkland, 50–76. London: Palgrave Macmillan.

Lecours, Andre, ed. 2005. *New Institutionalism: Theory and Analysis*. Toronto: University of Toronto Press.

Lecours, Andre, and Genevieve Nootens. 2009. *Dominant Nationalism, Dominant Ethnicity: Identity, Federalism and Democracy*. Brussels: P.I.E.-Peter Lang.

Leddy-Owen, Charles. 2013. "It Sounds Unwelcoming, It Sounds Exclusive, but I Think It's Just a Question of Arithmetic Really." *Sociological Research Online* 18 (3): 42–51.

REFERENCES

Leddy-Owen, Charles. 2014. "Reimagining Englishness: 'Race,' Class, Progressive English Identities and Disrupted English Communities." *Sociology* 48 (6): 1123–38.

Lee, Jayeon, and Young-shin Lim. 2016. "Gendered Campaign Tweets: The Cases of Hillary Clinton and Donald Trump." *Public Relations Review* 42 (5): 849–55.

Lévi-Strauss, Claude. 1963. *Structural Anthropology*. New York: Basic Books.

Lerman, Rachel. 2020. "Trump Says Twitter Is Trying to 'Silence' Conservatives. His Growing Number of Followers Suggests Otherwise." *Washington Post*, May 28, 2020. https://www.washingtonpost.com/technology/2020/05/28/trump-twitter-by-numbers/.

Lieven, Anatol. 2012. *America Right or Wrong: An Anatomy of American Nationalism*. New York: Oxford University Press.

Lipset, Seymour Martin. 1996. *American Exceptionalism: A Double-Edged Sword*. New York: W. W. Norton.

Liptak, Kevin, and Kristen Holmes. 2020. "Trump Calls Black Lives Matter a 'Symbol of Hate' as He Digs in on Race." CNN, July 1, 2020.

López-Alves, Fernando, and Diane Johnson. 2019. *Populist Nationalism in Europe and the Americas*. New York: Routledge. https://doi.org/10.4324/9780429437366-2.

Love, Erik. 2017. *Islamophobia and Racism in America*. New York: New York University Press.

Lucas, Jack, and Robert Vipond. 2017. "Back to the Future: Historical Political Science and the Promise of Canadian Political Development." *Canadian Journal of Political Science* 50 (1): 219–41.

Lucas, John. 1990. *England and Englishness: Ideas of Nationhood in English Poetry, 1688–1900*. Iowa City: University of Iowa Press.

Mahtesian, Charlie. 2016. "How Trump Won His Map." *Politico*, November 9, 2016.

Maksić, Adis, and Nihad Ahmić. 2020. "Constructing the Muslim Threat: A Critical Analysis of Marine Le Pen's Twitter Posts during the 2017 French Election Campaign." *Journal of Regional Security* 15 (1): 131–48. https://doi.org/10.5937/jrs15-25918.

Marcus, Jonathan. 1995. *The National Front and French Politics: The Resistible Rise of Jean-Marie Le Pen*. London: Macmillan.

Marston, S. A. 1990. "Who Are 'the People'?: Gender, Citizenship, and the Making of the American Nation." *Environment & Planning D: Society & Space* 8 (4): 449–58.

Maurer, Peter, and Trevor Diehl. 2020. "What Kind of Populism? Tone and Targets in the Twitter Discourse of French and American Presidential Candidates." *European Journal of Communication* 35 (5): 453–68. https://doi.org/10.1177/0267323120909288.

Maxwell, Angie, and Todd Shields. 2019. *The Long Southern Strategy: How Chasing White Voters in the South Changed American Politics*. Oxford: Oxford University Press.

Mayer, Nonna. 2013. "From Jean-Marie to Marine Le Pen: Electoral Change on the Far Right." *Parliamentary Affairs* 66 (1): 160–78.

Mazzoleni, Gianpietro. 2014. "Mediatization and Political Populism." In *Mediatization of Politics*, edited by Frank Esser and Jesper Stromback, 42–56. New York: Palgrave Macmillan.

McClarey, Donald. 2009. "The Devil and Andrew Jackson." *The American Catholic*, February 16, 2009. https://the-american-catholic.com/2009/02/16/the-devil-and-andrew-jackson/.

McLaren, Lauren, Hajo Boomgaarden, and Rens Vliegenthart. 2018. "News Coverage and Public Concern about Immigration in Britain." *International Journal of Public Opinion Research* 30 (2): 173–93.

McLaren, Lauren, and Mark Johnson. 2004. "Understanding the Rising Tide of Anti-Immigrant Sentiment." In *British Social Attitudes, 21st Report*, edited by Alison Park, John Curtice, Katarina Thomson, Catherine Bromley, and Miranda Phillips, 169–200. London: SAGE.

McLuhan, Marshall. 1964. *Understanding Media: The Extensions of Man*. New York: McGraw-Hill.

Meinecke, Friedrich. 1919. *Weltbürgertum Und Nationalstaat: Studien Zur Genesis Des Deutschen Nationalstaates*. Munich and Berlin: R. Oldernburg.

Mercieca, Jennifer. 2020. *Demagogue for President: The Rhetorical Genius of Donald Trump*. College Station: Texas A&M University Press.

REFERENCES

Merica, Dan. 2017a. "Trump—Once Again—Fails to Condemn the Alt-Right White Supremacists." *CNN*, August 13, 2017.

Merica, Dan. 2017b. "Trump Calls KKK, Neo-Nazis, White Supremacists 'Repugnant.'" *CNN*, August 14, 2017.

Miller-Idriss, Cynthia. 2020. *Hate in the Homeland: The New Global Far Right*. Princeton, NJ: Princeton University Press.

Mock, Steven. 2012. *Symbols of Defeat in the Construction of National Identity*. Cambridge: Cambridge University Press.

Moffitt, Benjamin. 2016. *The Global Rise of Populism: Performance, Political Style, and Representation*. Stanford, CA: Stanford University Press.

Moffitt, Benjamin. 2018. "Populism 2.0: Social Media and the False Allure of 'Unmediated' Representation." In *Populism and the Crisis of Democracy: Politics, Social Movements and Extremism*, edited by Gregor Fitzi, Juergen Mackert, and Bryan Turner, 2:30–46. London: Routledge.

Moffitt, Benjamin, and Simon Tormey. 2014. "Rethinking Populism: Politics, Mediatisation and Political Style." *Political Studies* 62 (2): 381–97.

Mondon, Aurelien. 2015. "Populism, the 'People' and the Illusion of Democracy: The Front National and UKIP in a Comparative Context." *French Politics* 13 (2): 141–56.

Morden, Michael. 2016. "Anatomy of the National Myth: Archetypes and Narrative in the Study of Nationalism." *Nations and Nationalism* 22 (3): 447–64.

Morgan, Edmund. 1975. *American Slavery, American Freedom*. New York: W. W. Norton.

Mudde, Cas. 2004. "The Populist Zeitgeist." *Government and Opposition* 39 (4): 542–63.

Mudde, Cas. 2016. *The Populist Radical Right: A Reader*. New York: Routledge.

Mudde, Cas, and Cristóbal Rovira Kaltwasser. 2013. "Exclusionary vs. Inclusionary Populism: Comparing Contemporary Europe and Latin America." *Government and Opposition* 48 (2): 147–74.

Mudde, Cas, and Cristóbal Rovira Kaltwasser. 2017. *Populism: A Very Short Introduction*. New York: Oxford University Press.

Myrdal, Gunnar. 1995. *An American Dilemma*. Vol. 1: *The Negro Problem and Modern Democracy*. New York: Routledge.

Nagel, Joane. 1998. "Masculinity and Nationalism: Gender and Sexuality in the Making of Nations." *Ethnic and Racial Studies* 21 (2): 242–69. https://doi.org/10.1080/014198798330007.

Narea, Nichole. 2020. "Trump Showed No Regret over Family Separations during Presidential Debate." *Vox*, October 22, 2020.

Nayak, Anoop. 2007. "Critical Whiteness Studies." *Sociology Compass* 1 (2): 737–55.

Newport, Frank. 2018. "Deconstructing Trump's Use of Twitter." Gallup.Com, May 2018.

Nguyen, Tina. 2016. "You Could Fit All The Voters Who Cost Clinton The Election in a Mid-Size Football Stadium." *Vanity Fair*, December 1, 2016.

Nieguth, Tim. 2020. *Nationalism and Popular Culture*. London: Routledge.

Nora, Pierre. 1996. *Realms of Memory: The Construction of the French Past*. New York: Columbia University Press.

Norris, Pippa, and Ronald Inglehart. 2019. *Cultural Backlash: Trump, Brexit and Authoritarian Populism*. Cambridge: Cambridge University Press.

O'Leary, Brendan. 2001. "An Iron Law of Nationalism and Federation?: A (Neo-Diceyian) Theory of the Necessity of a Federal Staatsvolk, and of Consociational Rescue." *Nations and Nationalism* 7 (3): 273–96.

Onishi, Norimitsu, and Constant Meheut. 2021. "In a Charged Environment, France Tackles Its Model of Secularism." *New York Times*, April 20, 2021.

Onuf, Peter S. 1998. "'To Declare Them a Free and Independant People': Race, Slavery, and National Identity in Jefferson's Thought." *Journal of the Early Republic* 18 (1): 1–46. https://doi.org/10.2307/3124731.

Orgad, Liav. 2015. *The Cultural Defense of Nations: A Liberal Theory of Majority Rights*. Oxford: Oxford University Press.

Orren, Karen, and Stephen Skowronek. 2004. *The Search for American Political Development*. Cambridge: Cambridge University Press.

Ott, Brian L. 2017. "The Age of Twitter: Donald J. Trump and the Politics of Debasement." *Critical Studies in Media Communication* 34 (1): 59–68.

Overing, Joanna. 1997. "The Role of Myth: An Anthropological Perspective, or: 'The Reality of the Really Made-Up.'" In *Myths and Nationhood*, edited by Geoffrey Hosking and George Schöpflin, 1–18. London: Routledge.

Painter, Nell Irvin. 2010. *The History of White People*. New York: W. W. Norton.

Pancer, Ethan, and Maxwell Poole. 2016. "The Popularity and Virality of Political Social Media: Hashtags, Mentions, and Links Predict Likes and Retweets of 2016 U.S. Presidential Nominees' Tweets." *Social Influence* 11 (4): 259–70. https://doi.org/10.1080/15534 510.2016.1265582.

Paxman, Jeremy. 1999. *The English: A Portrait of a People*. London: Penguin.

Peer, Shanny. 1998. *France on Display: Peasants, Provincials, and Folklore in the 1937 Paris World's Fair*. Albany: State University of New York Press.

Pegram, Thomas. 2011. *One Hundred Percent American: The Rebirth and Decline of the Ku Klux Klan in the 1920s*. Chicago: Ivan R. Dee.

Peterson, Tarla Rai. 1990. "Jefferson's Yeoman Farmer as Frontier Hero a Self Defeating Mythic Structure." *Agriculture and Human Values* 7 (1): 9–19. https://doi.org/10.1007/BF0 1530599.

Phillips, Kristine. 2017. "Timeline: How Growing Anger Finally Pushed Trump to Denounce White Supremacists." *Washington Post*, August 15, 2017.

Pierson, Paul. 2000. "Increasing Returns, Path Dependency, and the Study of Politics." *American Political Science Review* 94 (2): 251–67.

Pinheiro, John. 2014. 2014. *Missionaries of Republicanism: A Religious History of the Mexican-American War*. Oxford: Oxford University Press.

Polantz, Katelyn. 2021. "Capitol Riot Defendant Flips to Help Prosecutors against Proud Boys." CNN, April 7, 2021.

Pomain, Krysztof. 1996. "Franks and Gauls." In *Realms of Memory: The Construction of the French Past*, edited by Pierre Nora, 27–78. New York: Columbia University Press.

Poulat, Émile. 2003. *Notre Laïcité Publique: "La France Est Une République Laïque," Constitutions de 1946 et 1958*. Paris: Berg International.

Powell, Walter, and Paul DiMaggio. 1991. *The New Institutionalism in Organizational Analysis*. Chicago: University of Chicago Press.

Rambo, Eric, and Elaine Chan. 1990. "Text, Structure, and Action in Cultural Sociology." *Theory and Society* 19 (5): 635–48.

Rearick, Charles. 1997. *The French in Love and War*. New Haven, CT: Yale University Press.

Renan, Ernest. 1882. *Qu'est-Ce Qu'une Nation?* Paris: Ancienne Maison Michel Levy Freres.

Reynolds, Susan. 1997. *Kingdoms and Communities in Western Europe: 900–1300*. Oxford: Open University Press.

Richardson, Heather Cox. 2020. *How the South Won the Civil War: Oligarchy, Democracy, and the Continuing Fight for the Soul of America*. Oxford: Oxford University Press.

Roediger, David. 1991. *The Wages of Whiteness: Race and the Making of the American Working Class*. London: Verso.

Roediger, David. 2001. "Critical Studies of Whiteness, USA: Origins and Arguments." *Theoria: A Journal of Social and Political Theory* 98 (December): 72–98.

Roediger, David. 2006. "A Reply to Eric Kaufmann." *Ethnicities* 6 (2): 254–62.

Rogers, Alex. 2021. "Liz Cheney Loses House Republican Leadership Post over Feud with Trump." CNN, May 12, 2021.

Roshwald, Aviel. 2006. *The Endurance of Nationalism: Ancient Roots*. Cambridge: Cambridge University Press.

Saul, Jennifer M. 2017. "Racial Figleaves, the Shifting Boundaries of the Permissible, and the Rise of Donald Trump." *Philosophical Topics* 45 (2): 97–116.

Saxton, Alexander. 1990. *The Rise and Fall of the White Republic: Class Politics and Mass Culture in Nineteenth-Century America*. New York: Verso.

Scheckel, Susan. 1998. *The Insistence of the Indian: Race and Nationalism in Nineteenth-Century American Culture*. Princeton, NJ: Princeton University Press.

Schertzer, Robert. 2016. *The Judicial Role in a Diverse Federation: Lessons from the Supreme Court of Canada*. Toronto: University of Toronto Press.

Schertzer, Robert, and Eric Taylor Woods. 2011. "Beyond Multinational Canada." *Commonwealth and Comparative Politics* 49 (2): 196–222. http://resolver.scholarsportal.info/resolve/14662043/v49i0002/196_bmc.

Schertzer, Robert, and Eric Taylor Woods. 2020. "#Nationalism: The Ethno-Nationalist Populism of Donald Trump's Twitter Communication." *Ethnic and Racial Studies* 44 (7): 1154–73.

Schlesinger, Arthur. 1998. *The Disuniting of America: Reflections on a Multicultural Society*. New York: W.W. Norton.

Schmidt, Vivien. 2010. "Taking Ideas and Discourse Seriously: Explaining Change through Discursive Institutionalism as the Fourth 'New Institutionalism.'" *European Political Science Review* 2 (1): 1–25.

Schöpflin, George. 1997. "The Functions of Myth and a Taxonomy of Myths." In *Myths and Nationhood*, edited by Geoffrey Hosking and George Schöpflin, 19–35. London: Routledge.

Sewell, William. 1992. "A Theory of Structure: Duality, Agency, and Transformation." *American Journal of Sociology* 98 (1): 1–29.

Shear, Michael, Maggie Haberman, Nicholas Confessore, Karen Yourish, Larry Buchanan, and Keith Collins. 2019. "The Twitter Presidency." *New York Times*. https://www.nytimes.com/interactive/2019/11/02/us/politics/trump-twitter-presidency.html.

Shepard, Steven. 2017. "Poll: Trump Hit New Low after Charlottesville." *Politico*, August 23, 2017.

Shields, J. G. 2007. *The Extreme Right in France: From Petain to Le Pen*. Abingdon, UK: Routledge.

Shields, J. G. 2013. "Marine Le Pen and the 'New' FN: A Change of Style or Substance." *Parliamentary Affairs* 66 (1): 179–96.

Shulman, Stephen. 2002. "Challenging the Civic/Ethnic and West/East Dichotomies in the Study of Nationalism." *Comparative Political Studies* 35 (5): 554–85.

Silbey, Joel. 1985. *The Partisan Imperative: The Dynamics of American Politics before the Civil War*. New York: Oxford University Press.

Silver, Nate. 2016. "Education, Not Income, Predicted Who Would Vote for Trump." FiveThirtyEight, November 22, 2016. https://fivethirtyeight.com/features/education-not-income-predicted-who-would-vote-for-trump/.

Simmons, Harvey. 1996. *The French National Front: The Extremist Challenge to Democracy*. New York: Routledge.

Skelley, Geoffrey, and Anna Wiederkehr. 2020. "Trump Is Losing Ground with White Voters but Gaining among Black and Hispanic Americans." FiveThirtyEight, October 19, 2020. https://fivethirtyeight.com/features/trump-is-losing-ground-with-white-voters-but-gaining-among-black-and-hispanic-americans/.

Skey, Michael. 2010. "'A Sense of Where You Belong in the World:' National Belonging, Ontological Security and the Status of the Ethnic Majority in England." *Nations and Nationalism* 16 (4): 715–33.

Skey, Michael. 2011. "'Sod Them, I'm English': The Changing Status of the 'Majority' English in Post-Devolution Britain." *Ethnicities* 12 (1): 106–25.

Skey, Michael. 2020. "Nationalism and Media." *The State of Nationalism: An International Review*. https://stateofnationalism.eu/article/nationalism-and-media/.

Skey, Michael, and Marco Antonsich. 2017. *Everyday Nationhood: Theorising Culture, Identity and Belonging after Banal Nationalism*. London: Palgrave Macmillan.

Smith-Rosenberg, Carroll. 2010. *This Violent Empire: The Birth of an American National Identity*. Chapel Hill: University of North Carolina Press.

Smith, Anthony D. 1986. *The Ethnic Origins of Nations*. Malden, MA: Blackwell.
Smith, Anthony D. 1997. "The Golden Age and National Renewal." In *Myths and Nationhood*, edited by Geoffrey Hosking and George Schöpflin, 36–59. London: Routhledge.
Smith, Anthony D. 1998. *Nationalism and Modernism: A Critical Survey of Recent Theories of Nations and Nationalism*. London: Routledge.
Smith, Anthony D. 2003. *Chosen Peoples: Sacred Sources of National Identity*. Oxford: Oxford University Press.
Smith, Anthony D. 2006. "'Set in the Silver Sea:' English National Identity and European Integration." *Nations and Nationalism* 12 (3): 433–52.
Smith, Anthony D. 2009. *Ethno-Symbolism and Nationalism: A Cultural Approach*. London: Routledge.
Smith, Anthony D. 2010. *Nationalism: Theory, Ideology, History*. 2nd ed. Cambridge: Polity Press.
Smith, Rogers. 1993. "Beyond Tocqueville, Myrdal and Hartz: The Multiple Traditions in America." *American Political Science Review1* 87 (3): 549–66.
Smith, Rogers. 1997. *Civic Ideals: Conflicting Visions of Citizenship in U.S. History*. New Haven, CT: Yale University Press.
Sobolewska, Maria, and Robert Ford. 2020. *Brexitland: Identity, Diversity and the Reshaping of British Politics*. Cambridge: Cambridge University Press.
Solomos, John. 1993. *Race and Racism in Britain*. London: Macmillan.
Squires, Gregory, and Frank Woodruff. 2019. "Redlining." In *The Wiley Blackwell Encyclopedia of Urban and Regional Studies*, edited by Anthony M. Orum, 1–8. Hoboken, NJ: Wiley-Blackwell.
Stanley, Ben. 2008. "The Thin Ideology of Populism." *Journal of Political Ideologies* 13 (1): 95–110.
Stockemer, Daniel. 2017. *The Front National in France: Continuity and Change under Jean-Marie Le Pen and Marine Le Pen*. Cham, Switzerland: Springer International.
Stockemer, Daniel, and Mauro Barisione. 2017. "The 'New' Discourse of the Front National under Marine Le Pen: A Slight Change with a Big Impact." *European Journal of Communication* 32 (2): 100–115.
Taggart, Paul. 2000. *Populism*. Philadelphia: Open University Press.
Taggart, Paul. 2002. "Populism and the Pathology of Representative Politics." In *Democracies and the Populist Challenge*, edited by Yves Meny and Yves Surel, 62–80. London: Palgrave Macmillan.
Taifel, Henri. 1982. "Social Psychology of Intergroup Relations." *Annual Review of Psychology* 33 (1): 1–39.
Tharoor, Ishaan. 2015. "Donald Trump Tweets Image of Nazi Soldiers inside the U.S. Flag, Then Deletes Tweet." *Washington Post*, July 14, 2015.
Thompson, Debra. 2016. *The Schematic State: Race, Transnationalism, and the Politics of the Census*. Cambridge: Cambridge University Press.
Tilly, Charles. 1994. "States and Nationalism in Europe 1492–1992." *Theory and Society* 23 (1): 131–46.
Torpey, John. 2006. *Making Whole What Has Been Smashed: On Reparations Politics*. Cambridge, MA: Harvard University Press.
Trautsch, Jasper M. 2016. "The Origins and Nature of American Nationalism." *National Identities* 18 (3): 289–312. https://doi.org/10.1080/14608944.2015.1027761.
Travers, Len. 1997. *Celebrating the Fourth: Independence Day and the Rites of Nationalism in the Early Republic*. Boston: University of Massachusetts Press.
Triadafilopoulos, Triadafilos. 2011. "Illiberal Means to Liberal Ends? Understanding Recent Immigrant Integration Policies in Europe." *Journal of Ethnic and Migration Studies* 37 (6): 861–80.
Trump, Donald. 2017. "The Inaugural Address." January 20, Washington, DC.
Trump, Donald. 2018a. "Remarks by President Trump at Signing Ceremony for S. 3021, America's Water Infrastructure Act of 2018." October 23, Washington, DC.
Trump, Donald. 2018b. "Speech at Political Rally." March 10, Moon Township, Pennsylvania.

Trump, Donald. 2019. "Remarks by President Trump at Turning Point USA's Teen Student Action Summit." July 23, Washington, DC.

Tsang, Rachel, and Eric Taylor Woods. 2014. *The Cultural Politics of Nationalism and Nation-Building: Ritual and Performance in the Forging of Nation*. London: Routledge.

Turner, Victor. 1986. *Dramas, Fields, and Metaphors: Symbolic Action in Human Society*. Ithaca, NY: Cornell University Press.

Tyson, Alec, and Shiva Maniam. 2016. "Behind Trump's Victory: Divisions by Race, Gender, Education." Pew Research Center, November 9, 2016.

Urback, Robyn. 2017. "There Is No Moral Equivalency When It Comes to Neo-Nazi White Supremacy." CBC News, August 15, 2017.

Usherwood, Simon, and Katharine A. M. Wright. 2017. "Sticks and Stones: Comparing Twitter Campaigning Strategies in the European Union Referendum." *British Journal of Politics and International Relations* 19 (2): 371–88. https://doi.org/10.1177/1369148117700659.

Valentino, Nicholas, Carly Wayne, and Marizia Oceno. 2018. "Mobilizing Sexism: The Interaction of Emotion and Gender Attitudes in the 2016 US Presidential Election." *Public Opinion Quarterly* 82 (S1): 799–821.

van den Berghe, Pierre. 1981. *The Ethnic Phenomenon*. London: Praeger.

Valluvan, S. 2021. *The Clamour of Nationalism: Race and Nation in Twenty-First-Century Britain*. Manchester: Manchester University Press.

Vera, Amir. 2019. "James Fields, Who Plowed His Car through a Crowd at 2017 Charlottesville Rally, Gets Second Life Sentence." CNN, July 15, 2019.

Virdee, Satnam, and Brendan McGeever. 2018. "Racism, Crisis, Brexit." *Ethnic and Racial Studies* 41 (10): 1802–19.

Waisbord, Silvio. 2018. "The Elective Affinity between Post-Truth Communication and Populist Politics." *Communication Research and Practice* 4 (1): 17–34.

Waisbord, Silvio, and Adriana Amado. 2017. "Populist Communication by Digital Means: Presidential Twitter in Latin America." *Information, Communication & Society* 20 (9): 1330–46. https://doi.org/10.1080/1369118X.2017.1328521.

Warner, Michael. 2009. *The Letters of the Republic: Publication and the Public Sphere in Eighteenth-Century America*. Cambridge, MA: Harvard University Press.

Weber, Eugen. 1976. *Peasants into Frenchmen*. Stanford, CA: Stanford University Press.

Weber, Eugen. 1991. *My France: Politics, Culture, Myth*. Cambridge, MA: Harvard University Press.

Wellings, Ben. 2010. "Losing the Peace: Euroscepticism and the Foundations of Contemporary English Nationalism." *Nations and Nationalism* 16 (3): 488–505.

Wheaton, Sarah. 2008. "Bachman: Obama 'May Have Anti-American Views.'" *New York Times*, October 18, 2008.

Wiener, Martin. 2004. *English Culture and the Decline of the Industrial Spirit 1850–1980*. Cambridge: Cambridge University Press.

Wimmer, Andreas. 2004. "Dominant Ethnicity and Dominant Nationhood." In *Rethinking Ethnicity: Majority Groups and Dominant Minorities*, 35–51. London: Routledge.

Wimmer, Andreas. 2012. *Waves of War: Nationalism, State Formation, and Ethnic Exclusion in the Modern World*. Cambridge: Cambridge University Press.

Winock, Michel. 1998. *Nationalism, Anti-Semitism, and Fascism in France*. Stanford, CA: Stanford University Press.

Winter, Bronwyn. 2008. *Hijab and the Republic: Uncovering the French Headscarf Debate*. Syracuse, NY: Syracuse University Press.

Wodak, Ruth. 2015. *The Politics of Fear: What Right-Wing Populist Discourses Mean*. London: Sage.

Wolf, Zachary, Curt Merrill, and Daniel Wolfe. 2020. "How Voters Shifted During Four Years of Trump." CNN, November 7, 2020.

Woods, Eric Taylor. 2012. "Beyond Multination Federalism: Reflections on Nations and Nationalism in Canada." *Ethnicities* 12 (3): 270–92.

Woods, Eric Taylor. 2015. "Cultural Nationalism: A Review and Annotated Bibliography." *Studies on National Movements* 2: 1–26. https://repository.uel.ac.uk/item/85v76.

Woods, Eric Taylor. 2016. *A Cultural Sociology of Anglican Mission and the Indian Residential Schools in Canada: The Long Road to Apology*. New York: Springer.
Woods, Eric Taylor, Robert Schertzer, Liah Greenfeld, Chris Hughes, and Cynthia Miller-Idriss. 2020. "COVID-19, Nationalism, and the Politics of Crisis: A Scholarly Exchange." *Nations and Nationalism* 26 (4): 807–25.
Wuthnow, Robert. 2018. *The Left Behind: Decline and Rage in Small-Town America*. Princeton, NJ: Princeton University Press.
Wyn Jones, Richard, Guy Lodge, Ailsa Henderson, and Dan Wincott. 2012. *The Dog That Finally Barked: England as an Emerging Political Community*. London: Institute for Public Policy Research. https://www.ippr.org/publications/the-dog-that-finally-barked-england-as-an-emerging-political-community.
Yack, Bernard. 1996. "The Myth of the Civic Nation." *Journal of Politics and Society* 10 (2): 193–211.
Zesch, Scott. 2008. "Chinese Los Angeles in 1870–1871: The Makings of a Massacre." *Southern California Quarterly* 90 (2): 109–58. https://doi.org/10.2307/41172418.
Zimmer, Oliver. 2003. "Boundary Mechanisms and Symbolic Resources: Towards a Process-Oriented Approach to National Identity." *Nations and Nationalism* 9 (2): 173–93.
Zubrzycki, Geneviève. 2001. "'We, the Polish Nation': Ethnic and Civic Visions of Nationhood in Post-Communist Constitutional Debates." *Theory and Society* 30 (5): 629–68.
Zubrzycki, Geneviève. 2002. "The Classical Opposition between Civic and Ethnic Models of Nationhood: Ideology, Empirical Reality and Social Scientific Analysis." *Polish Sociological Review* 139: 275–95.
Zulianello, Mattia, Alessandro Albertini, and Diego Ceccobelli. 2018. "A Populist Zeitgeist? The Communication Strategies of Western and Latin American Political Leaders on Facebook." *International Journal of Press/Politics* 23 (4): 439–57. https://doi.org/10.1177/1940161218783836.

INDEX

For the benefit of digital users, indexed terms that span two pages (e.g., 52–53) may, on occasion, appear on only one of those pages.
Tables and figures are indicated by *t* and *f* following the page number

Académie Celtique, 117–18
Action Française, 118–19
Adams, John Quincy, 70
Adams, Sam, 58
Afghanistan, 83–84
African Americans, 56–57, 59–60, 66, 71–72, 78, 81–82, 182, 187
   Black Lives Matter, 93–94, 95–96
   "Great Migration" of, 79
   post-Civil War, 74–75
   Roosevelt (Franklin) and, 78
   Roosevelt (Theodore) and, 77
   scientific racism and, 69–70
   Trump and, 91–92, 96, 99, 106, 107
Agincourt, 126
agrarian society. *See* rural/agrarian society
Albania, 170–73
Alfred the Great, King of England, 58–59, 149–50, 160
Algeria, 119–20, 121–22, 139–40
Alternative for Germany, 3, 9
American ethnic nationalism, 4, 5–7, 9, 11, 14–15, 40–43, 46, 54–87, 156, 178–79, 180–81, 182–83
   cultural foundations of, 56–68
   current state of, 188–90
   development of, 68–85
   ethos and, 65–68
   form and content of, 185–87
   history and, 63–64
   homeland and, 64–65, 69
   people and, 58–61
   persistence and adaptability of, 180–81
   in presidential elections of 2016 and 2020, 91–92
   religion and (*see under* religion)
   resurgence of among conservatives, 80–85
   Trump brand, 92–98
   Trump brand continuity and change, 110–12
American exceptionalism, 104
American First Committee, 82–83
American Revolution, 56–58, 63–64, 66, 68
Anderson, Benedict, 33–34
Anglo-American identity, 56–58, 68–69, 71–72, 86–87, 150–51, 155, 157, 182
   Civil War and endurance of, 73–75
   ethos and, 65–66
   history and, 63–64
   homeland and, 64–65
   "new" immigrants and, 75–77
   peoplehood and, 58–61
   religion (Protestantism) and, 61–63, 72–73
   Trump and, 186–87
   whiteness and, 69–72, 77–80, 86
Anglo-Saxon ancestry myth, 40–43
   American ethnic nationalism and, 6–7, 58–59, 61, 62–65, 66, 68–69, 71, 182
   English ethnic nationalism and, 149–51, 154, 157, 158, 160, 183–84
Antifa, 95–96
anti-Semitism, 77, 120, 122, 129–30
Asians
   American ethnic nationalism and, 75, 76, 77, 78, 189
   Brexit Leave campaigns and, 162
   Trump and, 91–92

Asterix (cartoon), 117–18
Australia, 9, 166–67
Austria, 9
authoritarian populism, 9

Bachman, Michele, 85
banal nationalism, 19–20, 33, 35, 161
Barrès, Maurice, 119
Barth, Fredrik, 20, 32
Bede, 58–59, 63, 149–50
Belgium, 6–7, 29
Bell, David, 116, 119–20
Berlusconi, Silvio, 47–48
Bible, 155
Biden, Joe, 1–2, 188–89
Billig, Michael, 19–20
"birther" conspiracy theory, 84–85, 88, 97
birth on soil. See *jus soli*
Black Lives Matter (BLM), 93–94, 95–96
black peoples. *See also* African Americans
 Brexit Leave campaigns and, 162
 French ethnic nationalism and, 120, 121–22, 128
Blake, William, 154
Bland, Richard, 58
"Blood, Toil, Tears, and Sweat" (Churchill speech), 150–51
blood descent. See *jus sanguinis*
Blum, Edward, 74
Blumenbach, Johann Friedrich, 69
Bolsonaro, Jair, 9
Boulainvilliers, Henri de, 117–18
Boulanger, General, 119
Brazil, 9
"Breaking Point" billboard, 173
Brexit, 4–5, 14, 15, 47, 148–49, 158–59. *See also* Leave campaigns; Remain supporters
 English ethnic nationalism and, 160–74
 passing of, 189–90
 primary motivating factor for, 190
British Empire, 148–49, 151, 158, 160
British nationalism, 148, 175–76, 178
Brubaker, Rogers, 24, 31–32, 115
Buchanan, Pat, 83, 84
"burkinis," 141
Bush, George H. W., 83
Bush, George W., 83–84

Cameron, David, 164–65, 171
Canada, 29
"cancel culture," 189–90
capitalism
 consumer, 56–57
 print, 33, 44–45
Carlyle, Thomas, 156–57
Carroll, Charles, 58
Catalonia, 29

Catholicism, 28, 30, 112. *See also* Irish Catholics
 American ethnic nationalism and, 57, 61, 62, 71–73, 75–76, 80, 182, 186
 English ethnic nationalism and, 155–56, 158, 174–75, 186
 French ethnic nationalism and, 115, 116, 121–24, 129–30, 183
 Le Pen on, 132–33, 136–38, 144
Cavaliers, 74
Cheney, Liz, 189–90
Chinese Americans/immigrants, 75–76, 77
Chirac, Jacques, 123–24
"chosen people" myth
 American ethnic nationalism and, 61, 62–63, 64–65, 66
 Brexit Leave campaigns and, 171–73, 174–75
 English ethnic nationalism and, 155, 183–84
 French ethnic nationalism and, 122
Christianity, 187–88
 American ethnic nationalism and, 80, 82–83, 84, 86
 Le Pen on, 136–38, 145–46
 Trump on, 99, 100–1, 110–11, 182–83
Christian Right (US), 91
Churchill, Winston, 150–51
Church of England, 61, 155, 156–57, 160
citizenship
 American, 66
 English, 152–53
 French, 118–19, 122, 135, 140–41, 145–46
"city on a hill" myth, 40–43, 62
civic nationalism, 28, 31, 185
 American, 66, 68–69, 73, 74, 76–79, 80–82, 83–84, 86
 characteristics of, 20–26
 English, 148, 157
 French, 113–14, 115, 116, 125, 146, 178
 origins of, 21
civilizing mission. See *mission civilisatrice*
Civil Rights Act of 1964 (US), 79, 80–81
civil rights movement, 78–79, 86
Civil War (American), 72, 73–75, 81, 86, 182
Civil War (English), 74
Clay, Henry, 70
Clinton, Hillary, 46, 89–90, 91–92, 99–100, 104, 109, 110
Clinton Foundation, 109
colonialism
 American, 59, 68
 English, 148–49, 151–53, 168–69, 183–84
 French, 119–20, 121–22, 124, 128
Columbus Day proclamation (Trump), 92–93
Comey, James, 89–90
Commonwealth (British), 168–69, 176
communism, 2, 82–83, 115–16
communitarianism, 141–42, 144
Confederate monuments, 93–94

INDEX

Conservatives
    American ethnic nationalism and, 80–85
    Brexit Leave campaigns and, 162–63, 189–90
Constitution, US, 68, 74
COVID-19 pandemic, 90, 189, 190
critical junctures, 35
culture, 5–7, 10–11, 13–14, 16, 18, 31–33, 34–36, 37, 39–40. *See also* political culture
    American ethnic nationalism and, 56–68
    Le Pen on, 138
    overview of concept, 30–31
"culture wars," 24–25, 82–83, 188, 189–90

Daily Stormer (website), 94–95
Declaration of Independence, 63–64
Delacroix, Eugene, 18–19
democracy, 40–43, 179, 185–86, 191
    American ethnic nationalism and, 65, 66, 68, 73, 188–89
    English ethnic nationalism and, 150–51, 156, 157–58
Democratic Party (US), 80–81
Déroulède, Paul, 119
"dog whistles," 81–82, 188
Dole, Bob, 83
dominant ethnicity, 13–14, 16, 35–36, 37. *See also* white ethnic majorities
    overview of concept, 27–29
    Trump and, 101–2, 104, 109
Douglass, Frederick, 73–74
Dreyfus affair, 6–7, 116, 119, 120, 122
Durkheim, Émile, 18–19, 37–38, 39
Duterte, Rodrigo, 9

Ecclesiastical History of the English People (Bede), 58–59, 149–50
Economist, 184
economy, 11
    UK, 163–64, 168–69, 170
    US, 88–89, 100
Electoral College, 89
elites, 3, 21, 28, 31–32, 185
    Brexit Leave campaigns and, 163–65, 173–74, 175–76
    English ethnic nationalism and, 148–49
    ethno-symbolism and, 26–27
    French ethnic nationalism and, 117–18
    Le Pen on, 133
    modernism and, 26
    Trump on, 99–101, 104, 108–10, 111, 182–83
Elizabeth I, Queen of England, 155
Ellison, Keith, 84
Emancipation Park, 93–94
England, 21, 25–26, 58–59, 63–64, 147, 161. *See also* English ethnic nationalism
    French conflicts with, 61, 120, 122, 125–26, 151, 155–56, 174–75, 183–84
    German conflicts with, 151
    US culture influenced by, 56–57, 64
English ethnic nationalism, 4, 5–6, 9, 11, 15, 40–43, 46, 147–77, 178–79, 180–81, 183–84. *See also* Brexit
    British nationalism intertwined with, 148, 175–76, 178
    current state of, 189–90
    ethos and, 151, 156–58, 159*t*
    form and content of, 185–86, 187
    foundations of, 148–60
    history and, 158–60, 159*t*
    homeland and, 153–55, 159*t*
    people and, 149–53, 159*t*
    persistence and adaptability of, 180
    religion and, 155–56, 159*t*, 183–84
English exceptionalism, 156–57, 158, 160, 168
Erdoğan, Recep Tayyip, 9
ethnicity. *See* dominant ethnicity
ethnic myth-symbol complexes, 14, 30–31, 32–33, 35–36, 37. *See also* ethos; history; homeland; people; religion
    adaptability and persistence of, 180, 181–82, 184
    American ethnic nationalism and, 55, 67–68, 67*t*
    change in, 34–35
    defined, 30
    English ethnic nationalism and, 149, 183–84
    origins of, 32
    schema for mapping, 37–44, 41*t*
    Trump and, 88
ethnic nationalism. *See also* American ethnic nationalism; English ethnic nationalism; French ethnic nationalism; new nationalism
    characteristics of, 20–26
    current state of, 188–92
    mapping through social media, 44–53
    persistence and adaptability in the West, 180–84
    possible responses to, 190–92
    rise of in the West, 2–5
ethno-symbolism, 7–8, 13–14, 16, 18, 20, 26–35, 39–40, 179–80, 184
    core foci of (*see* culture; dominant ethnicity; history)
    development of, 26
    understanding ethnic nationalism via, 35–36
ethos, 40–43, 185–86
    American ethnic nationalism and, 65–68
    Brexit Leave campaigns and, 163
    English ethnic nationalism and, 151, 156–58, 159*t*
    French ethnic nationalism and, 124–25, 127*t*
    Le Pen and, 132–33, 138
    myths and symbols associated with, 41*t*
eugenicist movement, 76

215

European Union (EU), 133–34, 135, 136, 146, 148–49, 173–75. *See also* Brexit
evangelicalism, 82, 99
exceptionalism
American, 104
English, 156–57, 158, 160, 168
French, 132–33, 138
Exodus (Old English poem), 155

Facebook, 44–46, 47, 51, 191
Farage, Nigel, 9, 184
Fawkes, Guy, 155–56
Fichte, Johann, 22, 23
Fields, James, 93–94
"file S" (*fiché S*), 140–41
Fillon, François, 133
financial crisis of 2007-2008, 88–89, 160–61
First Great Awakening, 56–57
Floyd, George, 95–96
Fox News, 82–83
France, 3, 21–22, 25–26, 37, 44, 147, 157. *See also* French ethnic nationalism
English conflicts with, 61, 120, 122, 125–26, 151, 155–56, 174–75, 183–84
European Union and, 173–74
German conflicts with, 120, 125–26
France profonde, la, 128, 129, 136, 145–46, 183
France silencieuse, la, 135
Franco-German War, 120
Franklin, Benjamin, 58
Franks, 28, 117, 126, 128
Freedom Party (Austria), 9
French ethnic nationalism, 4, 5–6, 9, 15, 40–43, 46, 113–46, 156, 178–79, 180–81, 183
ethos and, 124–25, 127*t*
form and content of, 185–87
history and, 125–28, 127*t*
homeland and, 120–22, 127*t*
identity, political culture, and, 114–28
Le Pen and continuity and change in, 144–46
Le Pen and current state of, 128–44
people and, 117–20, 127*t*
persistence and adaptability of, 180
religion and, 122–24, 127*t*
French exceptionalism, 132–33, 138
French Resistance, 117–18, 126
French Revolution, 6–7, 18–19, 113–16, 117–18, 122–23, 125–26, 129

Gauls, 117–18, 120, 124, 125–26, 128, 129, 135, 183
Geertz, Clifford, 30, 181–82
Germania (Tacitus), 63
Germans, 63, 72, 75, 76
Germany, 3, 6–7, 9, 22, 23, 64, 113–14
English conflicts with, 151
European Union and, 173–74

French conflicts with, 120, 125–26
World War II and, 78, 173–74
Gildas, 153
globalization, 3
Brexit Leave campaigns and, 147–48, 163–64, 176–77
Le Pen on, 133–34, 135, 136, 146
Glorious Revolution (England), 63, 150–51
"golden age" myth
American, 59, 92–93, 103
English, 63, 158–59
Goldwater, Barry, 80–82
Goode, Virgil, 84
Good Friday Agreement, 156
Great Awakening, First, 56–57
"Great Migration," 79
Gunpowder Plot, 155–56

Haitian Revolution, 69–70
Hanson, Pauline, 9, 48
Henry, Patrick, 58
Henry VIII, King of England, 58–59, 155, 160
Herder, Johann Gottfried, 22
Hexigon, L', 121–22, 128
Heyer, Heather, 93–94
hijab, 123, 128
Hispanics/Latinos, 91–92, 99, 107, 180–81. *See also* Mexican migrants
history, 6–7, 13–14, 16, 37, 40–43
American ethnic nationalism and, 63–64
Brexit Leave campaigns and, 163, 168–69
English ethnic nationalism and, 158–60, 159*t*
French ethnic nationalism and, 125–28, 127*t*
myths and symbols associated with, 41*t*
overview of concept, 31–35
Trump on, 112
Hobsbawm, Eric, 31–32, 184
homeland, 40, 186–87
American ethnic nationalism and, 64–65, 69
Brexit Leave campaigns and, 163, 176–77
English ethnic nationalism and, 153–55, 159*t*
French ethnic nationalism and, 120–22, 127*t*
Le Pen on, 132–33, 136
myths and symbols associated with, 41*t*
Trump on, 106, 112
hot nationalism, 18–20, 28, 35
Hundred Years' War, 151

illiberal liberalism, 25–26, 54–55, 146, 186
Imagined Communities (Anderson), 33
immigration, 3, 9–10, 11, 25–26, 29, 179, 186, 190, 191
American ethnic nationalism and, 54, 68–69, 72–73, 75–77, 79, 82–83, 84, 182, 187
Brexit Leave campaigns and, 147–48, 160–62, 163–65, 166–67, 169–73, 174–77, 183–84, 187

English ethnic nationalism and, 148–49, 152–53, 154–55, 187
French ethnic nationalism and, 126, 128–30, 187
hot nationalism and, 20
Le Pen on, 130–31, 133–34, 135, 136, 139–42, 144–45, 146, 183
"new" immigrants, 75–77, 82–83
Trump on, 91–92, 97, 100, 102–4, 105–6, 107, 109f, 110
Immigration Act of 1971 (UK), 152–53
Immigration Acts (US), 75–76, 79
Independence Day (US), 57–58, 68, 73
Independence Party (UK), 9
India, 9
Indian Removal Act of 1830 (US), 70
Indigenous Americans, 56–57, 59–60, 68, 71–72, 78, 79, 151–52, 182
　forced removal from South, 66
　homeland and, 65
　religion and, 62
　Roosevelt (Theodore) on, 77
　scientific racism and, 69–70
　"Trail of Tears," 70
Industrial Revolution, 2, 154, 156–57
in-groups, 30, 34–35, 44, 180–81, 185, 186–87. *See also* "us"
　American ethnic nationalism and, 55, 56–57, 59–61, 71, 76, 77, 79–80, 81, 84–85, 86, 182
　Brexit Leave campaigns and, 169, 174, 175–76, 175t
　English ethnic nationalism and, 149–50, 152, 183–84
　French ethnic nationalism and, 126
　Le Pen on, 137f, 141–42, 144–46, 145t, 183
　Trump on, 90–91, 96, 97, 100–1, 111, 111t, 112, 182–83
Instagram, 44–45
institutional carriers, 33, 181
institutionalism, 32, 35
"invented traditions," 184
Iraq, 83–84, 169, 171
Ireland, 149. *See also* Northern Ireland
Irish Catholics, 6–7, 72, 75, 152, 156. *See also* Catholicism
ISIS, 107–8, 173
Islam, 186
　American ethnic nationalism and, 83–84
　Brexit Leave campaigns and, 147–48, 162, 163, 169, 171–76, 172f, 183–84, 187–88
　English ethnic nationalism and, 156, 158
　French ethnic nationalism and, 119–20, 121–22, 123–24, 125–26, 128, 129–30
　Le Pen on, 46, 130, 132–34, 136–38, 139–42, 144–46, 183, 187–88

Trump on, 97–98, 99, 100–1, 107–8, 108f, 110–11, 112, 182–83, 187–88
island nation mythology, 153–54, 156–57, 160, 173–74, 183–84, 186–87
Italian Americans/immigrants, 75–76, 82–83
Italy, 6–7, 9

Jackson, Andrew, 70, 71, 80–81
January 6 insurrection (US), 1–2, 94–95, 188–89
Japanese Americans/immigrants, 76, 78
Jay, John, 56
Jefferson, Thomas, 58, 59, 60, 63–64, 66
Jews, 23, 187–88. *See also* anti-Semitism
　American ethnic nationalism and, 75–76, 77, 78, 79–80, 85, 182
　French ethnic nationalism and, 118–19, 122–23, 125–26, 129–30
　Le Pen on, 146
　Trump on, 110–11, 182–83
Joan of Arc, 122, 125–26, 128, 129, 138–39
Johnson, Boris, 168–69
Johnson, Lyndon, 80–81
Judaism. *See* Jews
Julius Caesar, 117–18
jus sanguinis (blood descent), 118–19, 135
jus soli (birth on soil), 118–19, 129–30, 135, 146

Kaepernick, Colin, 95–96
Kipling, Rudyard, 149
Know-Nothing Party (US), 6–7, 72–73
Ku Klux Klan (KKK), 75–76, 94
Kumar, Krishan, 149, 154–55

Labour Party (UK), 162–63, 189–90
laïcité, 123–24, 130, 133–34, 136–38, 141, 146, 189–90
Law and Justice (Poland), 9
Law on the Separation of Churches and the State (France), 123
Leave campaigns (Brexit), 4, 9, 15, 113–14, 147–48, 160–62, 178–79, 183–84, 185, 186–88, 189–90, 192. *See also* Leave.EU; Vote Leave
　continuity and change in ethnic nationalism of, 174–77
　English nationalism of, 162–65
　factors influencing votes for, 161–62
　percent of vote won by, 161
　slogan of, 164–65, 167, 174–75
　Twitter and, 4–5, 44, 46, 48, 49–50, 51–52, 147, 148, 162–77
Leave.EU (Brexit campaign), 4–5, 44, 49–50, 51–52, 147–48, 162–70, 171–74, 176–77
Lee, Robert E., 93–94
Le Pen, Jean-Marie, 47–48, 125–26, 128–31, 145–46

Le Pen, Marine, 3, 4, 9, 14, 15, 47, 114, 178–79, 183, 184, 185, 186–88, 192
   ethnic nationalism continuity and change, 144–46
   ethnic nationalism today and, 128–44
   slogan of, 133
   on Twitter, 4–5, 44, 46, 48, 49–50, 51–52, 113–14, 131–34, 144–46
Lévi-Strauss, Claude, 37–38
Lewis, John, 106
LGBTQ rights, 88–89
liberalism, 2, 3, 9–10, 40–43, 44, 185–86
   American ethnic nationalism and, 55, 58–59, 66, 68, 73, 78, 188–89
   civic nationalism and, 21, 22
   English ethnic nationalism and, 157–58
   French ethnic nationalism and, 113–14, 146
   illiberal, 25–26, 54–55, 146, 186
liberty
   American ethnic nationalism and, 65, 66, 73
   English ethnic nationalism and, 150–51, 158
   French ethnic nationalism and, 127t
liberty, equality, fraternity (French revolutionary values), 115, 125, 186–87
Liberty Leading the People (Delacroix painting), 18–19
Limbaugh, Rush, 82–83
Lincoln, Abraham, 74, 96
Louisiana Purchase, 72–73

Macedonia, 170–71
Macron, Emmanuel, 114, 131, 132, 133, 189–90
Magna Carta, 63, 160
majority-minority cities, 29
"Make America Great Again" (#MAGA), 99, 103–4, 109, 182–83
"Manifest Destiny," 71
Manion, Clarence, 82–83
Maurras, Charles, 119
media, 33–34, 44–45, 82–83, 99–100. *See also* social media
Melting Pot, The (Zangwill), 76–77
Merovingian dynasty, 117
Mexican-American War, 71–73, 182
Mexican migrants. *See also* Hispanics/Latinos
   American ethnic nationalism and, 79, 82–83
   Trump on, 88, 97, 105f, 105–6, 111, 112, 187
Mexican territory annexation, 66, 71
mission civilisatrice (civilizing mission), 123–24, 132–33, 142, 145–46, 157, 183, 185–87
modernism, 26–27
Modi, Narendra, 9
Moffit, Benjamin, 47
Montenegro, 170–71
moral panic, 20
Morris, William, 154–55
Murdoch, Rupert, 82–83

Muslims. *See* Islam
myths, 5, 7, 10–11, 15, 37–39. *See also* ethnic myth-symbol complexes; ethno-symbolism
   American ethnic nationalism and, 55, 182
   Brexit Leave campaigns and, 163, 164, 165, 169, 174–77
   categories of, 41t
   defined, 37–38
   English ethnic nationalism and, 159t
   French ethnic nationalism and, 127t
   Le Pen's use of, 132–33, 138–39, 144, 145–46
   symbols and, 39
   Trump's use of, 99, 100–3, 104, 110–11, 112, 113

Napoleon I, Emperor of France, 117–18, 124, 173–74
Napoleon III, Emperor of France, 117–18, 124
nation (concept), 17, 18, 22, 24
National Front (France), 3, 4, 114, 128–32, 135, 146
National Healthcare Service (NHS; UK), 167, 170–71, 176–77
nationalism. *See also* banal nationalism; civic nationalism; ethnic nationalism; hot nationalism; new nationalism
   bad reputation of, 2
   defined, 17–18
   main tenet of, 17
   origin of, 17
   prevalence of, 17
   three goals of, 17–18
national populism, 9
National Rally (France), 3. *See also* National Front
National Recovery Agency (US), 77–78
national republicanism (French), 125, 129, 130, 146
Native American Party (US). *See* Know-Nothing Party
Nazi Party (Germany), 23, 78
neo-Nazis, 94–95
Netherlands, 3, 6–7, 9, 21, 26
Newbould, Frank, 154
New Deal, 77–78, 81
New France, 126
"new" immigrants, 75–77, 82–83
new nationalism. *See also* ethnic nationalism
   American, 86–87 (*see also* Trump, Donald)
   deep roots of, 5–8, 178–92
   defined, 2–3
   form and content of in the West, 184–88
   shift of focus from populism to, 8–13
New York Times, 52
Nixon, Richard, 80–82, 101–2
Nora, Pierre, 115–16
"Nordic" immigrants, 76, 82–83
Normans, 63–64, 150–51, 158, 174–75

Northern Ireland, 30, 147, 156, 161, 175–76
Nunavut, 29
NVivo, 50

Oath Keepers, 94–95
Obama, Barack, 84–85, 88, 97, 100, 107
Ocasio-Cortez, Alexandria, 98
Omar, Ilhan, 98
"one drop rule," 70
Orbán, Viktor, 9
Others, 32, 34–35, 86, 187–88, 191–92
   American ethnic nationalism and, 61, 69–70, 74, 84, 182
   Brexit Leave campaigns and, 162, 170, 174–76
   English ethnic nationalism and, 148–49, 155–56
   French ethnic nationalism and, 122, 135
   Le Pen's, 130
   Trump's, 107–8, 110–11
out-groups, 30, 34–35, 44, 180–81, 185. See also "them"
   American ethnic nationalism and, 55, 56–57, 59–60, 68–69, 71–73, 76, 79–80, 86
   Brexit Leave campaigns and, 174, 175t
   English ethnic nationalism and, 151, 152–53, 156
   French ethnic nationalism and, 126
   Le Pen's, 143f, 144–46, 145t
   Trump's, 90–91, 100–1, 111t, 182–83

paralipsis, 46
Paris International Exposition, 121
parliamentary sovereignty, 161–62, 163, 167–68, 174, 176, 186–87
Parscale, Brad, 52–53
Party for Freedom (Netherlands), 3
path dependence, 32, 35
patrie, 120–21, 128, 136
people, 40–43
   American ethnic nationalism and, 58–61
   Brexit Leave campaigns and, 163, 166
   English ethnic nationalism and, 149–53, 159t
   French ethnic nationalism and, 117–20, 127t
   myths and symbols associated with, 41t
   Trump on, 104, 110–11
perennialism, 26–27
Pétain, Philippe, 117–18, 125
Philippines, 9
phrenology, 69
Pieds-Noirs, 119–20, 121–22, 135
Poland, 9
political culture, 2, 8, 179, 181–82
   American ethnic nationalism and, 14, 54–55, 57–58
   French ethnic nationalism and, 114–28, 127t
   Le Pen and, 145–46

   Trump and, 90, 91, 94–95, 111–12, 113, 179, 181–82
populism, 2–3, 4, 6–7, 22–23, 47, 179, 185
   Brexit Leave campaigns and, 162, 163–65
   chameleonic nature of, 9–10
   debate over definition of, 9
   exclusive, 9–10
   inclusive, 9–10
   Jackson and, 70, 71
   Le Pen and, 130, 133–34, 135
   shift of focus to nationalism from, 8–13
   social media and rise of, 45–46
   Trump and, 46, 47–48, 88–89, 99–100, 104, 108–10
populist-nationalism, 9
populist radical right, 9
presidential elections (France)
   2017, 3, 49–50, 51–52, 113–14, 128, 131–34, 145t, 178
   2022, 189–90
presidential elections (US)
   1992, 83
   1996, 83
   2000, 83–84
   2008, 84
   2016, 3, 4, 46, 52, 88–92, 98–110, 111t, 178
   2020, 1–2, 88, 90–92, 178, 180–81, 188–90
Pressley, Ayanna, 98
primordialism, 26–27, 30
print capitalism, 33, 44–45
Protestantism, 6–7, 28, 30
   American ethnic nationalism and, 56–57, 60–63, 64, 68, 71–73, 80, 86, 182
   English ethnic nationalism and, 149, 155–56, 174–75
   French ethnic nationalism and, 122–23, 186
   persistence of, 72–73
   Trump and, 92–93, 112
Protestant Reformation, 26, 58–59, 61, 155, 156–57
Proud Boys, 94–95
Puerto Rico, 29
Putin, Vladimir, 9, 184

Quincy, Josiah, Jr., 58

"racial fig leaves," 46, 96
racism, 23, 27–28, 47, 189
   American ethnic nationalism and, 54, 55, 68–70, 71–72, 76, 79, 86, 180–81, 187
   American mobilization against, 93–94
   English ethnic nationalism and, 151–53
   French ethnic nationalism and, 119–20
   scientific, 68–70, 71–72, 76, 86, 151–52
Reagan, Ronald, 81–82
redlining, 79

religion, 40–43, 185–86. *See also specific religions*
  American ethnic nationalism and, 54, 55, 61–63, 74, 80, 82, 86
  Brexit Leave campaigns and, 163, 171–73, 174–75
  English ethnic nationalism and, 155–56, 159t, 183–84
  French ethnic nationalism and, 122–24, 127t
  Le Pen on, 132–33, 136–38, 140–42
  myths and symbols associated with, 41t
  Trump on, 99, 103, 107–8, 112
Remain supporters (anti-Brexit), 46, 161, 162, 171, 177
Renan, Ernest, 21–22, 115
republicanism (French)
  ethnic nationalism and, 114–15, 116, 123–24, 125, 129
  Le Pen on, 130, 132–33, 138, 141–42, 144–46, 183, 186–87
  national, 125, 129, 130, 146
Republican Party (US), 72, 80–85, 89, 91, 95, 189–90
Richard II (Shakespeare), 153
Robert E. Lee Park, 93–94
Romans (ancient), 117, 124, 126, 128, 135
Romanticism
  American ethnic nationalism and, 23, 58–59, 63
  English ethnic nationalism and, 154
  French ethnic nationalism and, 22, 116, 117–18, 124
Roosevelt, Franklin D., 77–78, 81
Roosevelt, Theodore, 76–78, 80
roundheads, 74
rural/agrarian society
  American ethnic nationalism and, 58, 59, 60–61, 65, 68
  Brexit Leave campaigns and, 161, 174
  English ethnic nationalism and, 153, 154–55
  French ethnic nationalism and, 121, 128
  Le Pen on, 132–33, 135–36, 142, 144–45, 183, 186–87
  Trump on, 92–93, 102–3, 110–11, 112, 182–83
Russia, 9
Russian Revolution, 76

sacredness, 18, 64–65, 155, 156–57
Salvini, Matteo, 9
sang reçu, le, 129–30
sang versé, le, 129–30
Scavino, Dan, 52–53
scientific racism, 68–70, 71–72, 76, 86, 151–52
Scotland, 147, 161, 175–76
secularism (French)
  ethnic nationalism and, 115, 122–24
  Le Pen on, 132–33, 136–38, 141, 142, 144, 145–46, 183, 186–87
September 11 terrorist attacks, 80, 83–84, 97–98

Serbia, 170–71
Seven Years' War, 126
Shakespeare, William, 153–54, 157, 160, 173–74
silent France, 135
"silent majority," 3
  Le Pen on, 132–33, 135
  Nixon on, 81–82
  Trump on, 99, 100–3, 102f, 104, 110–11, 182–83
slavery, 57, 69–70, 71, 72, 73, 74
Smith, Anthony, 8, 16, 17–18, 20–21, 24, 28, 34, 40, 153–54, 184
social Darwinism, 69, 151–52
social drama, 35
socialism, 9–10, 12, 179
social media, 4–5, 6–7, 11–12, 14, 37, 191. *See also specific platforms*
  mapping ethnic nationalism through, 44–53
  populism rise and, 45–46
Sodhi, Balbir Singh, 84
South (US), 66, 69–70, 71, 72–73, 79, 80–81, 82. *See also* Civil War (American)
South Downs (Newbould painting), 154
Southern Baptist Convention, 82
"southern strategy," 80–81
Sovereign Debt Crisis, 160–61
Spain, 6–7, 29
"Squad, the," 98
St. George's Cross, 160
St. John, Hector, 76–77
Stasi commission, 123
Steinle, Kathryn, 105–6
symbolic border guards, 39, 70, 79, 102–3, 121–22
symbols, 5, 7, 10–11, 15, 37–38, 39. *See also* ethnic myth-symbol complexes; ethno-symbolism
  American ethnic nationalism and, 55, 182
  Brexit Leave campaigns and, 163, 164, 165, 169, 174–77
  categories of, 41t
  Le Pen's use of, 132–33, 138–39, 144, 145–46
  myths and, 39
  Trump's use of, 99, 100–3, 104, 110–11, 113
Syrian refugees, 97–98, 107–8, 110, 160–61, 169, 171

Tacitus, 63, 65, 157
Tea Party (US), 85
terroir, 121–22, 145–46
terrorism
  Brexit Leave campaigns and, 163–64, 169, 171–73, 174–75
  Le Pen on, 130, 133–34, 139–41, 142, 144, 183, 187–88
  September 11 attacks, 80, 83–84, 97–98
  Trump on, 91–92, 97–98, 100–1, 107–8, 110, 111, 182–83, 187–88

INDEX

"them," 20, 21–22, 53, 180–81, 185, 188. *See also* out-groups
   Brexit Leave campaigns and, 163, 164, 165, 169–75, 176
   English ethnic nationalism and, 153–54
   Le Pen on, 139–44
   Trump on, 100–1, 104–10, 111
Tlaib, Rashida, 98
"Trail of Tears," 70
Trump, Donald, 1–38, 46, 48, 86–87, 88–112, 113, 178–79, 180–81, 182–83, 184, 185, 186–88, 192
   approval ratings of, 88, 92, 95
   "birther" conspiracy theory and, 84–85, 88, 97
   contestation of election results, 1–2, 189–90
   ethnic nationalism brand, 92–98
   ethnic nationalism brand continuity and change, 110–12
   impeachment of, 92
   Inaugural Address of, 92–93, 110–11
   spending on digital campaign, 52–53
   on Twitter, 4–5, 44, 46–47, 48, 49–50, 51–53, 90–91, 98–110, 112
   Twitter ban, 1–2, 51–52, 191
   votes for (2016), 91, 92
   votes for (2020), 88, 90, 178, 188–89
Turkey, 9, 163, 164–65, 166–67, 169, 170–73, 172*f*, 174–75, 176–77, 187
Twitter, 33–34, 37, 39, 44–46, 47, 184, 185
   breadth and depth of tweet analysis, 48–50
   Brexit Leave campaigns on, 4–5, 44, 46, 48, 49–50, 51–52, 147, 148, 162–77
   Le Pen on, 4–5, 44, 46, 48, 49–50, 51–52, 113–14, 131–34, 144–46
   reasons for focusing on, 50–53
   Trump banned from, 1–2, 51–52, 191
   Trump on, 4–5, 44, 46–47, 48, 49–50, 51–53, 90–91, 98–110, 112
Tyndale's Bible, 155

UK Independence Party (UKIP), 162–63, 173
United Kingdom, 6–7, 28–29, 37, 44, 113–14, 147. *See also* England; Northern Ireland; Scotland; Wales
United States, 1–2, 25–26, 28–29, 37, 44, 147. *See also* American ethnic nationalism
"Unite the Right" rally, 93–96
universal basic income, 190
"us," 20, 21–22, 53, 180–81, 188. *See also* in-groups
   Brexit Leave campaigns and, 163, 164, 165–69, 174–75, 176
   English ethnic nationalism and, 153–54
   Le Pen on, 134–39
   Trump on, 100–4, 111

Vercingetorix, 117–18, 125–26, 128, 129

Vichy regime (France), 116, 117–19, 121, 125, 126, 129, 146
Vote Leave (Brexit campaign), 4–5, 44, 49–50, 51–52, 147–48, 162–74, 176–77

Wales, 29, 147, 161, 175–76
Wallonia, 29
Wall Street Journal, 82–83
War of the Roses, 21
Washington, George, 57–58
WASPs (White, Anglo-Saxon, Protestants), 78 (*see also* Anglo-Americans)
Weber, Eugene, 121
Weber, Max, 25
welfare chauvinism, 139–40, 146, 170–71
welfare system
   in France, 133–34, 139–40, 144, 146, 183
   in the UK, 170–71, 174–75
   in the US, 81–82
Whig historiography, 58–59, 150–51, 157, 158–59
white ethnic majorities, 3, 5, 6, 17–18, 27–29, 35–36, 178, 180–81, 185, 188, 191. *See also* dominant ethnicity
   American ethnic nationalism and, 14–15, 77–83, 180–81
   Brexit Leave campaigns and, 166–67, 171–73, 186–87
   English ethnic nationalism and, 180–81
   French ethnic nationalism and, 129–30, 180–81
   Le Pen and, 135, 186–87
   Trump and, 90–91, 92–93, 94, 95, 100–3, 105–6, 109, 110–12, 113, 178, 182–83, 186–87
   in US presidential elections of 2016 and 2020, 91–92
"white flight," 79
White Man's Burden, The (Kipling), 149
whiteness, 180–81
   American ethnic nationalism and, 59–61, 68–73, 74–76, 84–85, 86
   ascendance of, 69–72
   English ethnic nationalism and, 149, 151–53
   French ethnic nationalism and, 116, 117, 118–20, 121–22, 128
   Trump and, 100–1, 112, 186–87
"whiteness studies," 27–28
white supremacy, 74–75, 93–94
Wilders, Geert, 3, 9, 48
Winglesworth, Michael, 65
Winock, Michel, 116
Winthrop, John, 62
World War I, 76, 150–51
World War II, 78, 126, 150–51, 173–74

xenophobia, 9–10, 119, 189

Zangwill, Israel, 76–77